Regarding Ellen Glasgow

Regarding Ellen Glasgow
Essays for Contemporary Readers

Edited by
WELFORD DUNAWAY TAYLOR
& GEORGE C. LONGEST

THE LIBRARY OF VIRGINIA • 2001

Library of Congress Catalog Card Number: 00-112049
Standard Book Number: 0-88490-188-2

Library of Virginia, Richmond, Virginia
© 2001 by The Library of Virginia
All rights reserved. First Edition 2001
Printed in the United States of America.

Earlier versions of chapters eleven and thirteen appeared in *The Mississippi Quarterly* 49, no. 2 (spring 1996). A version of chapter three appeared as "Ellen Glasgow's *The Battle-Ground:* Civil War Richmond in Fiction and History" in *Rewriting the South: History and Fiction,* ed. Lothar Hönnighausen and Valeria Gennaro Lerda (Tübingen und Basel: A. Francke Verlag, 1993), 185–196. All used by permission.

This book is printed on acid-free paper meeting requirements of the American Standard for Permanence of Paper for Printed Library Materials.

Jacket illustration: Miniature portrait by I. Carregi of Ellen Glasgow in her twenties taken from a photograph reproduced in *The Woman Within* (New York, 1954). Miniature on ivory, 3¾ x 3 in., POR946.2, Virginia Historical Society, Richmond.

Jacket design: Sara Daniels Bowersox, Graphic Designer, The Library of Virginia.

TABLE OF CONTENTS

LIST OF ILLUSTRATIONS

All of the small woodcuts that appear throughout this volume are by Julius John Lankes (1884–1960). They appear courtesy of the children of J. J. Lankes.

Preface & Acknowledgments

 ON THE DAY AFTER ELLEN GLASGOW DIED an editorial tribute in the *Richmond Times-Dispatch* opened by stating, "The greatest woman Virginia has produced is dead." These simple, definitive words, appearing in Virginia's largest newspaper, left no doubt as to the esteem in which Glasgow was held at the time. It would seem to follow, therefore, that a figure of such repute should be memorialized down the years. This is not necessarily the case. History in general—local, regional, national, hemispheric—has undergone serious reexamination during the last two decades. Individuals who shaped past events in significant ways have been subjected to reevaluation by present standards of acceptability. Some of the most prominent of them have all but disappeared from the historical record. Although these developments have been met with charges ranging from narrow self-interest, to arrogance, to outright distortion, they have left a clouded picture of the past.

Despite this upheaval, the image of Ellen Glasgow and her fictional legacy shows little tarnish. Since she herself had challenged received notions of history in her own day, it may be that she had won a certain immunity from modern-day revisionists. Or perhaps her depictions of Virginians' being liberated from past stereotypes—seen as quite advanced in their time—have become reality in our own. Whatever the reasons, in the five decades since her death Ellen Glasgow's achievements have attracted hosts of scholars, editors, and critics. As a result, today we may claim to know more about her life, and better understand her work, than her contemporaries did.

These efforts seem to continue with increasing momentum. New studies appear frequently, as do reprint editions of her novels and other works. Glasgow is a frequent subject in college courses in American literature, Southern literature, and women's studies. A society honoring her has existed since 1974; she is accorded exclusive sessions at regional and national meetings of the Modern Language Association of America. Her work continues to attract academic and general readers alike. One gauge of this appeal is that an Ellen Glasgow Festival, held in Richmond in the autumn of 1993, was well attended by representatives of both groups. A number of the essays in *Regarding Ellen Glasgow: Essays for Contemporary Readers* derive from presentations made at this event. These have been supplemented, however, by commissioned pieces in an effort to achieve thematic roundedness and symmetry.

Though occasioned by the half-century anniversary of Glasgow's death, the current volume is intended to be more than a memorial. Rather, it is designed to convey a sense of how she is perceived by the present generation. This is reflected in the variety of topics represented, by a roster of contributors containing both veteran scholars and their younger counterparts, and by interviews with several individuals who knew her.

In addition to the authors who have contributed to this volume, we wish to thank a number of other individuals, institutions, and organizations who have assisted in various ways. First among these is Marvin Heffner, who conceived the idea of the Ellen Glasgow Festival sponsored by the Virginia Writers Club and implemented much of its design and who, as president of Virginia Writers' Special Projects, Inc., has provided generous support to this volume. Similar thanks go to Sarah Bird Wright, a former president of the Virginia Writers Club and a prime mover in that organization's Ellen Glasgow Festival. The following librarians and libraries are equally deserving of thanks: Paul Porterfield, Nancy Vick and Nancy Woodall, Boatwright Memorial Library, University of Richmond; Ray Bonis, James Branch Cabell Library, Virginia Commonwealth University; Bill Simpson, Richmond Public Library; and various staff members of the Photography Division of the Library of Congress and Special Collections at the University of Virginia Library. Special thanks also go to Paul Di Marie of the Washington and Lee University Journalism Department, to Betty Dementi of the Dementi-Foster Studio, and to the children of J. J. Lankes for allowing the reproduction of their father's woodcuts.

We would also like to thank Edward D. C. Campbell, Jr., director of Collection Management Services at the Library of Virginia for his early interest in publication of the essays, and the following Library staff members, especially Gregg D. Kimball, John T. Kneebone, Stacy G. Moore, Emily J. Salmon, and Brent Tarter, of the Publications and Educational Services Division, for their editorial work; Edward Harcourt, of Vanderbilt University, for preliminary copyediting; Sara Daniels Bowersox, the Library's lead graphic designer, for her design of the book; and Elizabeth Gushee, of the Picture Collection, Paige Buchbinder, of Photographic Services, and Sara B. Bearss, of the Publications and Educational Services Division, for their assistance with images to illustrate the volume.

WELFORD DUNAWAY TAYLOR
GEORGE C. LONGEST

INTRODUCTION

WERE IT POSSIBLE FOR THEM TO COMMENT, ELLEN Glasgow's Presbyterian ancestors might contend that the time of her death, like most events of her life, was predetermined. If so, the appointed date, 21 November 1945, could hardly have been more symbolic, coming as it did on Thanksgiving Day and in the final year of World War II. Glasgow's passing itself represented an end to conflict, of course—namely, to the myriad personal struggles that had marked her seventy-two years. As to the termination of global fighting, while it appeared to resolve hostilities among nations, it would become a precursor to a new and vastly different era to follow. The war in the Pacific had been won with a force mightier than the traditional intellect could comprehend, and it soon became apparent that once unleashed this power would pose a constant and permanent threat to the entire world population. One wonders how Glasgow's fictional heroines, who functioned in a devastated post–Civil War Virginia, might have reacted to the new angst. It is also interesting to speculate on how they would have responded to the social and political order that evolved under this insidious influence. As vague fears galvanized into Cold War posturings, there emerged a redefined world in which political boundaries were realigned and battle lines redrawn. Beyond the watershed of the war itself, families, politics, economics, religion, and morality would all undergo dramatic changes.

How Glasgow herself might have accommodated to this altered state of being we can only imagine. For, practically speaking, a lifetime of intense engagement with her times was now cast into the static mold of history, and with it her fictional chronicle of a formidable segment of Virginia life (1860–1940). Although this record would be extended slightly by the posthumous publication of her autobiography, *The Woman Within* (1954), and by the novelette *Beyond Defeat* (a sequel to *In This Our Life* published in 1966), her literary legacy was essentially fixed. It would become hostage to whatever fortunes might obtain in a time of change, to be remembered, forgotten, or reevaluated.

In eras such as the second half of the twentieth century and the beginning of the twenty-first, when change is continual, rapid, and unrelenting, memory suffers proportionally. How is it, then, that more than fifty years after Ellen Glasgow's death she is celebrated by a new generation of readers, scholars, and critics? It is assuredly not because the intervening decades have shown a fondness for the past. Period reputations greater than her own have been forgotten long since. Nor can the reason be isolated to admiration for Glasgow the woman, as frequently expressed by an emerging feminist hegemony. As most of the following essays indicate, the current attraction to Glasgow and her work grows out of an on-going interest that, though admittedly limited in scope, has slowed only occasionally (and then only briefly) since her death.

The publication of this volume, however, denotes more that a landmark in recent history. It makes its appearance at the beginning of a new century and, more important, a new millennium. Just as Glasgow's writing career, begun on the cusp of the nineteenth and twentieth centuries, addressed the present and future by successfully subsuming the past, we believe that the current work is also forward-looking. For, as surely as our contributors are poised to continue their efforts into the future, the issues they engage here will attract further exploration and comment in the years ahead. As these efforts continue, we predict that Glasgow and her achievement will prove relevant to the new millennium. In short, like the "vein of iron" that characterizes many of her fictional beings and became the title of one of her novels Glasgow, woman and author, has proved—and continues to prove—remarkably durable. Moreover, the essays also demonstrate that this durability derives not from a single strength, but from an alloy consisting of many "veins."

The following contributions offer a representative array of these elements beginning with Catherine Rainwater's survey of Glasgow's literary reputation during the five and a half decades since her death. In addition to tracing salient trends in criticism during the period, Rainwater gives an accounting of why the scholarly approaches remained limited, how they came to be expanded, and what may lie ahead. The final essay regarding Glasgow's life and work also surmises on the appeal to future readers, while stimulating renewed interest in one of the most intriguing riddles in Glasgow scholarship. Its author is Julius Rowan Raper, whose judgments are based on more than two decades of active scholarship on Glasgow. Her readers should be gratified by his optimistic forecast.

The Rainwater and Raper essays serve as brackets for eleven others that represent the ways in which modern scholars see Glasgow's standing in the current literary milieu. Given the sociohistorical design of her fiction, Glasgow's connections to Southern history continue to engage scholarly interest. E. Stanly Godbold, a respected historian and Glasgow biographer, assesses the uniqueness of the woman and her work within this framework. His analysis serves to remind modern readers that Glasgow's rebellion against the entrenched sentimental novel, and her outspoken defiance of the received image of the Southern Belle, should not be taken for granted. To the contrary, such attitudes and actions were remarkable for a woman of her station and time.

Although most of the novels deal with the post–Civil War era, Ellen Glasgow did set one—*The Battle-Ground*—during the war. Dorothy Scura treats its

Richmond-based episodes as a gauge of Glasgow's ability to synthesize history in the realization of her own thematic and philosophical ends. Another major component of Southern history, the Calvinist tradition, is the subject of Susan Goodman's essay. Focusing first on *The Woman Within*, Goodman charts Glasgow's attempts to come to terms with the overarching religion of her father, Francis Glasgow. Goodman sees the ultimate resolution of this multifaceted conflict expressed in *Barren Ground*. Still, Glasgow's rebellion against historical tradition continues to draw attention. For example, Catherine Peaslee explores her contributions to the woman suffrage movement, both as an active participant and through the novel *The Romance of a Plain Man*.

Of more immediate concern to the 2000s, perhaps, are Glasgow's perspectives on gender. They are emphasized in the contributions of Pamela Matthews, Benita Muth, Helen Fiddyment Levy, and Mark Graves. Utilizing the heroines of two short stories, Matthews develops a coherent articulation of Glasgow's convictions regarding the static role of Southern women during the Civil War and fifty years later. Their struggle for individual status against an entrenched male establishment is shown to have yielded little. Glasgow is saying, according to Matthews, that Southern women can hope to achieve greater independence and power within the prevailing order only through their collective efforts. Glasgow did not portray this condition as insurmountable, however. Focusing on Dorinda Oakley, the protagonist of *Barren Ground*, Benita Muth discusses this extraordinary woman's victory over natural forces and personal tragedy. Nevertheless, Muth's interpretation runs somewhat counter to modern feminist readings of this novel in that she sees Dorinda's choice of entrepreneurial success over love as transforming her life into an "emotional winter."

Helen Fiddyment Levy, on the other hand, offers a more positive depiction of feminine strength in her discussion of *Vein of Iron*, Glasgow's penultimate novel. Levy presents a modern South possessing a latent vitality. This force is successfully energized by an indomitable feminine tradition and is freely expressed through "the speech of the heart." With its open-ended plot suggesting a resolve toward the future, this later novel indicates, according to Levy, a much more positive and hopeful outlook for women—and the South itself—than that found in some of Glasgow's earlier work. In structuring her argument Levy also draws on *Barren Ground*, which she sees as forming, with *Vein of Iron*, a kind of developmental matrix in which defiance against nature ripens into acceptance, and an objectified feminine role is replaced by a more-nurturing maternal one.

Glasgow's concern for gender issues was not confined to women, however, as Mark Graves shows in his study of her average Southern man. The author emphasized in several novels the theme of the nonaristocratic male and his rigidly defined position in the hierarchy of the Cavalier South. In its own way, this status was as unempowered as that of the Belle in the same society. Glasgow's modern Southern males, who are able to achieve a greater upward mobility, often come from the lower social orders—and are the stronger for it.

While the veins of history, religion, and gender run far and deep in many of the aforementioned interpretations, other selections present newly discovered (in some cases rediscovered) elements. For instance, in what may be the most thorough treatment of the short fiction to date, Edgar MacDonald demonstrates how the selections of *The Shadowy Third and Other Stories* reflect an evolving pattern of introspection and self-discovery that began in 1916, a time of creative uncertainty for Glasgow. This development was made possible by her many-faceted relationship with Henry Anderson, whom she met that year and whose influence MacDonald traces allegorically through several stories.

Another much neglected title is *The Descendant*, which, in addition to being the first of Glasgow's score of novels, was composed while her hearing was fast deteriorating. Drawing on recent discoveries in audiological research, Linda Kornasky sheds unexpected light on this text, while at the same time establishing yet another analogy between Glasgow's life and art. David W. Coffey likewise explores a new artistic dimension by treating the film of *In This Our Life*. Although this final novel is not usually considered one of Glasgow's best, Coffey's assessment of its transformation into a motion picture intended for racially segregated audiences calls particular attention to Glasgow's (and Hollywood's) sensitivity to this issue.

Still, despite these new expressions of interest in several little-explored areas of Glasgow's work, the popularity of certain time-honored titles continues and is obvious in a significant number of the essays. For example, *Barren Ground*, probably the most famous and characteristic of the novels, is given primary emphasis in three selections. *Vein of Iron* is the centerpiece of another. In addition, *The Woman Within* continues to prove its sturdiness as a primary resource for biographical as well as textual analysis.

The first thirteen essays are followed by two chapters that offer different, yet basic information. Tricia Pearsall's "Ellen Glasgow's Richmond" attempts to re-create the Richmond environment in which Glasgow lived and from which she drew in her novels. Pearsall reproduces in prose and photographs Richmond buildings prominent in Glasgow's life and fiction. Many of these edifices are still standing, a further reminder of the direct connection between Glasgow's era and our own. Scattered throughout *Regarding Ellen Glasgow* are numerous other images, some of which portray a very different Glasgow from the one found in the usual publicity pictures. Also included are illustrations of her house and garden, taken in the 1930s by Frances Benjamin Johnston as part of the Architectural History of the South project, sponsored by the Carnegie Foundation.

Punctuating the volume are a number of woodcuts by Virginia artist Julius John Lankes. Glasgow and Lankes first collaborated during production of *Barren Ground* in 1925. Lankes's depiction of a rather dilapidated structure, evoking the era, region, and social class of the novel's main characters, set the right tone as a title page and cover illustration. Lankes went on to produce three more original works for the author: an illustration for *The Romantic Comedians* in 1926, though never published in the novel; the Glasgow house at One West Main Street, which Glasgow used for her Christmas card in 1927; and the image for the dust jacket of *The Deliverance* in 1929. A year later in 1930, Lankes cut a new block of the Glasgow house, with a less-textured facade, for his own *Virginia Woodcuts*. Although small in number, this body of work constitutes the largest single group of graphic designs inspired by Ellen Glasgow's two Virginias—the one in which she resided and the one she re-created in her fiction. With the addition of several other works by J. J. Lankes, this volume of essays visually represents Glasgow's critical understanding of the timeworn world of her Virginia.

The final chapter, "Remembering Ellen Glasgow," consists of interviews with seven individuals who knew her. These interviews underscore the fact that Glasgow is not a relic from an inaccessible past but is still, if only vicariously, part of the present—close enough to our own time for us to make connection through direct ties. Moreover, the reminiscences of the seven subjects represent a variety of perspectives, some of which have little to do with Glasgow's artistic life. These exchanges feature relatives, admirers, friends, and associates. The details they offer of her social, professional, and domestic life form part of the intimate material of which oral history is made. It is often the kind of detail that "professional" historical studies fail to include.

Taken as a whole, these essays demonstrate that scholars and critics writing in the present—whether on Glasgow or any other literary subject—are equipped with substantially more analytical implements than their counterparts of a half century ago. For instance, the historical-biographical, formalist, and psychological approaches, seen as current fifty years ago, have been supplemented by innovations such as feminist theory, deconstructionism, and the new historicism. The latter three schools inform many of the studies in this volume, especially the essays of Matthews, Levy, and Goodman. However, many of the traditional methodologies are found here as well. Graves, Kornasky, and Muth offer close formalist readings of their subject texts, while Peaslee, Coffey, and Godbold draw in various ways from a historical context.

It is our conviction that this eclecticism should not be taken as an indication that Glasgow studies have become fragmented into so many divisions, or "schools." Rather, it reflects the broad scope of her appeal. Moreover, her ability to attract diverse methodologies and points of view is a reflection of the liberal spirit with which, by personal as well as artistic example, she herself resisted the strictures of parochialism and conformity. The fact that she continues to attract the traditional and the avant-garde alike testifies to the breadth and depth of her substance.

Part of the strength of this appeal is to be found in the skill and dedication of the interpreters she has attracted. Any student of the secondary literature will recognize among our contributors individuals who have made Ellen Glasgow's name and reputation a vital presence in American literature over the past twenty-five years. Not only have these scholars helped fix Glasgow more securely in the literary consciousness, they have also inspired others to continue such efforts. Indeed, names such as Raper, MacDonald, Scura, Matthews, Rainwater, and Godbold have become synonymous with Glasgow studies. Their pioneering works have formed a foundation for subsequent scholars. Still, these ranks cannot be limited to the veterans. This volume introduces the work of a number of young scholars, several of whom are new to Glasgow criticism. The quality of their work is, we feel, clear indication of an emerging generation that promises to carry on, and even to rival, the achievements of the present one.

Despite this array of subjects, works, approaches, and contributors, we cannot pretend that the volume is a comprehensive treatment of its subject. Ellen Glasgow was a complex individual, who hid much of her private self from public view. She lived a long and many-faceted life. No single work can hope to do justice to such variety. We can, however, make one broad and consistent claim for these offerings. Although they appear fifty-six years after her death, each and every one contains new facts or insights. Moreover, given the rich and varied texture of Glasgow's work, we predict more of the same for the decades ahead.

Perhaps Anne Virginia Bennett had such prospects in mind when she selected as Ellen Glasgow's epitaph the final line of John Milton's *Lycidas:* "Tomorrow to fresh woods, and pastures new." It is as if she were directing us to Catherine Rainwater's opening essay, "Through a Gate and into Another Life: Ellen Glasgow After 1945."

Ellen Glasgow: A Chronology

1873   Ellen Anderson Gholson Glasgow born 22 April at 101 East Cary Street, Richmond, Virginia, ninth of the ten children of Francis Thomas and Anne Jane Gholson Glasgow

1880   Composes her first literary work (a brief five-line poem)

1887   Francis Glasgow purchases One West Main Street, a Greek Revival residence, where he and family move

1889   Begins to experience difficulty with hearing

1890   Makes debut at Saint Cecilia Ball in Charleston, South Carolina; completes some 400 pages on first novel, *Sharp Realities;* refuses to make debut in Richmond

1891   Begins writing *The Descendant*

1892   Destroys manuscript of *Sharp Realities* after traumatic session with New York publisher

1893   Mother dies on 27 October; Ellen Glasgow destroys part of *The Descendant*

1894   Is deeply distressed by the death of George Walter McCormack, one of her intellectual mentors and husband of her favorite sister, Cary McCormack

1895   Returns to remaining portion of *The Descendant,* completes the novel

1896   Travels during summer in England, Scotland, and France

1897   *The Descendant* published (anonymously) in January by Harper and Brothers

1898   *Phases of an Inferior Planet* published in March, with title page stating "by Ellen Glasgow, Author of '*The Descendant*'"

1899   Travels with two of her sisters to Europe and Middle East (4 February–5 September); falls in love with "Gerald B——," a still-unidentified married man

1900   *The Voice of the People* published

1902	*The Battle-Ground* (Civil War novel) published in March; *The Freeman and Other Poems* published in August
1903	Travels in Europe with sisters Rebe Glasgow and Cary McCormack
1904	*The Deliverance* published in January; returns to Europe with Rebe Glasgow
1905	In Europe; "Gerald B——" dies late in summer
1906	*The Wheel of Life* published in January
1907	Summers in Italy
1908	*The Ancient Law* published in January; travels in England and Italy
1909	*The Romance of A Plain Man* published in January; brother Francis (Frank) Glasgow dies 7 April; vacations in Colorado late in summer
1910	Travels in France and Italy with Cary McCormack, whose health is rapidly declining; Anne Virginia Bennett comes to One West Main to nurse McCormack
1911	*The Miller of Old Church* published; Cary McCormack dies on 19 August
1913	*Virginia* published
1914	In England until just prior to outbreak of World War I; meets Thomas Hardy, John Galsworthy, Arnold Bennett, Joseph Conrad, Henry James
1916	Father dies on 29 January; *Life and Gabriella* published; on Easter Sunday meets Henry Watkins Anderson (called "Harold S——" in *The Woman Within*)
1917	Becomes engaged to Henry W. Anderson
1918	On 3 July quarrels with Anderson; she attempts suicide with sleeping pills
1919	Breaks engagement to Henry W. Anderson; *The Builders* published
1920	Becomes honorary member of Phi Beta Kappa at the College of William and Mary
1922	*One Man in His Time* published

1923	*The Shadowy Third and Other Stories* published
1924	Becomes president of Richmond Society for the Prevention of Cruelty to Animals
1925	*Barren Ground* published in April
1926	*The Romantic Comedians* (first novel in comedy of manners trilogy set in Queenborough)
1927	In England; visits Thomas Hardy, Hugh Walpole, Frank Swinnerton
1929	*They Stooped to Folly* (second Queenborough novel) published; Doubleday, Doran and Company begins publication of eight-volume *Old Dominion Edition of the Works of Ellen Glasgow* (completed 1933)
1930	Awarded Doctor of Letters degree by University of North Carolina; travels in England, France
1932	Elected to National Institute of Arts and Letters; *The Sheltered Life* (last installment of trilogy) published
1935	*Vein of Iron* published; summers in Castine, Maine, to which she will return during each of her remaining summers
1937	Makes final trip to Europe
1938	Charles Scribner's Sons publishes twelve-volume *Virginia Edition of the Works of Ellen Glasgow*; receives honorary degrees from Duke University and University of Richmond; elected to American Academy of Arts and Letters
1939	Receives honorary Doctor of Laws degree from the College of William and Mary; suffers heart attack in December
1940	Suffers second heart attack in spring; receives Howells Medal from American Academy of Arts and Letters in autumn
1941	*In This Our Life* (final novel) published; on 5 April receives *Saturday Review of Literature* Award for Distinguished Service to American Literature
1942	Awarded Pulitzer Prize for fiction; on 6 April, Warner Brothers releases film of *In This Our Life,* starring Bette Davis and Olivia de Haviland

1943	*A Certain Measure* (collected prefaces from the *Virginia Edition* of her works) published
1945	Dies on 21 November at One West Main; is buried in Hollywood Cemetery on 23 November
1954	Henry W. Anderson dies; *The Woman Within* (autobiography) published
1958	*The Letters of Ellen Glasgow* (edited by Blair Rouse) published
1963	*The Collected Short Stories of Ellen Glasgow* (edited by Richard K. Meeker) published
1966	*Beyond Defeat: An Epilogue to an Era* (edited by Luther Y. Gore)—a brief clarifying sequel to *In This Our Life*—published
1988	*Ellen Glasgow's Reasonable Doubts: A Collection of Her Writings* (edited by Julius Rowan Raper) published
1994–1995	University Press of Virginia brings back into print *The Romantic Comedians* (1995), *The Sheltered Life* (1994), *Vein of Iron* (1995), and *The Woman Within* (1994).

Regarding Ellen Glasgow

ONE

Through a Gate and into Another Life:
Ellen Glasgow After 1945

CATHERINE RAINWATER

Contemplating her own mortality and Jason Greylock's imminent death, Dorinda Oakley near the end of Ellen Glasgow's *Barren Ground* (1925) imagines herself walking through a gate and "into another life," while Jason looks down the road to "starry fields of the life-everlasting."[1] If an enduring literary reputation amounts to starry immortality, then Glasgow herself, when she died on 21 November 1945, walked into another life of posthumous critical acclaim that now spans more than half a century.

Though her fame has endured, Glasgow, like many of her devotees, might not be completely satisfied with the trajectory of her reputation if she could assess it today. Glasgow self-consciously monitored her rising-star status in the American literary sky and apparently resented twinkling above the horizon while contemporaries such as Edith Wharton and Willa Cather rose higher and brighter by comparison. If we could interview Glasgow today, we might find her still justifiably irked that, in the fifty years since her death, she has yet to win what she (and many others) doubtless believed to be her rightful place in twentieth-century literature as a star of greater magnitude.

The perennial underappreciation of Ellen Glasgow's art is indeed intriguing. On the one hand, a century's worth of steady attention to Glasgow's fiction seems to belie all claims of neglect. Edgar E. MacDonald and Tonette Bond Inge's *Ellen Glasgow: A Reference Guide*, for example, shows only one year (1901) between 1897 and 1981 when there were apparently no publications of any type on Glasgow or her works, and in every year since 1981 scholarly publications have diversified and increased.[2] Critical and even popular attention to Glasgow's art has prevailed despite the general unavailability of most of her books over the past forty years. On the other hand, a nagging sense that a great American writer has yet to receive her due has haunted many noteworthy American scholars, among them C. Hugh Holman, a tireless apologist for Glasgow's art. Off and on for approximately three decades until his death in 1981, Holman wrote about Glasgow and encouraged the academic community to discover the depth and the wide-ranging scope of her mind, not to mention the frequently disregarded aesthetic richness of her fiction.[3] Over equally as many years, Holman's sentiments have echoed throughout the pages of *American Literary Scholarship* in the voices of critical reviewers complaining of Glasgow's relative neglect among major American literary figures.[4]

Regarding this overall lack of adequate critical appreciation, one might argue that until fairly recently most female writers have been routinely neglected, or at least relegated to marginal, noncanonical status. This argument fails to explain why Glasgow in particular, even among her exclusively female contemporaries, is so conspicuously absent from the revised twentieth-century pantheon of major authors. A more likely explanation comes from recognizing the way that Glasgow's works are situated in relation to three intertwined, literary historical developments: the "Southern renascence" movements of the early twentieth century, the New Critical hegemony during the middle years of the century, and a narrowly defined Modernist aesthetic that has prevailed throughout most of the century. Each of these developments implies perceptual and evaluative frames of reference that are ill-matched to Glasgow's achievement. In short, as so much contemporary critical theory reveals, our ways of seeing literature are also ways of *not* seeing, and our insights as well as our blindness have frequently operated at Glasgow's expense.

GLASGOW'S UNEASY LOVE AFFAIR WITH THE SOUTH

Despite her bold, often scathing critiques of Southern social and aesthetic traditions, Glasgow always thought of herself as a Southern writer. So has nearly everyone else, partly to her advantage and partly to her disadvantage. Undoubtedly, the focus during Glasgow's life on regional writing helped win her and others some well-deserved attention that might not otherwise have been paid to female authors. However, as she suggested throughout her novels and in her 1928 essay, "The Novel in the South," Glasgow saw herself as part of a new wave of Southern writers defining themselves against their antebellum and Reconstruction-

Ellen Glasgow, ca. 1930. Though she saw herself as a Southern writer, Glasgow reached beyond strictly regional portrayals in her novels to touch on universal human themes.

era predecessors. She called for an end to her forebears' "complacency, self-satisfaction, [and] ... blind contentment with things as they might be: all these cheerful swarms ... stifle both the truth of literature and the truth of life [and] settle ... like a cloud of honey bees over the creative faculties" of Southern people. She called for "a literature of revolt" with a broad, national and even "international attitude of mind" as well as a "detached and steadfast point of view."[5]

Such are the attitude and point of view that she so admirably develops in philosophically astute, mature works such as *Barren Ground* (1925) and *Vein of Iron* (1935); but we must also recognize the same in her earlier, less-commonly appreciated works such as *Virginia* (1913). On the surface, this novel is a study of the post–Civil War "Southern lady," but like Wharton's *House of Mirth* (1905) and *The*

Age of Innocence (1920), *Virginia* transcends its temporal and regional bounds. As critical examinations of mindless traditions and contemporary trends, *Virginia* and other Glasgow novels are certainly as perceptive as Wharton's fiction even if, stylistically, they lack Wharton's cool, surgical precision; also obscuring the "universality" of Glasgow's writing as a "literature of revolt" are her settings in towns and cities of the South as opposed to Wharton's cosmopolitan New York City.

Certainly, critical and popular response to Glasgow's art has noted her "revolutionary" stance in *Virginia* and other novels. Glasgow, however, has been more consistently treated as a writer (unlike some of her younger contemporaries such as William Faulkner, Robert Penn Warren, and Katherine Anne Porter) who fails to transcend the insularity of the South, perhaps partly because her career developed simultaneously with a long and self-conscious campaign to define Southern literature, a campaign in which Glasgow herself participated.[6] Though the Southern dimensions of Glasgow's art obviously merit the attention they have received, regionalist criticism has nevertheless constituted a vise holding Glasgow studies in place, despite the insistence of Holman, Jay B. Hubbell, Maxwell Geismar, Van Wyck Brooks, and other notables on Glasgow's wider appeal.

Even her own proclaimed objections did not forestall misreadings of her books as narrow statements of regional themes and views. For instance, as Blair Rouse explained in 1962, "Her delight in nature and her interest in the possibilities of life on the land have been misunderstood as expressions of the [Nashville Agrarian] doctrine."[7] Even less perceptive than these misreadings, one book on American literature published in 1945 described her works as portrayals of "farm and village life" in the United States, and Henry Bamford Parkes in 1947 declared her work too narrow to address larger American themes.[8]

For close to thirty years after her death, even those who appreciated Glasgow often could not escape the imprisoning intellectual discourse that trained the critical eye habitually on Southern social and historical issues. Raising questions about Glasgow's "traditionalism" (as opposed to mere "provincialism"), for example, the prominent voice of Allen Tate in a 1945 issue of the *Virginia Quarterly Review* helped confirm the regionalist idiom of Glasgow studies for years to come.[9] Throughout the 1940s and 1950s, critics also perpetuated James Branch Cabell's widely publicized view of Glasgow as chiefly a social historian. These perspectives were in turn enshrined in the various editions of Robert E. Spiller's monumental *Literary History of the United States* (1948). Ironically, even C. Hugh Holman, among the first to object to Glasgow's narrow classification as "Southern writer," reinforced her regionalist status by including her in his *Virginia in History and Tradition* (1958).[10]

No doubt sparked by the interest in Glasgow as Southern iconoclast, however, inklings of future, alternative trends in Glasgow criticism appeared as early as

Celebrated literary contemporaries Edith Wharton (*left*) and Willa Cather (*right*)

1948. A small but steady trickle of doctoral dissertations, beginning with Josephine Jessup's, concentrated on Glasgow's "feminists" and remarked on features of her mind and art that transcended regional interests.[11] Despite these countertrends, the political and ideological conservatism reflected in Anglo-American literary critical discourse of the 1950s was far from conducive to the serious study of female authors, especially those with feminist and other unorthodox concerns (for instance, Glasgow's fascination with Darwin's implied ethos concerning animals). And the liberal agendas of the tumultuous 1960s celebrated primarily a male-dominated Modernist and Postmodernist vision. With a few indisputable exceptions (for example, the work of Frederick P. W. McDowell and Julius Rowan Raper), it was not until the late 1970s that Glasgow criticism finally began to diversify. Until this time, approaches to Glasgow's work tended to be either regionalist or formalist, and, ironically, critics taking the latter approach frequently devalued her works even as they attempted to reach beyond Glasgow's Southern concerns toward the purely aesthetic features of her art.

Must a Novel Be "As Formally Perfect as a Poem"?

If for years a perpetually regionalist view shaped critical response to Glasgow's fiction, the New Criticism amounted to an even more tightly circumscribed perceptual frame because it was, in the long run, ill-suited to Glasgow's art. On the one hand, formalist "close reading" is extraordinarily sensitive to language and form; on the other hand, it tends to marginalize works not resembling the rhetorically flamboyant poetry that inspired the method in the first place. Like most other interpretive practices, the New Criticism both enables and constrains inquiry. Its dogmatic emphasis on the aesthetic unity and verbal pyrotechnics of great art derive not only from its founders' preference for poetry, especially Metaphysical and Romantic verse, but also from the Modernist poems that some of the New Critics themselves (John Crowe Ransom, Robert Penn Warren, Allen Tate, and others) were writing. Indeed, Ransom, Tate, Cleanth Brooks, William Empson, R. P. Blackmur, and other titans of Anglo-American formalism developed the New Critical method (and its characteristic vocabulary of architectural terms) primarily within a practical critical discourse devoted to readings of poems written by Donne, Keats, and others. Consequently, the New Criticism, for all its brilliant insights into the poetics of form, is best suited for explications of concretely imagistic, lyric poetry. As a critical method, the New Criticism cannot help but define a narrow view of "great art." (Indeed, it was partially in response to this limitation that the Neo-Aristotelians, led by Ronald S. Crane and others at the University of Chicago during the 1950s, developed a broader formalist poetics more suitable to a wider variety of genres.) Throughout the 1950s, the New Critical bias plagued Glasgow scholarship. Complaints about the formal imperfections of Glasgow's works proliferated and, unfortunately, predominated until Frederick P. W. McDowell, in his groundbreaking book *Ellen Glasgow and the Ironic Art of Fiction* (1960), demonstrated persuasively that Glasgow's works "can be as cogently discussed in aesthetic terms as in any other."[12]

A fascinating exchange in 1952 between Blair Rouse and John Edward Hardy in the *Hopkins Review* shows how firm adherence to a retrenched formalism can blind one to the richness of Glasgow's works. In a letter to the journal's editor, Blair Rouse challenged Hardy's negative assessment of Glasgow's fiction.[13] Considering Hardy's opinion of Glasgow as not even a good storyteller, much less a serious artist, one wonders why he bothered to write about her at all. Hardy's distaste revealed more about the limitations of his own critical vision than about any aspect of Glasgow's fiction, yet his essay marks a significant moment in the history of Glasgow criticism. Proceeding on the assumption that a novel ought to be "as formally perfect as a poem,"[14] Hardy bludgeoned Glasgow for her alleged formal ineptitude, particularly with literary symbols.

Hardy's view of art was narrow even within formalist strictures; nevertheless, he showed precisely the kind of dissatisfaction that other critics of his era felt when they attempted to account for their interest in Glasgow. Again and again, major critics such as Alfred Kazin, Louis D. Rubin Jr., and Maxwell Geismar accorded Glasgow qualified, sometimes downright grudging, praise; rather than persuading us to overlook Glasgow's alleged deficiencies, however, their commentaries reveal the lack of a critical discourse suited not only to discussion but also to full discovery of precisely what attracted them to her works.[15] Dissatisfaction led to a dismissal of Glasgow by critics such as Hardy who most staunchly adhered to New Critical principles and who, therefore, were usually the most frustrated with Glasgow's elusive texts. Though her novels exhibit many more of the formalist virtues than Hardy apparently perceived, her narrative practices and implied poetics are best understood through alternative critical frames of reference.

The difficulties besetting Glasgow criticism of the 1950s and 1960s were further compounded by the prevailing Modernist aesthetic; this aesthetic was, in the first place, inextricably bound up with formalist analytical methods. Ezra Pound, T. S. Eliot, and other architects of Modernist poetry had, almost by manifesto in the early years of the century, demanded a poetics of form best suited to Imagist poetry. Modernism, as it came to be defined by midcentury, posited aesthetic norms that did not seem germane to Glasgow's fiction; indeed, New Critical and Modernist credos in effect expelled Glasgow from the twentieth-century avant-garde to which she felt she belonged as a writer.

So, What Was Modernism?

In "The Novel in the South," Glasgow calls herself a Modernist writer: "To those of us who are and have been always in accord with the artistic impulse we are pleased to call Modernism it is a relief to find that the horizon even of the American novel is fluid, not fixed, and that there is a way of escape from the artificial limitations of material and method."[16] Obviously, Glasgow understood Modernism as a development that included rather than excluded her art. Her sophisticated engagement with the ideas of Freud, Jung, Darwin, Spencer, Schopenhauer, Marx, Nietzsche, and others, even in her earliest works, certainly places

A Modern Glasgow in 1938

her squarely within the community of Modernist thinkers. Moreover, her narrative strategies, sometimes camouflaged by an effusive style, are far more in line with Modernist experimentation than has yet to be fully appreciated today. Critical failure to recognize the nature and extent of Glasgow's Modernism is another key factor in the underappreciation of her art.

Marianne DeKoven, a perceptive contemporary critic, argues that New Critical modernism's narrow construction "not only omitted from its canon works . . . by white women, and works by the black writers of the Harlem Renaissance, but also valorized, at the expense of the progressive implications of its forms, modernism's reactionary features: . . . totalizing myth, externally imposed order, ahistoricity, deadlocked irony, [and] the idea of 'well-wrought,' perfectly balanced form as an end in itself, the only interesting end of art." Far from constituting "some transhistorical, essentialist modernism," DeKoven believes that such characteristics "*construct a version of modernism* [*emphasis added*] that, in history, as a result of unpredestined outcomes of cultural-political struggles, modernism has become."[17]

Adherence to this version of Modernism effectively screens Glasgow's works from mainstream critical vision throughout much of the twentieth century. Her views on many issues, such as the significance of history, the relative meaning of human experience, and the plight of the individual in the universe, do not seem to conform to those perspectives most commonly deemed Modernist; furthermore, her narrative technique appears conventional rather than Joycean or Faulknerian. To let go of a too-narrowly conceived idea of Modernism, however, is to realize that her works explore in depth and with considerable sophistication what DeKoven calls the "progressive implications" of Modernist form. Modernism was characterized primarily by numerous, agonized conflicts and contradictions rather than by any of the "essentialist" or consensus positions with which it has frequently been equated. As I have attempted to show in my own discussions of Glasgow's novels, her dialectical narrative strategies frequently amount to a search for authority and epistemological grounding; they epitomize the revolutionary, iconoclastic spirit of Modernism itself rather than the reductive view of the movement that prevailed by midcentury.[18]

Indeed, Glasgow's Modernism and her deceptively "conventional" narrative technique are subjects long overdue for further study. Regrettably, we have heard too little from critics such as Wayne Lesser and J. E. Bunselmeyer who, in 1979 and 1984 respectively, published potentially groundbreaking essays on Glasgow's narrative manner.[19] One hopes that recent developments in narrative theory, together with a fuller understanding of Modernism, will lead to a new era of Glasgow criticism in this new century. A time of recognition is at hand when we are beginning to see Glasgow as she saw herself—not behind, but ahead of her time as a writer.[20]

The State of Glasgow Studies at Century's End

Writing in 1979, Judith B. Wittenburg remarked on the disorderly state of Glasgow studies. She lamented a lack of direction, on the one hand, and a failure to develop promising trends on the other.[21] Subsequent scholarship, however, has produced important changes, including new attention to previously underexplored or ignored aspects of Glasgow's thought and art. Moreover, as E. Stanly Godbold Jr. has recently observed, Glasgow scholarship is no longer exclusively in the hands of male critics.[22] Indeed, since 1980, female scholars have generated most of the commentaries on her work. Female and male scholars alike currently pursue an array of long-overdue arguments on such diverse subjects as Glasgow's feminism, her treatment of gender and racial issues, the ways in which her knowledge of psychology and philosophy inform her narrative strategies, and especially her notions of self and art as revealed in her autobiography, *The Woman Within*.

Bonnie, one of the many and much-loved dogs that Glasgow owned throughout her life

Though it was published in 1954 and generated much discussion during the late 1950s, *The Woman Within* is only now beginning to receive the serious consideration that it merits. During the 1980s and 1990s, critical discourse on autobiography (especially of women) came of age. Informed by complex psychological, linguistic, and other types of theory, this contemporary discourse affords greater appreciation of Glasgow's oddly self-concealing, self-inventing document that she constructed during the last years of her life. Julius Rowan Raper and Susan Goodman, in particular, have introduced appropriate psychological frames of reference within which to consider Glasgow's autobiography, both by itself and in connection with the autobiographies of some of her female contemporaries, including Edith Wharton.[23]

Overall, like Dorinda in *Barren Ground* when she saves the family farm using "scientific farming" principles of crop rotation, Glasgow scholars are at last cultivating the seeds of new growth.[24] Since many of these same scholars are members of the Ellen Glasgow Society, one might reasonably conclude that the society has contributed to the growth and maturation of Glasgow studies over the past twenty years. Certainly, this was a major aim of Edgar MacDonald, Dorothy

Scura, Josephine Glasgow Clark, Emma Gray Trigg, Thomas Inge, and Maurice Duke when they met in August 1974 to found the society at the Glasgow House in Richmond, Virginia. Another of the society's announced missions was to help keep Glasgow's works in print. Though there have been sporadic attempts by several presses to introduce a line of Glasgow's works, most of Glasgow's novels have been out of print for many years. The University Press of Virginia has recently brought out editions of *The Sheltered Life* (1932), *The Romantic Comedians* (1926), *Vein of Iron* (1935), and *The Woman Within* (1954), and promises to reprint more of her works over the next few years.[25] Let us hope that they will, for if all or most of Glasgow's works were in print again we would no doubt see an even greater increase in the number and variety of critical studies devoted to this long-underestimated, frequently misunderstood American author.

TWO

Ellen Glasgow and Southern History

E. STANLY GODBOLD, JR.

llen Glasgow belongs to the history of Richmond, of Virginia, and of
the New South just as surely as she belongs to the annals of Southern
and American literature. Indeed, before professional historians were writing viable accounts of Virginia between the Civil War and World War II, Ellen
Glasgow was doing it herself in her novels. As late as the 1970s, historians and
literary critics alike looked to Ellen Glasgow as a realist who wrote good history
that was also good literature. Now, more than half a century after her death,
Ellen Glasgow has taken a long road from chronicler of her native Richmond
and of Virginia to an indelible figure in its history. Let us look at her journey.

It began, as did virtually all scholarship related to the history of the New
South, with C. Vann Woodward—a failed novelist who had to reconcile himself
to being a distinguished historian. Woodward's appreciation of literature remains
a salient and distinctive characteristic of his enduring histories. In *Origins of the
New South, 1877–1913*, Woodward notes that of the twelve Southern historical
novelists of her generation, only Glasgow remained in her native South, and only
Glasgow discovered something new in the South.[1] What she discovered, of
course, was that in the post–Civil War era, the old class structure had been scram-
bled; a new generation of industrialists and businessmen had risen to power;
some women were demanding the right to vote; and the fluid relations between
whites and blacks were moving in new and unpredictable directions. Ironically—

a word one must always use when speaking about Woodward *and* about Glasgow
—Woodward reached similar conclusions about the South in *Origins*, a book he
published six years after Glasgow's death. Young scholars have attempted to build
their reputations by taking Woodward to task, but the old master still stands as the
Aristotle of New South history. But I wish to propose a brazen question: Is it
possible that from his reading of Glasgow, the great historian absorbed the thesis
for which he became famous? Was the novelist, ironically, the mentor to the historian? Woodward backed away from a full evaluation of Glasgow in 1951 with
the disclaimer that the rebellion of the novelist could "as yet, only be recorded,
not explained," thus leaving her fate to the next generation of scholars. They
were more than willing to take it up.

Two historians of Virginia who published late in the 1960s unabashedly noted
that up until that time Glasgow was the person who had written the best
account of Virginia and Virginians. Glasgow herself had given them the clue by
proclaiming that her novels should be judged as a social history of Virginia.
Grateful for the prompt, they took her at her word. On the very first page of *Old
Virginia Restored, 1870–1930*, Raymond H. Pulley quoted General Bolingbroke
from Glasgow's 1909 work, *The Romance of a Plain Man*, to demonstrate how
important the history of Virginia was to Virginians.[2] Likewise, Allen W. Moger, in
Virginia: Bourbonism to Byrd, 1870–1925, acknowledged the historian's debt to
Glasgow in the very first line of his preface. He agreed with her that to present "a
true view" of history, complete with the unpleasant and the painful, meant that
an author took a great risk.[3] By the time professional historians went to work on
Virginia, Ellen Glasgow was already famous, sometimes infamous, for the "blood
and irony" she had injected into the veins of her Virginians. Her courage and
example have helped to make it possible for the history of Virginia to be so well
written.

The dawn of the Age of Ellen Glasgow came in 1971 when Julius R. Raper
published his *Without Shelter: The Early Career of Ellen Glasgow*.[4] Building on the
insights and discoveries of his predecessors in Glasgow studies, Raper attempted,
with a good measure of success, to integrate biographical detail with the novelist's
artistic accomplishment. Noting that the "central drama" of Glasgow's early career
had been to break free of the restraints of being Southern, a lady, a Virginian, and
of holding a particular religious or political viewpoint, he took her image of herself as a philosopher more seriously than did earlier critics. Raper contends, and I
think correctly, that Glasgow retained some peculiar form of Jeffersonian agrarianism as well as the Scots-Irish fortitude she called "a vein of iron," but she was
also deeply affected, as she herself said, by Darwinian philosophy.[5] He thus took
up the gauntlet thrown down by C. Vann Woodward and explained Glasgow's
rebellion despite her sheltered Richmond rose garden existence.

Ellen and Rebe Glasgow flank the front portico of their birthplace, at the corner of First and Cary Streets in Richmond's Monroe Ward neighborhood.

Following in the steps of Woodward, New South historians have always thought that Ellen Glasgow is too valuable to be surrendered entirely to the literary critics. Thus, in 1972, one of them—the present author—produced a full biography entitled *Ellen Glasgow and the Woman Within*.[6] It remains my belief that both Ellen Glasgow and C. Vann Woodward were indeed correct about the ways class, race, gender, and power relations evolved in the New South.

Like so many other Southerners, place and history were extremely important to Ellen Glasgow. She was rooted in Richmond, in Virginia, in the South, at a time when painful but creative change was taking place after the Civil War and Reconstruction. She belonged to a place that was and is conscious of its history. After all, living in a state that began as the first permanent English colony in North America and residing in a city that became the capital of the Confederacy imposes a certain burden of knowledge and accumulated experience on generation after generation. In her effort to escape her heritage and her private demons through Darwinian science and short flights to the North and the literary world of England, Ellen Glasgow became much like Brer Rabbit kicking and flailing at the tar baby: The more she kicked and flailed and butted her head against her own history, the more she became stuck in it. The happy result is a body of fine novels set in Virginia, a dynamic life that still instructs and inspires us, and a chapter of her own in the history books.

To contribute to that chapter I worked as I was told historians must, examining the primary evidence, assimilating the secondary sources, and treading insofar as possible where the subject once trod. After devouring the novelist's own writings and reading everything I could find about her in the Duke University Library, I took to the road. In Charlottesville I read her incoming correspondence, and in Baltimore, Washington, New York City, New Haven, and Boston, I read her letters. I drove through the glorious White Mountains of New Hampshire in the fall, as she had done, and in Maine I talked to her doctor and to others who had known her. By then, since winter was setting in, I headed for Florida and the treasure of notes on interviews with her contemporaries that Marjorie Kinnan Rawlings had collected. Now I thought I was sufficiently prepared for my encampment at Richmond.

Richmond welcomed me with grace and good manners. At the Henrico County courthouse I read the Glasgow family wills. I mourned at the grave of Miss Ellen in Hollywood Cemetery. I walked softly among the ghosts of One West Main Street. I traveled the streets that were familiar to me from her novels. In antique shops and churches and elegant condominiums I listened and took notes as people told me about one of their city's most famous citizens.

The highlight of my Richmond adventure came one memorable afternoon when Mrs. James Branch Cabell invited me to a cocktail party at her home on

Ellen Glasgow's garden at One West Main, photographed by Frances Benjamin Johnston in the 1930s. Jeremy's headstone is visible among the pansies close to the house.

Glasgow's headstone at Hollywood Cemetery is inscribed, "Tomorrow to fresh woods and pastures new," from Milton's *Lycidas*.

Monument Avenue, where she had assembled friends and relatives of the late novelist. I learned marvelous and contradictory things about Ellen Glasgow. I remember that when Mrs. Cabell introduced me to a Virginia gentleman as a student from North Carolina, he recoiled. Sensing the situation, she quickly said, "He is a student in North Carolina. He's from South Carolina." "Well, that's so much better," came the gentleman's reply. And how remarkable it was to have Ballard Cabell, the son of James Branch, give me a boy's memory of Miss Ellen and of her dogs. I also remember Mrs. Cabell's parting words to me at the door of her Victorian home. "When you get to the end of the walkway," she said, "please be sure to close the gate, because there are little dogs in the neighborhood who are not named Jeremy." That was more than twenty-five years ago, and I still do not remember whether or not I closed that gate!

Safely back in Durham, I attempted to bring it all together. I decided that both Ellen Glasgow and C. Vann Woodward were correct. There was indeed a New South, and Ellen Glasgow had told its story as well in her novels as Woodward did in his history. Maybe she did it better. How could we understand the New South if Ellen Glasgow had not given it to us, alive and full of blood and irony in her pioneering fiction? How could we have understood what the ending of slavery meant if Ellen Glasgow had not given us Uncle Ish in *The Voice of the People* (1900) who said, "freedom, it are a moughty good thing"; or Parry Clay, the young black man in the Richmond of *In This Our Life* (1941) who wanted to become a lawyer but had his spirit broken by a false charge of hit-and-run driving[7]?

Could we have understood the male of the species and how he coped with the new era without Cyrus Treadwell, the hero of *Virginia* (1913), who improved his station by marrying an aristocrat but subordinated all human compassion to his driving ambition to rebuild the tobacco industry and control the railroad in

Petersburg[8]? Surely the decline of the aristocracy would remain in obscurity had not Glasgow given us Judge Gamaliel Bland Honeywell, "a great lawyer but a perfect fool" in *The Romantic Comedians* (1926), who placed the Episcopal Church, the Democratic Party, and the allure of young women all on the same pedestal.[9] The mysteries of life and of history, as Ellen Glasgow filtered them through the memory of eighty-three-year-old General Archbald in *The Sheltered Life* (1932), her best character, show us that the spirit of humanity transcends history.

What the New South meant to women has never been told better than by Ellen Glasgow. Her novels are populated with females, both black and white, who changed with the times as well as those who did not. The black conjure woman, Aunt Mehitable Green, in *Barren Ground* (1925), and her granddaughter Fluvanna indicate that each new generation is a bit more free than the previous one. Few women of fiction can rival the stark accomplishments of the determined Dorinda Oakley in *Barren Ground*, a book with more irony than blood driving its plot. In case her readers had missed it in her earlier novels, with the publication of *They Stooped to Folly: A Comedy of Morals* (1929), Ellen Glasgow nailed her theses about women and their rights to the door of the capitol of the old Confederacy. Three generations of "ruined" women parade through those pages, revealing what H. L. Mencken delighted in calling "the Southern attitude toward fornication."[10] There is the old maid Agatha Littlepage, who was ruined just because a suitor jilted her half a century earlier; the middle-aged widow Mrs. Dalrymple, of good birth but easy virtue, who redeemed her reputation by rendering service to the Red Cross during World War I; and the twentieth-century girl Milly Burden, who experienced little regret or social disgrace as the mother of an illegitimate baby. The most tragic figures of the New South were the Virginia Pendletons and the Eva Birdsongs who were so bound by tradition that they could not function in the twentieth century. The pain and the promise of change was much to be preferred, according to Glasgow, over clinging to a system that no longer worked.

Last, and certainly not least, how could we understand the New South if Ellen Glasgow had not given us herself? She lived on Main Street in Richmond, she was heiress to all the traditions of the Old South, and she labored with her unique psyche and her physical limitations. Yet her mind was so alive that she dissected the history of her region, her own personality, and the thinking of her favorite philosophers to create a set of novels that integrated history with life and literature. The complexities of the human soul and of the history of her region she did not destroy. She celebrated them, made them comprehensible, and gave them blood and words in the persons of Uncle Ish and Dorinda and General Archbald and Ellen herself.

To shelve Ellen Glasgow as nothing more than the first Southern realist, a social historian of Virginia, would not do her justice. Her fiction remains full of

A scene illustrating Glasgow's *Romantic Comedians* by Virginia artist J. J. Lankes conveys the author's familiar theme of the Old South's meeting the New.

truth. Her life and her work whet the appetites of biographers, critics, writers, and historians. New books and articles about her appear almost every year. Notable recent additions to the Glasgow bookshelf include Pamela R. Matthews's *Ellen Glasgow and a Woman's Traditions* (1994), editor Dorothy Scura's *Ellen Glasgow: New Perspectives* (1995), and Susan Goodman's *Ellen Glasgow: A Biography* (1998).[11] Ellen Glasgow has her own newsletter. The Virginia Writers Club celebrated its seventy-fifth anniversary with a conference in her honor.

A 1992 history of the New South, *The Promise of the New South: Life After Reconstruction*, by Edward L. Ayers, a student of C. Vann Woodward, assigns Glasgow a preeminent place in the people's history of the South.[12] He gives her ten pages and a photograph. I think that he could not have written such a fine history had he not been possessed of the wisdom to give so many of its pages to Ellen Glasgow, of Richmond, Virginia.

The challenge given to us by Vann Woodward to explain Glasgow is a continuing one. Those who take it up will discover a truth not generally known half a century ago. And that truth is this: Ellen Glasgow has come a long way from being a chronicler of Virginia in the New South to a vital resident herself in the pages of its history. I believe that she has arrived in those pages to stay.

THREE

Ellen Glasgow's Civil War Richmond in *The Battle-Ground*

DOROTHY M. SCURA

In his history of Confederate Richmond, Emory Thomas explains that through sacrifice the capital city came to "feel herself the very embodiment of the Confederacy."[1] More than a century and a quarter after Appomattox, Richmond still bears countless reminders of the Civil War. Statues of Jefferson Davis, Robert E. Lee, Stonewall Jackson, J. E. B. Stuart, and Matthew Fontaine Maury line Monument Avenue, the most beautiful street in the city. Stained-glass windows memorialize Lee and Davis in Saint Paul's Episcopal Church, still referred to as the Cathedral of the Confederacy. The Lee Bridge joins North and South Richmond. More than 35,000 Confederate soldiers lie in Oakwood and Hollywood Cemeteries; among those in Hollywood are twenty-two generals. The Museum of the Confederacy, Jefferson Davis's home during the war years, holds countless Civil War mementos, including a military jacket stained with Stonewall Jackson's blood.

In addition to these palpable reminders of the war, there is a vast literature on the subject that includes novels, diaries, memoirs, and histories. Among these volumes are a 1902 novel, *The Battle-Ground*, by Virginia's most distinguished novelist, Ellen Glasgow; a journal—generally considered to be the best diary of the period—kept by the South Carolinian Mary Chesnut during the war years, much of which she spent in Richmond; the 1971 standard historical study by Emory Thomas of *The Confederate State of Richmond*; and a massive three-volume work, published between 1958 and 1974, *The Civil War: A Narrative*, by the novelist Shelby Foote, who explains that in writing of the war, he has accepted the "historian's standards without his paraphernalia" and "employed the novelist's methods without his license."[2]

An analysis of Glasgow's treatment of Richmond during the Civil War compared with that of a historian, a diarist, and a novelist-historian will show how she dealt with the facts in transposing reality into fiction. It will also show that Glasgow, who necessarily had to be selective in the depiction of detail, did not compromise fidelity to fact in her portrayal of Civil War Richmond.

Published when she was twenty-nine years old, *The Battle-Ground* is Glasgow's fourth novel. Born in Richmond eight years after the close of the Civil War, she grew up hearing about the wartime from members of her family and from her governess, Virginia Rawlings. In her autobiography, *The Woman Within*, Glasgow recounts the story of General David Hunter's burning of Mount Joy, her grandaunt's ancestral home in the Valley of Virginia. Given an hour to remove her belongings, Glasgow's aunt chose to save family portraits.[3] This house provided the name of the protagonist, Dan Montjoy, in *The Battle-Ground*, and Dan's grandparents saved only a portrait of the beauty of the family, Aunt Emmeline, when their home was burned by Union troops. Thus, Glasgow adapted family experiences in her fiction about the war.

Not only did she include incidents from actual participants, but Glasgow also read diaries, letters, and copies of three newspapers printed between 1860 and 1865—the *Richmond Enquirer*, the *Richmond Examiner*, and the *New York Herald*— and she visited the Valley of Virginia, going over all of the scenes of the novel. In her research, as she later explained, she was "collecting impressions, rather than facts." Glasgow designed her novel to be the "chronicle of two neighbouring families," the Amblers, including the heroine Betty Ambler, and the Lightfoots, grandparents of the hero Dandridge Montjoy.[4]

Glasgow explained in *A Certain Measure* that she consciously rejected the sentimental costume romances that purported to tell the story of the 1860s and from the beginning of her career considered herself a writer in "solitary revolt against the formal, the false, the affected, the sentimental, and the pretentious, in Southern writing." She noted, however, that "one cannot approach the Confederacy without touching the very heart of romantic tradition." She attempted in *The Battle-Ground* "to portray the last stand in Virginia of the aristocratic tradition . . . shallow-rooted at best, since, for all its charm and its good will, the way of living depended, not upon its own creative strength, but upon the enforced servitude of an alien race." Glasgow saw the Confederacy as "the expiring gesture of chivalry."[5]

Glasgow considered the whole body of her work to be "in the more freely interpretative form of fiction, a social history of Virginia" from 1850 to 1939.[6]

A girlish Ellen Glasgow poses for a publicity photograph for her 1902 novel, *The Battle-Ground*.

The Battle-Ground is, therefore, the first book in this chronology, covering the earliest years from 1850 to 1865. Because she defined the controlling theme in her work as the decline of the Virginia aristocracy and the rise of the middle class, *The Battle-Ground* appropriately begins her long story of Virginia by depicting what she saw as the "last stand" of the landowning old order.

The Battle-Ground is a big novel, more than 500 pages long, divided into four books, two taking place before the war and two during the war. The plot focuses on two families: the Amblers of Uplands and their daughters Betty and Virginia, and the Lightfoots of Chericoke and their grandnephew Champe and their grandson Dan Montjoy. The novel yokes together a romance that takes place in the happy, well-ordered days before the war and a realistic account of the terrible hardships of the war experienced primarily by Dan as an infantryman but also by those at home.

The first book, entitled "The Golden Years," tells of the growing-up years of the young people, and the second book, "Young Blood," opens with a great Christmas party at Chericoke, the obligatory social occasion in the plantation novel that depicts the grace and elegance of the antebellum aristocratic way of life. Although this half of the book appears to be a traditional romance, Glasgow subtly undercuts many of the romantic elements. Brown-haired Virginia Ambler is the perfect Southern lady, but the heroine is red-headed Betty Ambler, who does not conform to the model of behavior exemplified by her sister and her mother. When Betty is thirteen and must hem tablecloths, she "would weep until her needle rusted."[7]

Hanging on the parlor wall at Chericoke is the portrait of Great-aunt Emmeline, "the beauty and belle of two continents," who had danced with General Washington. Emmeline had married a man for love, one who had neither money nor fame, and refused an English earl who had both. She had written with her diamond ring on the window pane "Love is best."[8] Set against the image of this household goddess is the life of Jane Lightfoot, the Major's daughter and Dan's mother, who had eloped with her great love, Jack Montjoy. Her miserable life at the hands of Montjoy, who physically abused her, ended in death at an early age.

The account of the war years, which begins in the third book, entitled "The School of War," is realistic. Although Dan participates in the action from First Manassas to Appomattox, the focus is on an infantryman's experience, his perceptions, the sight and sound and smell of battle. Dan suffers from aching limbs, painful feet, chilling cold, and intense hunger. As he experiences life in the military, the women at home suffer the privations and losses of civilians during wartime.

When the war is over after four years, Dan is left with a "wrecked body and blighted mind," with "maimed and trembling hands, and limbs weakened by starvation as by long fever," his youth wasted, his energy sapped: "and at last he saw himself burned out like the battle-fields, where the armies had closed and opened, leaving an impoverished and ruined soil." He comes to realize that the army was not the worst he had to face but rather "what came afterward, this sense of utter failure and the attempt to shape one's self to brutal necessity." For the future he could see "only a terrible patience," and to replace "the old generous existence, he must from this day forth wring the daily bread of those he loved, with maimed hands from a wasted soil." He comes home to find the hills unchanged, but his house, Chericoke, in ashes and himself "a beggar, a failure, a wreck."[9]

Betty—having lost her father, sister, and brother-in-law in the war—is in control of both farms, has matured with her hardships, and has actually thrived with her great responsibilities. When the war ends, she is healthy and energetic, ready to face the future, while Dan is exhausted, maimed, and physically "burned out."[10] Betty and Dan will marry, and they will begin again, but the happy ending is modified by the destruction of their old comfortable world and the bleak future they face.

The novel is briefly set in Richmond in the spring and early summer of 1862. Two chapters, only twenty pages, allow Glasgow to characterize the capital of the Confederacy and to advance her plot. She brings to Richmond several characters—principally Virginia Ambler Morson, her husband Jack, and Dan Montjoy. One chapter focuses on Virginia and depicts her death along with that of her unborn child. The second chapter allows Dan Montjoy to come to terms with the memory of his long-estranged father.

In the chapter entitled "The Altar of the War God," Virginia and her child are the human sacrifices taken on the hellish "altar" of the capital of the Confederacy. Because Virginia is the very image of her mother, and both women are the embodiment of the beautiful, gentle lady of the aristocracy, Virginia's death suggests that this figure is too fragile mentally and physically to survive the demands of the war.

Glasgow's irony is evident in her treatment of the suffering and death of the innocent Virginia. The narrator explains about Virginia that "there was in her heart an unquestioning, childlike trust in the God of battles—sooner or later he would declare for the Confederacy and until then—well, there was always General Lee to stand between."[11] Virginia's naive faith in the God of Battles and in General Lee is misplaced; neither can save her from destruction on the very altar of the God of War.

Also ironic is Glasgow's use of the magnolia, the beautiful, white, sweet-smelling flower so often connected to Southern romances. A large magnolia tree stands next to the piazza at the back of Virginia's house, and she places a rustic bench and a flower garden under this tree. A setting designed to replicate in a small way her home, Uplands, in the Valley of Virginia, the spot contrasts with the back garden that features vegetables rather than flowers, and, especially, with the view from her front window, which reveals the busy passing parade that is the overcrowded city of Richmond. But the scent of the magnolia becomes connected with the heat, clamor, and dust of the city, and Virginia sickens of the smell. She is pleased when a rainstorm sends the petals to the ground, but new blossoms open, and she associates their perfume with the sound of cannons. On the night of her death when her mind wanders in a delirium, the "odour of the magnolia filled her nostrils" reminding her of the "scorching dust" and "the noise that would not stop." Thus, the flower's scent is intermingled with the sound and heat of war as Glasgow makes it a symbol not of romance, but of death.[12]

In the chapter "The Montjoy Blood Again," Dan Montjoy's blood is shed at Malvern Hill, and there is blood both on the battlefield and in the warehouse that serves as a hospital. A surgeon, getting some air at the window near where Dan lay, tells him of the bravery of a patient who has just died. The man had both legs removed surgically, but he never cried out. When Dan realizes that the man, who had served as a scout with Jeb Stuart, is his father, he feels first "a wave of repulsion" for the man he had always regarded as "a braggart and a bully," but then he acknowledges his father's bravery and loses "his old boyish shame of the Montjoy blood." The narrator explains: "With the instinct of his race to glorify physical courage, he had seen the shadow of his boyhood loom from the petty into the gigantic. Jack Montjoy may have been a scoundrel,—doubtless he was one,—but, with all his misdeeds on his shoulders, he had lived pure game to the end."[13] And the chapter closes with more Montjoy blood as Dan feels faint at the onset of fresh bleeding, but suppresses his impulse to groan as he remembers his father's stoic silence.

Glasgow's depiction of the city of Richmond in the spring and early summer of 1862 features a careful selection of revealing details. In the first chapter she describes the life of a cavalry officer's wife and in the second the experience of a wounded infantryman. When Virginia, Jack, and Mammy Riah arrive in Richmond to board in the house of a widow with three sons dead in the war and three others away fighting, they find the streets crowded, food expensive, and houses wearing a "festive air." While her husband is in Richmond, Virginia feels "an almost feverish gayety," and attends parties "where the women wore last year's dresses, and the wit served for refreshment." Her beauty is appreciated and her hairstyle copied; verses about her are published in the newspaper and reprinted in England. Gentlemen notice her "with warming eyes" as she walks home from church. When her husband goes to battle, however, the pregnant Virginia stays home and sews for her baby. Her landlady visits occasionally and explains that she has lost three sons and sent the other three to fight. With the "fire of the South" burning "in her veins," she spends her days caring for the sick and wounded soldiers.[14] As Virginia looks out her front window, she sees the "whole overcrowded city passing through sun and shadow":

> Sometimes distinguished strangers would go by, men from the far South in black broadcloth and slouch hats; then the President, slim and erect and very grave, riding his favourite horse to one of the encampments near the city; and then a noted beauty from another state, her chin lifted above the ribbons of her bonnet, a smile tucked in the red corners of her lips. Following there would surge by the same eager, staring throng—men too old to fight who had lost their work; women whose husbands fought in the trenches for the money that would hardly buy a sack of flour; soldiers from one of the many camps; noisy little boys with tin whistles; silent little girls waving Confederate flags.[15]

Then, too, there were battalions of soldiers "marching to the front," and the "single soldier riding, with muffled drums, to his grave in Hollywood." The contrast of "quick step" and "slow gait of the riderless horse," of "wild cheers" and "silence," of flying flag and "banners furled with crepe," made Virginia realize that "life and death walked on within each other's shadow." Always there were the wounded—in ambulances, on litters, in market wagons, walking—and no room left for them in the makeshift hospitals. And then a clergyman gives Virginia the false report that her husband has been wounded, and she goes out into the "fur-

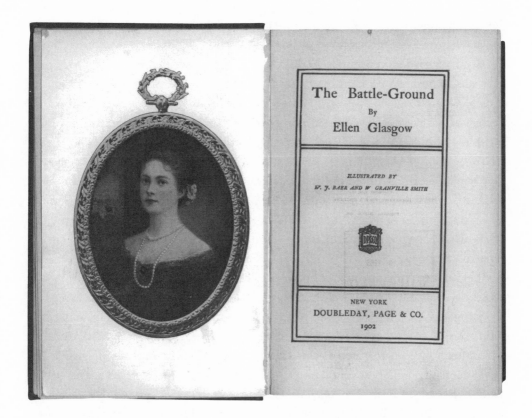

The title page for the first edition of *The Battle-Ground* features a portrait of the character Betty.

nace" of a city, accompanied by Mammy Riah, to search fruitlessly for him. Returning home from the "rude hospitals" with "the memory of open wounds and red hands of the surgeons," she sinks into delirium and dies with her unborn child.[16] A month later Dan is brought wounded to Richmond in a dump cart. Big Abel, Dan's devoted slave who had accompanied him to war, rescues him under fire, protected only by a bucket on his head, and carries him from the cornfield at Malvern Hill where he lay with a rifle ball through his leg and with fingers missing from one hand. Big Abel saves his life—finding him, struggling to get him in a vehicle, reaching a hospital only after a three-hour search in Richmond. That makeshift hospital is hot, full of flies, and short of supplies, the men tended by women and children.

Thus, Glasgow depicted wartime Richmond in a small part of her only novel that focused on the Civil War. When that novel was published in 1902, it received positive reviews. William Payne of *Dial* called it one of the best Civil War novels ever written; the reviewer for *Athenaeum* compared it to Stephen Crane's "vividly impressionistic work"; *British Weekly* praised the war scenes and pointed out that the "campaigns as seen from the private's point of view, with all their blood, rags, and starvation, were probably never better described."[17]

Two later critics were not as enthusiastic in their assessment of the book. For example, Edmund Wilson, in his 1962 work, *Patriotic Gore: Studies in the Literature of the American Civil War,* ignored Glasgow, concentrating on only four fiction writers of the postwar South—Albion Tourgeé, George W. Cable, Kate Chopin, and Thomas Nelson Page. Daniel Aaron, in another general study in 1973, *The Unwritten War: American Writers and the Civil War,* dismissed *The Battle-Ground* as an "apprentice work," pointed out that Glasgow later "acquired a deeper understanding, compassionate and ironic, of the War's significance," and placed her in a transition position between "the period of mindless commemoration" and the "critical school of Southern writing"—in other words, between Thomas Nelson Page and Allen Tate.[18]

Sheldon Van Auken, however, in an article in *Journal of Southern History* (1948), noted that 378 historical novels had been published in this country between 1895 and 1912. Of these 378, Van Auken selected 72 novels, based on popularity and inclusion in histories of American literature, for further study. Twelve Southern authors were represented in this sample, and Van Auken ranked Glasgow's *The Battle-Ground* as "the best single book . . . on the war, both as a novel and as social history." Ernest Leisy, in *The American Historical Novel* (1950), placed *The Battle-Ground* with novels that "really fuse history and life"; he called it "the first realistic treatment of the war from the Southern point of view." Robert A. Lively, who studied 512 novels for *Fiction Fights the Civil War* (1957), included Glasgow's novel in a list of the fifteen "best Civil War novels" along with works by Cable, Crane, Faulkner, and Tate.[19]

In a lengthy critical discussion of the work, C. Hugh Holman called it a novel of manners, one in which the author "has been interested primarily in the social change that occurred as a result of the Civil War," and he placed it in the context of all her work. Holman pointed out that Glasgow's depiction of Dan Montjoy's confused and bewildered "initiation into the realities of war" at First Manassas and in the enforced march to Romney "have some of the characteristics of an impressionistic painting." Frederick P. W. McDowell praised Glasgow's treatment of the "malignant power" of war and proposed that her portrait of Richmond was more successful than her rendition of the military campaigns.[20]

In a recent appraisal of *The Battle-Ground,* R. H. W. Dillard calls the novel rich and "complex." He argues that Glasgow deliberately appropriated the traditional form of the historical novel, which ordinarily romanticizes and idealizes the Old Order, to "analyze and subvert the values of that very order, and in particular to reveal the sources and transformations of power within the Old Order as it passed through the Civil War." After the war, according to Dillard, the old ruling class was still supported by the "awesome force" of "Southern chivalry and the myths of the Old Order" that "continued to empower the old ruling class at the expense of blacks, poor whites, and women."[21]

Glasgow's fictional treatment of Richmond in *The Battle-Ground* is condensed, and it is realistic, undercutting romantic myths about the war. Turning to other sources—Mary Chesnut's record, Emory Thomas's historical account, and Shelby Foote's 3,000-page narrative of the war—we can verify the accuracy of Glasgow's fictional account. We can also find much material not included by Glasgow, whose portrayal was necessarily selective.

Mary Chesnut was an intelligent, observant, and insightful recorder of the Civil War years. Her record of those years has been published in four editions, but this paper draws primarily on *The Private Mary Chesnut*, an edition of her original diary entries, which survive only for the years of 1861 and 1865, and also on *Mary Chesnut's Civil War,* which reprints Chesnut's rewriting of the original diary some two decades after the war.[22] Chesnut's husband held important positions with the Confederacy during the war, eventually as a brigadier general, and she was a member of the small "public-spirited and well-educated" ruling class, as Edmund Wilson explained. Wilson based his evaluation on a reading of a poor early edition—heavily edited and cut—of Chesnut's rewriting of the journal in the 1880s. In *Patriotic Gore*, he called her diary an "extraordinary document," "a masterpiece," and he praised "the brilliant journal of Mary Chesnut, so much more imaginative and revealing than most of the fiction inspired by the war." Her biographer, Elizabeth Muhlenfeld, termed Chesnut "the preeminent writer of the Confederacy."[23]

Chesnut's record of the Civil War era provides documentation for Glasgow's description of Richmond. Chesnut writes of the hot Richmond summer, of overcrowding, of soldiers marching through the city, of sick and wounded soldiers, of hospitals, and of the muffled drums of funerals. In the summer of 1861, she writes, "Saw *hundred & fifteen* sick soldiers yesterday—the saddest sight these poor eyes have ever encountered. . . . I am to do all I can to help them." In August she tells of visiting all day in hospitals, one in which "I saw there, dirt & discomfort & bad smells enough [for] the stoutest man." She notes on 13 August 1861, that "Nine funerals passed here on Sunday."[24] In December 1863, some eighteen months after Glasgow's characters were in the city, Chesnut reports that a barrel of flour cost $115, and that she had paid $75 for a little tea and sugar.[25]

Abounding with references to flirtations and romances, Chesnut's journal documents the attention paid by men to such Confederate beauties as Hetty Cary and Sally Buchanan "Buck" Preston. Her account of the rector of Saint Paul's being summoned from a church service by his distraught wife after she had been erroneously informed that their son was at the railroad station in a coffin is reminiscent of Virginia's being mistakenly informed by a clergyman that her husband had been wounded in battle.[26] A darkly comic story contrasts with Glasgow's account of Big Abel's heroic rescue of Dan Montjoy at Malvern Hill: Chesnut tells in July 1861 of a black servant dashing onto the battlefield to "take his Master a tin pan filled with rice & ham, screaming, 'Make haste and *eat*. You must be *tired* & hungry, Massa.'"[27] Chesnut's poignant account of the death on Christmas Eve 1863, of the twenty-two-year-old Charlotte Wickham Lee and her baby while her husband, William Henry Fitzhugh "Rooney" Lee, the son of Robert E. Lee, was a war prisoner is reminiscent of Virginia's and her child's death when her husband was in battle. Chesnut wrote that "General Lee had tears in his eyes when he spoke of his daughter-in-law just dead."[28]

Although Chesnut's journal supports the accuracy of Glasgow's fiction, her account includes very much more than Glasgow's. Those "distinguished strangers" in "black broadcloth and slouch hats," the erect, slim, grave president, and the "noted" beauties who passed by Virginia's window were all members of Mary Chesnut's social circle. Her friendship, for example, with the Jefferson Davises and the Robert E. Lees, as well as others in important positions in the Confederate government, opened the world of society, the military, and the government to her observant eyes. Her opposition to slavery because it undermines the morality of white men as well as her linking of slavery with the institution of marriage are ideas that make her an extraordinary thinker and observer of her time. On 18 March 1861, she writes:

> I wonder if it be a sin to think slavery a curse to any land. Sumner said not one word of this hated institution which is not true. Men & women are punished when their masters & mistresses are brutes & not when they do wrong—& then we live surrounded by prostitutes. An abandoned woman is sent out of any decent house elsewhere. Who thinks any worse of a Negro or Mulatto woman for being a thing we can't name. God forgive *us*, but ours is a *monstrous* system & wrong & iniquity.[29]

Although Glasgow's novel includes subtle and ironic views against slavery, she did not mention miscegenation in this Civil War novel. Not until her 1913 novel *Virginia* did she depict the results of the relationship of a white man and a black woman, and she chose to make perhaps her worst villain, the industrialist Cyrus Treadwell, the indifferent father of a mulatto son.

Emory Thomas, the historian, also confirms Glasgow's picture of wartime Richmond. Like Mary Chesnut, he includes much more in his account than did the novelist. Thomas documents the crowded condition of the city, the difficulty in finding rooms to rent, the high prices of food. He writes of the omnipresence of soldiers and of the casualties that hit the city in three waves after a battle—the walking wounded, the dead, and then the seriously wounded. He tells of the generosity of Richmonders in setting up hospitals all over the city.

He quotes the French consul as calling the city "a hell" during the spring of 1862 when Glasgow's characters were there. General George B. McClellan's forces threatened the city, and Richmond was not in a proper state of defense. Jefferson Davis declared martial law, and a conscription of men aged eighteen to thirty-five was instituted. The president's family moved to North Carolina, and War Department records were removed from the city. After Richmond's baptism of fire at Seven Pines—the battle in which Glasgow's Jack Morson was fighting when Virginia died—ambulances came into Richmond for five days bringing 5,000 wounded soldiers who filled the sixteen hospitals. A month later, on 1 July, the retreating Union army beat off the Southern charge at Malvern Hill—where Glasgow's Dan Montjoy was wounded. On 26 June, McClellan had been a mere four miles from Richmond, but 1 July ended with his army twenty-five miles away at Harrison's Landing. The capital was safe, but July 1862 was an "awesome month," according to Thomas.[30] Dead soldiers would swell and burst their coffins before the gravediggers could get them buried. Glasgow chose a critical and appropriate time for setting two chapters in the city of Richmond, a time when her characterization of it as a hellish place fit the facts.

Just as Chesnut depicts the social life of Richmond during the war in far more detail than Glasgow's fictional version, there was, as Thomas reveals, an underside of the capital that did not find its way into Glasgow's fiction. Thomas quotes a description of the city as a "true mecca of prostitutes" with venereal diseases widespread. He quotes the *Richmond Examiner* in calling Richmond a "bloated metropolis of vice" with much lawlessness, gambling, and thieving.[31]

In telling the story of wartime Richmond, the historian Thomas draws on available primary and secondary sources including Mary Chesnut's work and two of the Richmond newspapers that Glasgow used. His narrative is necessarily comprehensive and carefully documented, rich with dates and statistics, a contrast to Glasgow's impressionistic approach to the material.

Shelby Foote not only draws a comprehensive view of Richmond, but also creates a panoramic narrative of the war itself. He calls on a wide range of sources, including fifty volumes of official records from the war, telling the whole story from both Union and Confederate points of view from Manassas to Appomattox. His focus—primarily on the battlefields, the officers, and the fighting troops—contrasts with Glasgow's. In her account the hero and officer Dan

Montjoy takes center stage on the battlefield, but Foote takes the point of view of the unsung infantrymen. The reader knows the foot soldiers' confusion, exhaustion, pain, and hunger intimately. Foote's work sheds light and detail on Glasgow's novel by telling what was happening militarily.

Foote recounts the full story of each of the battles that touch the lives of Glasgow's characters while they are in Richmond. Seven Pines, the battle in which Jack Morson was engaged while his wife and child were dying, is called by Foote "a Donnybrook of a battle" and "unquestionably the worst-conducted large-scale conflict in a war that afforded many rivals for that distinction." It was "a military nightmare." He counts 6,134 Confederates dead or wounded.[32]

The Battle of Malvern Hill, where Dan Montjoy was wounded, was also described by Foote. The battle took place on a wheatfield with McClellan's troops placed 150 feet above the Confederates. "It was not war," Foote quotes Confederate general Daniel Harvey Hill as saying, "it was murder." Foote uses the account of an unidentified Union cavalry colonel to describe the battlefield where Big Abel rescues Dan Montjoy: "Down there on the lower slope, the bodies of five thousand gray-clad soldiers were woven into a carpet of cold or agonized flesh. 'A third of them were dead or dying, . . . but enough of them were alive and moving to give the field a singular crawling effect.'"[33] The casualties for seven days of fighting totaled 36,463 Americans, killed, wounded, and captured. Union troops were driven from the "gates of Richmond," but the cost was high. An interesting detail added by Foote is that after the fierce battles that concluded on 31 June 1862, some soldiers from each side laid down their arms on the Fourth of July to meet together in an open field. According to a Confederate private, the men "gathered berries together and talked over the fight, traded tobacco and coffee and exchanged newspapers as peacefully and kindly as if they had not been engaged for the last seven days in butchering one another."[34]

Foote explained in a "Bibliographical Note" at the end of volume one of his narrative that

> the novelist and the historian are seeking the same thing: the truth—not a different truth: the same truth—only they reach it . . . by different routes. Whether the event took place in a world now gone to dust, preserved by documents and evaluated by scholarship, or in the imagination, preserved by memory and distilled by the creative process, they both want to tell us *how it was*: to re-create it, by their separate methods, and make it live again in the world around them.[35]

Foote is willing, then, to accept the truth of history as well as the truth of fiction; he would evaluate a work not on the basis of method, technique, and approach, but rather on the result in terms of its truthfulness in re-creating the past. Ellen Glasgow, on the other hand, had argued for the fiction writer's primacy in the search for the truth of the past: "From its rudimentary outlines and embryonic flutters in a firelit cave, the art of fiction has remained the most accurate mirror of the different stages in the pilgrimage of humanity."[36]

Analyzing Glasgow's depiction of a limited place and time during the great crucial event of both Southern literature and Southern history shows that the novelist had to be extremely selective in writing her account based on the demands of plot and point of view and space. In her brief story of Richmond in the spring of 1862, she does an excellent job of telling readers *how it was* for her characters. A comparison of her account to a sampling of other accounts in different genres suggests that the young novelist with limited historical resources chose an appropriate time during the war to bring some of her characters to the Confederate capital and that she selected valid details to characterize the setting. She produced a novel that is an apprentice work, but it is a work of fiction that is—in many respects—true to history.

FOUR

From Joan of Arc to Lucy Dare:
Ellen Glasgow on Southern Womanhood

PAMELA R. MATTHEWS

D uring her lifelong residence in Richmond, Virginia, Ellen Glasgow frequently assumed an insider's privilege and criticized her native South,
often for an uncongenial climate that had failed to nurture its women.[1]
In a 1913 *New York Times* interview, for example, she described the limits placed
on Southern women in the past and the prospects for the future. While she
acknowledged that Southern women's burdensome household responsibilities
before and after the Civil War in some ways prepared them for independence,
she also recognized the limited range of that preparation. If modern consciousness recognized that granting full personhood to women is nothing less than "an
obedience to the laws of growth," she remarked, in the previous generation a
Southern woman suffered her imposed dormancy with a "mind [that] lay fallow." In imagining those earlier lives, Glasgow was "horror-stricken at the loneliness and depression they must have endured." Women were captives of a
"condition which shrieks loudly enough, surely, for redress and remedy." Her
own generation's increasingly prominent image of women working together for
what Glasgow described as "feminist growth and unfolding" was to her "as
inspiring as a battle cry."[2]

Glasgow's comments on Southern women point to an overriding concern
that surfaced early and remained constant throughout her writing career: the traditions of womanhood available to her as a white, upper-middle-class, Southern

woman. Two of her most transparently Southern stories—one written in her youth and the other in her maturity—illustrate Glasgow's continued engagement with defining herself as Southern and female. The unpublished brief story, "A Modern Joan of Arc," was probably written during the late 1880s when Glasgow was in her teens.[3] "Dare's Gift" was written when Glasgow was in her mid-forties. First published in *Harper's Magazine* in 1917, "Dare's Gift" was included in *The Shadowy Third and Other Stories* (1923), the only volume of short stories Glasgow ever published; in Britain this was the title story. Despite the thirty-odd years that separates these stories, in both "A Modern Joan of Arc" and "Dare's Gift" female protagonists share qualities associated with the ideal of the Southern lady—sexual purity, self-sacrifice, inner strength masked by outward fragility.[4] Glasgow's youthful work, "A Modern Joan of Arc," is an exercise in recognizing that exalted female heroism, even if possible in the past, has limited use for modern Southern women (and, indeed, that exalted femininity is part of the problem rather than the solution). Her adult vision in "Dare's Gift" shares and extends the pessimism of the earlier story: The past actions of heroic women can even help to bind modern women into a cyclic pattern of powerlessness. Though both stories flirt with the possibility that female cooperation can empower women to reject male prescriptions for women's behavior, both also assert that the patriarchal power structure is too strong to circumvent completely. The lives of Joan of Arc and Lucy Dare do provide historical models of female strength and determination for the protagonists who look to them for guidance. But Joan and Lucy ultimately serve to emphasize the futility of those heroic qualities in an actual world gendered male.

Exploiting the opportunity provided Southern women by the Civil War to range outside their usual domestic sphere, Glasgow sets her two stories during wartime to suggest the potential for women's active public roles.[5] But the setting also highlights the split between public and private worlds that enables a structure where gender determines appropriate separate spaces. The title of her early Civil War story, "A Modern Joan of Arc," announces that the protagonist, a "dainty wee lassie" named Sally, represents modern possibilities for the heroism exhibited by her historical counterpart, Joan of Arc.[6] The bifurcated structure of "Dare's Gift," with the first section set in the present during World War I and the second in the past during the Civil War, allows Glasgow a double perspective as she examines both past and present opportunities for female agency. Both stories end by reinforcing the inevitability of separate spheres even while criticizing the attitudes and structures that make them possible.

In "A Modern Joan of Arc," Sally's story of female development turns on several themes—female role models, the confinements of domesticity, female power accessible by way of traditionally male pursuits, and the ultimate realization of

Glasgow at about the time she penned "A Modern Joan of Arc"

that power's failed possibility. Drawing on the late nineteenth century's preoccupation with the story of Joan of Arc as a woman's story, Glasgow simultaneously suggests Sally's unrealized potential and her, as yet unrecognized, limitation—her gray homespun dress is at once Joan's armor, her father's Confederate uniform, and her mother's beautiful gown. Intuitively understanding the social and sexual significance of costume, Sally, though proud of the homespun necessitated by wartime shortages, nevertheless knows what it signifies: "I can't fight 'em like I am," she thinks. "They wouldn't be 'fraid of a little girl in a short dress." She takes a sword and a "gray slouch hat" from the wall and sets out.[7] Conflating the power of Joan's armor and Sally's father's uniform with the powerlessness of the mother's dress, Glasgow reminds us that Sally's foray into the sphere of public action will take more than a change into the clothes of the woman warrior.

When Sally, worn out and seated by the side of the road, meets the Union soldiers she had sought, her original plan to "scare them awfully" in imitation of Joan of Arc, fails pitifully as, frightened and trembling, she announces in a "childish treble" that the soldiers are "bad" and "must go 'way."[8] Sally's verbal footstomping elicits not fear but pity from her adversaries. An officer tenderly picks her up; she falls asleep on his shoulder; he carries her home to her mother. On one hand, the scene enacts a caring, surrogate father's gentle understanding; on the other, it describes female powerlessness in the face of masculine authority. The natural order is presumably restored when Sally, safe in her domestic space once more—thanks to the heroics of "this kind gentleman," as her mother says— "sedately" offers her hand to the officer and "politely" thanks him "for not burnin'" her.[9]

But, like Joan, Sally *is* burned, though hers is a metaphorical stake rather than a literal one. Near the end of the story, when Sally confronts the soldiers, she stands bravely, just as the actual Joan of Arc is said to have stood against her accusers:

> There, bathed in the sunset light that flashed over her like liquid fire, stood a tiny girl, a huge sword in her baby hands. An old slouch hat fell over her sunny curls and her coarse frock was red with dust.[10]

The sun's rays bathing her like "liquid fire," her "sunny curls," her now "red" dress—the picture reinforces the resemblance between Sally's fate and that of her namesake, but with an important difference. Joan of Arc's burning testifies to the seriousness with which her enemies regarded her, while Sally's testifies to the ease with which her enemies dismiss her as inconsequential. In the failure of Sally's mission and the necessity of her return to a domestic life of passive waiting, Glasgow suggests that Sally, like other women, is metaphorically burned as she is sacrificed to a cultural order that relegates her to a woman's sphere, burned as her potential, heroic self is destroyed. Part of her growth to adult womanhood, Glasgow further implies, is dependent on her successful capitulation to the role others have already assigned to her. E. Stanly Godbold's assessment that the story's conclusion reaffirms Glasgow's belief that happy endings depend on a young girl's "assuming the gentle attitude expected of a young lady of Ellen Glasgow's class" misses the mark.[11] Glasgow's point is that the "gentle attitude expected" of women is precisely the problem in the first place. If the tradition of womanhood represented by Joan of Arc's exceptional heroism has limited modern usefulness, the tradition of renunciation represented in Sally's story is hardly a happy substitute.

By the time of "Dare's Gift," Glasgow represents Sally's restricted sphere as further circumscribed by language; consequently, the importance of women finding a voice to articulate their own experience becomes a central issue of the story. Language is a medium through which women potentially gain power, and the necessity of women's united efforts in telling their own stories is evident even across historical boundaries. Both sections of this two-part tale tell of women betraying the men they love. In Part I, Mildred Beckwith, while living in the Dare house, publicly exposes her husband's complicity in withholding information that implicates the company for which he is the legal counsel. Part II tells the story of Lucy Dare fifty years earlier. In her loyalty to the South, Lucy leads Confederate soldiers to her escaped Union lover; they kill him as he attempts to flee from her house, Dare's Gift. The parallel structure of "Dare's Gift" reproduces the identification between Mildred and Lucy even across the barrier of time as Mildred reenacts in the present the Civil War story of Lucy. But the women do not tell their own stories. Rather, they are encased in versions of them told by male narrators. Harold Beckwith's limited perspective is announced at the outset; nevertheless, he will tell the story that properly belongs to his wife, just as Dr. Lakeby later will tell the story that belongs to Mildred's precursor, Lucy Dare. Both women are inscribed in some male's version of their female experience.[12]

Harold Beckwith's unreliability as narrator, which is evident as the story opens, is even clearer in retrospect. From wondering a year after the events whether "the thing actually happened" to asserting that "every mystery" has its "rational explanation" ("I admit it readily!" he says) to believing with equal assurance that "the impossible really happened," Harold's Poe-esque vacillation from almost hysterical assertion to quavering doubt destabilizes the narrative and seriously undercuts his ability even to tell his own story, let alone someone else's.[13] Harold states from the beginning that the story will be about Mildred's "erratic behaviour," as he calls it, at Dare's Gift, where she had been sent on the advice of her physician to recuperate from her "first nervous breakdown" (Harold's words) a year earlier.[14] Sequestered in the private, domestic sphere, away from her husband's public male world of corporate enterprise, Mildred will be reminded of her proper place and emotional health will follow.

Mildred clearly knows her place only too well, and it is more likely that adhering to it, not fleeing from it, has brought on any emotional instability that exists.[15] Her place is to be silent. Harold's friend Harrison says of Mildred's imagined response to Harold's proposal to move her to Dare's Gift: "As if Mildred's final word would be anything but a repetition of yours!" Harold takes this as testimony to the "perfect harmony" of their marriage rather than to the perfect subordination of his wife, which is described in terms of her silence. When Harold hears in the night the "thousand voices" spoken by "the old house" after he has told his legal secrets to Mildred, he does not realize that they are giving voice to his "quiet" wife; they are trying to tell the stories that she cannot. Significantly, when she betrays him, it is by telling *his* story to the newspaper; she reveals the damaging evidence he has covered up. The exposé, headlined in "one of the *Observer's* sensational 'war extras'" highlights the extent to which Harold and Mildred's relationship itself, like that of Lucy and her lover, has become a battle zone of sorts.[16] Instead of "news of the great French drive," he reads Mildred's version of his confessions to her, a declaration of war by Mildred on Harold through her appropriation of his story and through her public telling of it. When

Harold confronts Mildred, her words are Lucy Dare's words, as we discover in Part II. As Mildred repeats that she "had to do it" and would "do it again," Harold concludes that if she defied him and is without remorse, she must be crazy: "I knew," he says, "that Mildred's mind was unhinged."[17] The very thrust of Glasgow's story—structurally, narratively, and thematically—is the inherent insufficiency in the telling of women's stories by those other than themselves.

Part II moves to the Civil War scene of Lucy Dare's identical words as she similarly betrays her fiancé. Like Mildred, Lucy was assumed to be unhinged, and her male physician, Dr. Lakeby, narrates her story. Lakeby ascribes both Mildred's and Lucy's behavior to supernaturalism; his interpretation that the house is "saturated by a thought" and "haunted by treachery" denies the women their assertions of will.[18] Lakeby's assessment of what he sees as Lucy's "one instant of sacrifice" captures in essence the historical version of the silencing of women. Lucy, he says,

> has not even a name among us to-day. I doubt if you can find a child in the State who has ever heard of her—or a grown man, outside of this neighbourhood, who could give you a single fact of her history. . . . She is forgotten because the thing she did, though it might have made a Greek tragedy, was alien to the temperament of the people among whom she lived. . . . She missed her time; she is one of the mute inglorious heroines of history.[19]

FROM JOAN OF ARC TO LUCY DARE

Lucy is "mute," Mildred "quiet"; both are inscribed in and circumscribed by male versions of the stories they are not allowed to tell. Both, exiled from the public realm, have recourse only to the heroics of betrayal. Lucy literally still lives, and her continued existence confirms the story's sense that not much has changed from Lucy's story to Mildred's, from the conditions of a woman's life during the Civil War to World War I and the concurrent gendered battles waged in individual homes. Lucy, "never much of a talker," sits in her nursing home and knits mufflers for the war effort. In parodic reminder of a woman's natural place in a domestic sphere, Lucy comments: "It gives me something to do, this work for the Allies. It helps to pass the time, and in an Old Ladies' Home one has so much time on one's hands." No sentimental belief in the good of self-sacrifice keeps Lucy "knitting—knitting," but the boredom of a woman's life—of an old *lady's* life—literally confined in a domestic prison.[20]

But just as Lucy and Mildred in speaking identical words—"I had to do it. I would do it again"—indicate that at least *their* stories overlap in a unified female voice, so does Glasgow use her own heroines and her heroines' heroines as the material for rewriting the stories that they did not see as possible. In Glasgow's own act of writing fiction, that is, she reclaims for herself and other women the female heroism denied in the context of the fictional worlds of Sally and of Mildred Beckwith. Thus, even as Glasgow points out the limitations of historical role models for female behavior, she rewrites those limitations into a tradition of female cooperation that closes the gap between women as historical models, fictional characters, authors, and even readers.

In the 1913 *New York Times* interview, Glasgow called for women's united efforts, and her words strike a note of optimism in a world she saw, from as early as her teenage years, as uncongenial to women: "Even to this day we are not wholly out of the woods, though we have made an incredibly vast stride. The point of value is that we have realized our plight and have set ourselves to abolish it, and that we have stumbled on the important truth that co-operation is strength. That will lead us out of the wilderness."[21]

FIVE

Mining the *Vein of Iron:*
Ellen Glasgow's Later Communal Voice

HELEN FIDDYMENT LEVY

From the beginning, I had known that I was engaged upon a family chronicle, that I was studying, not a single character or group of characters alone, but the vital principle of survival, which has enabled races and individuals to withstand the destructive forces of nature and of civilization.[1]

Ellen Glasgow, *A Certain Measure*

Ellen Glasgow's *Vein of Iron* (1935) emerged from the same era and region as William Faulkner's *Light in August* (1932), Thomas Wolfe's *Look Homeward, Angel* (1929), James Agee's *Death in the Family* (published posthumously in 1956, but composed in the 1930s), and Robert Penn Warren's *All the King's Men* (1946). Those books by male authors have long been considered canonical works of modern Southern literature; Glasgow, however, has suffered a certain measure of "benevolent neglect."[2] In contrast to those writers' male protagonists who mourn the lost father, the long-gone days, and the forgotten language, Glasgow proposes a forward-looking countermyth. Refuting "melodramas of beset manhood," Ellen Glasgow undertakes a revolutionary revision of Southern history.[3]

Written late in Glasgow's career, *Vein of Iron* transforms the fictional narrative of America's settlement, a story at the heart of much of the national literature deemed canonical. The novel's revolutionary intent appears both in its characterization and in its origins. In contrast to tales of heroic individual authorship, Glasgow insists that her creative process for *Vein of Iron*, like the novel's own account of Virginia's homemaking, is a "family chronicle" inspired by the voice of her Aunt Rebecca relating the story of their family.[4] And unlike male narratives of the defeated or dead patriarch, the isolated son, and a consequently diminished Southern present, this novel places three generations, male and female, in a vital social context. Even more, the female narratives that form so central a part of the first pages of Glasgow's novel emerge with the force of a fourth collective character. Composed of women's orally transmitted histories, these narratives are shaped by Glasgow into a constant presence

Rebecca Anderson Glasgow, whose recollections were the inspiration for *Vein of Iron*

actively influencing the working out of events in the fictional present and, by suggestion, into the future.[5] In *Vein of Iron*, Glasgow's process of composition and the narrative's fictional contents parallel and reinforce one another.

Refusing to evoke the blasted mansion and abandoned fields of much Southern literature, Glasgow here presents in their stead an abiding Virginia home that stands, by implication, until the present. Expressed through the growth of the children, the fertility of the gardens, and the conservation of the community's memories, the ongoing Virginia civilization created by Grandmother receives its finest expression in the strong foundation and sturdy walls of the manse. At the novel's end, Glasgow portrays Ada Fincastle, the female founder of the latest generation, returning to Shut-In Valley with her children, intending to revive the family ancestral home. The manse still stands despite the ravages of the Great Depression and urbanization, and Ada's return will renew its vitality.[6] Glasgow points to the centrality of this physical artifact when she remembers that "the whole family dropped dead at my feet as soon as I started to pull down the manse."[7] Moreover, through the manse's identity as the community's spiritual home for both Grandmother's hard-edged Calvinism and father John Fincastle's abstract philosophy, Ada's reclamation of the family seat suggests that a new female faith holds residence. Freed from both the hold of Grandmother's patriar-chal deity and the insubstantiality of John Fincastle's mental constructs, this "em-bodied" belief claims a sure immortality that is exemplified by the wise women's physical and spiritual creativity. Through her representation of the Virginia home, Glasgow refutes the myths of the bygone aristocratic days, suggesting that the real South resides in the Shut-In Valleys, among the plain people, conserved by the homemakers who remember the community's tales and who bear and nurture the new generations. As an examination of the plot indicates, all members of the community exist at once, free from death and time, in the memories and narra-tives of the female family.

Unlike an earlier protagonist, Dorinda Oakley of *Barren Ground* (1925), who wages a lonely, constant, and often desperate battle with the forces of nature, the wild broomsedge, and her own sexual desire, Ada Fincastle accepts the inevitabil-ity of personal aging and death within the stable social context of family and neighborhood. Unlike Dorinda, Ada considers herself a part of the Virginia land-scape. In contrast, despite her identification with the cycle of life, Dorinda's atti-tude toward the earth of necessity keeps her outside as observer, an attitude quite similar in intent toward nature as that of the phallic gaze toward its female object. Dorinda objectifies and judges the land to effect her modernization, and she shapes it to her own ends. To Dorinda, the natural landscape always retains a sym-bolic identity referential to the course of her own individual life. In contrast, Ada and Grandmother Fincastle discover and experience a microcosm of the entire natural cycle in their physical and imaginative life as women. Underlining the emphasis on all aspects of female creativity in this novel, including the biological identity, an unmarried Glasgow protagonist carries a pregnancy to term for the first time.[8] Thus, both women understand, imaginatively, intellectually, and instinctively, the twin processes of growth and decline, of sowing and harvesting.

Anne Goodwyn Jones delineated Glasgow's relationship to that distant inhu-man being, the Southern Lady, in the early works of her career, but here we see the author venturing even further. By insisting on the equality of the powerful female body engaged in physical labor, including the biological functions, Glasgow counters the forever young, asexual Southern Belle. In *The Sheltered Life* (1932), Glasgow had shown the fate of this mannequin-ideal; now she replaces that barren figure with the grandmother, a figure very often portrayed as missing or inconsequential in male American literature. Grandmother has nothing of the lovely feminine coquette in her nature as the first description of her makes clear:

> Grandmother was the kind of person you saw better when you were not
> looking straight at her. Even when she was young, Mother said, she could
> never have been handsome; but she had the sort of ugliness that is more

impressive than beauty. Her figure was tall, strong, rugged; her face reminded the child of the rock profile at Indian Head; and her eyes, small, bright, ageless, were like the eyes of an eaglet that had peered out from a crevice under the rock.[9]

Grandmother Fincastle's participation in "birthing labor" and nurture refutes the very idea of individual self-creation implicit in the notion of the belle as artifice, as a crafted being intended for display. Grandmother displays in the same strong but aging body the inevitability of time passing, resulting in a death that is denied by the forever young, forever virginal belle. By replacing the sterile figure of male desire and female competition—the belle—with the character of the strong, vital wise woman, Glasgow further emphasizes the communal nature of her narrative.

Grandmother's immense stature suggests the resonance of Willa Cather's prairie heroines or Sarah Orne Jewett's Almira Todd of *The Country of the Pointed Firs* (1898). By their identification with the land, and its flora and fauna, these strong female figures stand for the vitality of their respective homelands. And like those other seers, Grandmother has a wisdom transcending the physical, a voice beyond mere language, and a body seemingly shaped of the Virginia landscape. Her body seems carved from the earth, but her spirit soars with intelligence, belief, and bravery.[10] Her attendance at Ada's lying-in signifies the passing of the chain of life to the new generation, and John's vision of her at his death suggests a figure approaching the divine. This maternal figure becomes the keeper of the history of Ironside, the source of the family, and the soul of the manse.

Glasgow's depiction of Grandmother Fincastle also shares crucial similarities with other fictional female seers such as Katherine Anne Porter's Aunt Eliza of *The Old Order* (1944), Gloria Naylor's titular *Mama Day* (1988), and Eudora Welty's Grandmother "up home" in *The Optimist's Daughter* (1972). Most notably, the narratives in which these figures occupy the fictional center emphasize the elder women's wisdom in natural lore. Like those other fictional heroines, Grandmother knows the healing properties of the plants around her. Through their work with nature and through their participation in the rites of birth and death, these elder wise women as a group are immersed in the natural world and its cycles; through their homemaking they magnify the earth's abundance even as they bring each of the daughters to her own highest abilities.

Vein of Iron offers no simple-minded essentialist pleading, nor does it propose that women retreat to conventional restricted gender roles. The woman's body in "birthing labor," Sara Ruddick's apt phrase for the woman's reproductive capacity, offers only one type of immortality, and the Fincastles and Grahams have had neither the privilege nor the desire to live as idle belles. (The one person who exemplifies that aristocratic tradition is the fragile, half-mad Mary Evelyn, who

Green Forest in Rockbridge County, the Glasgow family manor built about 1780 by Arthur Glasgow

scarcely has the ability to function as a mother to Ada.) At the same time, *Vein of Iron* refuses to diminish the social contributions of women who have served in maternal roles.

As Glasgow shows from the history found in the novel's earliest pages, Grandmother and Ada are only the latest heirs of a venerable and continuing female tradition. The emblematic maternal figure of Grandmother Fincastle brings forth the strength and creativity of the early Scots-Irish pioneers as it extends into the present. Through the creation of this powerful character, the author not only reclaims the history of her region but also the history of her own family. In *A Certain Measure*, Glasgow explicitly connects the history of her father's family with the writing of *Vein of Iron*, "For the three full years while I was writing this book, I projected my consciousness, without effort, into that resolute breed from which my father had sprung."[11]

From the early settler and first grandmother Martha Tod, who suffers captivity for seven years, to Grandmother Fincastle, who creates the Virginia homeland, to Ada, who returns home at the height of the Great Depression, Glasgow insists

A plan of Glasgow's Ironside, reproduced as endpapers in *Vein of Iron*, shows "The Manse" standing solidly and securely just outside the center of town.

that the Scots-Irish women create the actual material body as well as the soul at the center of the manse, the homeland of Virginia. As she establishes her continuing new Southern history, Glasgow presents an array of female pioneers who precede Grandmother and Ada. For each John Fincastle, the series of patriarchs sharing the same name, there exists a parallel woman's story of heroism and daring. In the ancient human work with the elements and the earth, the women settlers in Virginia, laboring alongside the men, raise the church, meet the native people, and found the settlement. Ada's female ancestors, Margaret Graham and Martha Tod, achieve equal importance to the first John Fincastle, just as Grandmother, and later Ada, share the novel's center with the present John Fincastle.

One of Ada's ancestors, Margaret Graham, for example, is defined as fully by the life of the mind as that of the body. The highborn Margaret indeed possesses so striking a physical presence that the elders ask her to wear a veil in church, but through Margaret's example, Glasgow insists that the community is built in equal parts of woman's physical, mental, and imaginative labors. Margaret, for example, props a book on the counter as she kneads her bread dough, educating herself in history and languages. By this integration of intellect and physical labor, she is empowered to protect the family. When she is widowed at the young age of thirty-eight, she educates her three sons, sends them to college, and inspires all three to useful lives. Moreover, despite her long physical absence from the manse, Margaret Graham still exerts a daily influence. Through the reliable testimony of the latest John Fincastle, readers understand that her legacy has been passed down in both its intellectual and physical manifestations. His physical appearance, interest in education, and perseverance all come from this determined female individual who unashamedly greeted the church elders in her bare feet.

As Grandmother brings the history of the female community to life through her voice, which bears a "thrilling quiver" of emotion, she tells the granddaughter that "men and women worked together building the walls, and every grain of sand to make mortar was brought by the women on horseback." Drawing her granddaughter into the family history explicitly, she concludes, "Remember, my child, you have strong blood."[12] Grandmother passes the stories of the settlers directly to her granddaughter, readying the girl to take her place as seer, healer, and physical founder as the older woman had earlier come into her own full powers. Her story will join those of other early women who built and kept the manse, and her salvation of the home is intended by Glasgow to be fully as heroic an event as the exploits of Grandmother or Margaret Graham. The stories of the community, the narratives of the Fincastles, the Craigies, and the Grahams, male and female, emerge in the opening pages directly from Ada's own memory. By evoking the oral tradition as well as the interior states of memory and emotion, Glasgow hopes to reproduce in written literature the bonding effect that is integral to ritual.[13]

Many of the assumptions underlying the novel, especially those directed toward socially marginalized groups, cause indignation—the condescension toward the lower classes, the identification of the Shawnee with sexuality and nature, and the somewhat patronizing attitude toward the black character Aunt Abigail Geddy. (Nonetheless, the depiction of Aunt Abigail Geddy's personality and the description of her cabin creates a far more complete character than Fluvanna in *Barren Ground*, who exists mainly to serve and support Dorinda.) Because our social order valorizes individual autonomy and competition, many critics also find uncomfortable, if not infuriating, Glasgow's emphasis on the diminution of the individual in favor of the social group and the insistence—so like that of the later Willa Cather—that actual physical and familial inheritance shapes individual fate. Given these characteristics, then, what raises the novel to the forefront of Glasgow's work? Its historical scope, its often lyrical language, and its cultural depth allow it to challenge the assumptions of the canonical male works of the South. *Vein of Iron* covers the period from the settlement of Virginia to the Great Depression and beyond, and it represents a further refinement in the Southern agrarian vision that Glasgow promulgated in *Barren Ground*.

The novel rests on a new language, represented by passages such as the following excerpt describing Grandmother Fincastle's mystical, spiritual, and physical connection with land, family, and manse:

Suddenly, without warning, descended upon her a sleep that was not sleep as yet. Her eyes saw; her ears heard; and in her stiff fingers the needles did not slacken. But she was immersed in profound stillness; she rested upon an immovable rock. And about her she could feel the pulse of the manse beating with that secret life which was as near to her as the life in her womb. All the generations which had been a part, and yet not a part, of that secret life. The solid roof overhead, the solid floor underfoot, the fears of the night without, the flames and the shadows of flames within, the murmurs that had no voices, the creepings that had no shape, were all mingled now. Weaving in and out of her body and soul, knitting her into the past as she knitted life into stockings, moved the familiar rhythms and pauses—now— of the house; and moved as a casual wave, as barely a minute's ebbing and flow, in the timeless surge of predestination.[14]

Yet it is important to note that although the family is but a part of Grandmother's "secret life," it does ultimately define it. Glasgow insists on balancing individual consciousness with the claims of the community in this crucial passage. Moreover, Glasgow here states the living connection of the woman and the ancestral home.

Such passages, with the collapsing of time into the immediate, physical present, with the reaching for mythic reverberations, suggest an attempt to give literature the social centrality and consequence of communal ritual. In addition, Glasgow's discussion of the relation of thought rhythms to characterization shows her intent to defeat the isolating linear pattern of conventional history: "I have treated the past and the present as co-existent in time, and time itself as a subjective medium."[15] By moving toward the conventional symbolism of cycles of human life and the seasons of the landscape, by attacking the conventional linear narrative, and by using repetition and emphasizing rhythm, Glasgow hopes to capture the social bonding implicit in the ritual community.

By using the body of the matriarch, and its symbolic representation, the manse, as the creative source of both physical and emotional reality, Glasgow reaches toward an embodied language, a female language with the force and presence of actual breathing life.[16] And through Glasgow's emphasis on the central importance of the female body, she addresses a difficult problem for authors and theoretical feminists alike. In a rationalized, competitive, individualistic, large-scale society, the fact of the female body, often functionally immersed in the life of the group, comes in conflict with the notion of the completely autonomous, social free-agent. By connecting her own creativity in authorial labors with the very different creativity of Grandmother Fincastle, Glasgow attempts to reconcile this female dilemma; the split between bodily and mental labors is healed as are the divisions between generations of women.

In contrast to the male narratives of lost patriarchal domains, Glasgow's narrative of Virginia's continuing creation centers on the "good people"—the villagers, small merchants, farmers, and such who exist hidden far away from the events of the great public world. In this retelling, Glasgow depicts women as equal creators of Virginia's early settlement. And by her insistence on the female family as the conservators and equal creators of the life of this vital neighborhood, she grants the forgotten women an importance missing in standard, canonical literary works.

Unlike the female tradition in *Vein of Iron*, the male Fincastle line seems unable or unwilling to accept the demands of homemaking. It is the succession of John Fincastles who suffer disillusionment for their demand that life conform to abstract pattern—in the repetition of the single name through the generations, we glimpse not only the assertion of paternalistic ego, but also, ironically, the diminution of individuality usually suffered by the anonymous wives of history and fiction. From the first John Fincastle who moves "west" because of his disgust with his flock to the latest John Fincastle who realizes at death that his belief in philosophy is a "tale told by an idiot," the men of Ironside find themselves retreating from their fellows' messy, limited human lives.

John Fincastle has been cited by commentators from Linda Wagner to Julius R. Raper as an authorially self-identified figure; John has spent his whole life immersed in the elaborated language and the abstract patterns of a search for truth, as had Glasgow. Like Glasgow, Fincastle first questioned and then rejected orthodox Calvinism, journeying on to other beliefs and arguments. Indeed, in her notes on the novel, Glasgow stated that "for twenty years, in my early youth, my chief interest was the study of philosophy; and all that I read and thought was embodied in my favorite character [John Fincastle]."[17] John moves further and further away from his Virginia background and his family until in the end he can only communicate through his writings to a handful of his fellows through the mails—here Glasgow's own life, her deafness, her closeness to her pets, suggests a parallel despite her active social life. Glasgow herself calls John's return to the manse one of her most deeply felt passages, and by the circumstances of his passing, we may glimpse the author's own acceptance of her female lineage. John's death may well suggest Glasgow's final destination on her long metaphysical search.

Finally, John Fincastle's search ends in isolation, a circumstance underlined by his inability to communicate with the German philosopher who journeys to meet with him. Although he brings the benediction of intellectual immortality, the philosopher and his concerns seem distant to John:

> Then, as they settled themselves in the two pine chairs with rush bottoms, John Fincastle realized that the power of speech, as he had once known speech, had deserted him. He was out of touch, it seemed to him, with two hemispheres. Downstairs, he had completely missed the idiom of facts. Up here, alone with a visitor who spoke his own language, the streams of metaphysics seemed as vague as the lapping of surf on a beach. Beyond time and space, nothing that men thought of eternity was either important or unimportant. Speculation? Philosophy? Had these realities failed him? Or were they at last resolved into the only element that endures? He was more at home with the humble folk, like old Midkiff or Otto Bergen, who spoke, neither the hollow idiom of facts nor the dead tongues of the schools, but the natural speech of the heart.[18]

Instead of attending to his guest's words, John looks at Maggie and thinks of his grandmother, Margaret Graham, and his own mother. He remembers how these women had shaped and been shaped by the Virginia land: "The frontier, for all its savage impulses and brutal habits, had created, if only now and then, characters that rose superior to destiny."[19] This reminder of his family's female line prepares us for the conclusion of John's quest.

At the end of his life, dying, he leaves behind his family and his books so that he can undertake a pilgrimage to the mother's home as the source of his life and his philosophy. As the weakened philosopher makes his final return, he has a horrific vision of the loss of words that have ordered his life. He dreams his way back to a nightmare childhood, a representation of the confusion to which his long search has condemned him.[20] As his mother and he undertake a mission of mercy up to Panther's Gap, a place of instinct and lack of human order, the loss of meaning experienced during the German philosopher's visit returns fourfold. Waiting for his mother, who has entered the cabin, he is surrounded by "a world of idiots," jeering and dancing around him. A jumble of human instinct and senseless words separate him from his mother. Now he knows that his long search for the ultimate source of creation has led him homeward. As he thinks back, he forgets all since his childhood. In between there has been only loneliness as his quest takes him away from *seeing* the female source. On seeing the manse, he experiences "a peace too deep for happiness, too still for ecstasy."[21]

His search for language ends where it first started, with the face of his mother "dark and stern and bright."[22] With the explicit identification of the mother and her home as the source of language and civilization, and with the insistence on

Glasgow's publicity photo for *Vein of Iron*

the importance of the abiding ancestral female narratives, Glasgow leaves behind the pattern of assumptions underlying *Barren Ground*. As the author insists, this is a communal story of a family and a civilization, not an individualistic narrative of a completed, personal quest.

As befits her new plot, Glasgow recounts a new method of composition, one that allows her, like the aged John Fincastle, to hear and heed the "speech of the heart." Glasgow wrote, "And so the speech of the heart, not the language of the mind, must serve as the revealing medium for my narrative." This novel therefore represents a significant turning point for Glasgow's work as she eschews the progressive, individualistic assumptions of her earlier writings, and this change is directly tied to her creation of the ongoing homeland presided over by the grandmother. To tell this female story, Glasgow knew she needed a language devoid of her usual sophisticated irony.[23] Like John Fincastle, Glasgow found her inspiration by going back to her childhood remembrance of her Scots-Irish aunt Rebecca, who first brought alive literature and religion through the "magical tones of [her] voice."[24] The author states in *A Certain Measure* that she had almost forgotten the influence her aunt had exerted on the child Ellen Glasgow's developing literary sensibility and intellect until she turned to this communal narrative (a circumstance that suggests John's Fincastle's last pilgrimage). Now she finds her own emotion-imbued speech through the memory of the voice of her Aunt Rebecca, who represents her female family and the oral tradition of storytelling. Her family and its narratives inspire the fictional outlines of Grandmother Fincastle and her memories in *Vein of Iron*; by this use of her own personal background, she may well at last have redeemed the memory of her Scots-Irish heritage from the looming shadow of her father, Francis Glasgow.[25] The novel abandons Glasgow's usual tripartite thesis–antithesis–synthesis organization, a pattern that suggests resolution and closure, one appropriate to the author's intention that this novel should open up to the future. In keeping with the plot, linguistic, and structural changes she proposed to make in the work itself, Glasgow changed her publisher.[26] Clearly, this was a new direction for the author, one that challenged previous assumptions on many fronts.

To those critics who attempted to place her writing within a limited historical context, Glasgow in *A Certain Measure* responded that such events as World War I and the Great Depression "were scarcely more than an incident in the larger drama of mortal conflict with fate."[27] *Vein of Iron* and its continuing Virginia community does not present history as completed, objectified, possessed. The manse is most emphatically not lost and gone. Thus, Glasgow tells a story that intends to have an impact on the Southern present and its future.[28] Glasgow retells Virginia history, attacking cultural stereotypes, focusing on the female contribution, and attempting to draw all members of her region, living and dead, male and female, together in an ongoing tradition. Unlike male narratives of lost Southern glory and fallen fathers, Glasgow creates a Virginia community that includes both genders as crucial members. Moreover, through her connection of her own creativity with that of the grandmother, Glasgow valorizes all aspects of female inspiration.

To limn the outlines of her new Southern community, Glasgow reaches toward a different language; in a time of individualistic, artistic competition and of rationalizing, isolating language, the author evokes a communal, ritualistic language, one she calls the "speech of the heart." Through this language, this pattern of characterization, and this ideal homeland, Glasgow creates a feminist, regional critique of modernization of great depth and complexity. In *Vein of Iron*, Ellen Glasgow moves away from the male ideal of the son's continuing search for the lost father, to the abiding Southern center of the wise woman's home—the artist daughter's resting place.

SIX

Novelist Ellen Glasgow's Feminist Rebellion in Virginia—the Suffragist

CATHERINE G. PEASLEE

A rebel who sought equality for the sexes, intellectual freedom, and literary reform, Virginia novelist Ellen Glasgow must be included with those who have successfully revolted against what H. L. Mencken called "the immovable certainties of the nation."[1] Her feminist sympathies were rooted in her youthful compassion for those who were abused or shortchanged by society. Early in life she developed a passion for justice.

Glasgow's sympathies for the social outcasts and oddballs of her era show clearly in her novel, *The Romance of a Plain Man* (1909). She sympathetically portrays a courageous suffragist, Miss Matoaca Bland, the younger of two Bland sisters. Matoaca had decided to remain single and not marry her faithless lover, General Bolingbroke. As a result of this traumatic decision, she often thought about not only her own but also other women's lives and what they lacked. She wanted women to enjoy the rights that men had, including the right to vote, to run for public office, and to help write the laws.

Matoaca, wrote one critic, was Glasgow's "most splendidly drawn portrait of an aristocratic old lady who defied the conventions of her family in order to read a daily newspaper and who died of exhaustion after participating in a move for women's rights."[2] Matoaca insisted that taxation without representation was tyranny, while her conservative sister Mitty despised such dangerous sentiments. In one scene the General baits Matoaca by asking her, "But what would you do with a vote, my dear Miss Matoaca? Put it in a pie? . . . A woman who can make your mince pies, dear lady, need not worry about her rights."[3]

Faithful to her convictions, on the day when the suffragists marched in Richmond, Matoaca, to the dismay of her sister and the General, joined the parade, defying both the heat and the crowds in the streets. Walking primly at the end of the line dressed in a black poke bonnet and mantle, she ignored hooting boys and carried her white banner aloft. Her unseasonably heavy garments and the long walk, however, were too much for the frail, elderly Matoaca. She collapsed. A doctor arrived in time to pronounce her dead. Years later, Matoaca's niece Sally acknowledged that "poor Aunt Matoaca was right. . . . Right in believing that women must have larger lives—that they musn't be expected to feed always upon their hearts."[4]

In reviewing the story later in life, Glasgow revealed that she modeled the portrait of Matoaca from her childhood memories of Elizabeth Van Lew, a passionate abolitionist and a Union spy during the Civil War. The old woman lived alone in a large antebellum mansion on Richmond's Church Hill, where her neighbors shunned her both because of her reputation as a traitor to the Southern cause and because she was a suffragist who annually protested paying taxes because she had no representation. "When I inquired about her at home, I was told that she was not only suspected of spying for the Yankees, but that she was known . . . to be the first woman suffragist in the South." When Glasgow asked what a "suffragist" was, she was told it "meant having a vote, but not ever, ever . . . having a man offer you either his arm or a chair."[5]

Growing up in post–Civil War Richmond, "a city in thralldom to its past,"[6] where ancestral ways prevailed, how did this privileged daughter of a prominent Virginia family become a feminist and suffragist? Her mother was related to the Tidewater Randolphs. Her Scots-Irish father's cousin, General Joseph Reid Anderson, owned the great Tredegar Iron Works, and Francis Glasgow was one of his managers. The tale begins in Glasgow's earliest memories of a home ruled by a stern patriarch that was a battleground for mental and emotional hostilities. Her feminist sympathies developed as her experiences grew in ever-widening circles from a center in Richmond. As she matured, she visited and lived in New York City and traveled in the American West and Europe.

As a small child, Glasgow had heard from a friend of her mother how a Federal officer during the Civil War had protected her mother and her small children when they were living on a farm in the Valley of Virginia while Francis Glasgow was in Richmond manufacturing arms for the Confederacy. The Union officer spent the night outside their farmhouse guarding the woman and her children from the pillaging of Union general David Hunter. After that experience, Glasgow's mother could never condemn the Northern soldiers. At war's end,

Anne Glasgow was thankful when she heard the slaves were free. She remembered the auction block, the slave traders, and the broken families of the slavery era. Her daughter, hearing these tales, was sure that, if she had lived then, she would have been an abolitionist, whose successors were her generation's suffragists and feminists. As with like-minded women in the North, Southern women who had held abolitionist sympathies often transferred these to the cause of woman suffrage after the Civil War.

Before Glasgow and her older sister Cary took up the feminist cause of suffrage in Virginia in 1909, woman's rights in the commonwealth hardly existed. These two daughters of one of Richmond's gentry families helped to establish a movement for woman's rights where others' efforts had either failed or left only faint traces.

The right to vote, the "cornerstone of every emancipation program, its denial the central and most visible symbol of women's subordination,"[7] was not explicitly denied to females by law in Virginia's earliest years. Before 1699, the right to vote was based on ownership of property, not gender. When the highborn Margaret Brent arrived in Westmoreland County from Maryland in 1651 and was denied the right to vote she had enjoyed in Maryland, she lodged a formal complaint with the General Assembly demanding that right.[8] But in 1699, Virginia was the first colony to pass a law that deliberately disenfranchised women. This

Francis Glasgow (*fourth from left*) at Tredegar Iron Works, where he was a manager

Cary Glasgow McCormack, Ellen's sister and a like-minded suffragist

initiated a long tradition of legal discrimination.

In 1778, Hannah Lee Corbin, also of Westmoreland and sister of Richard Henry and Francis Lightfoot Lee, asked her brother Richard why she could not vote. "Why should widows pay taxes when they have no voice in making the laws or in choosing the men who made them?" Corbin, a wealthy widow who managed her own plantation, believed and applied to herself the slogans that had precipitated the American Revolution. Her brother agreed with her, but she was never allowed to vote. After the Revolution, the position of American women compared to men declined and concern for women's equality was heightened.[9]

Almost a century later, Orra Gray Langhorne, of Lynchburg, a journalist concerned with the rights of women and blacks, wrote to the General Assembly "praying" for female suffrage in presidential elections plus an equal rights amendment to the United States Constitution "to establish the equal rights of all citizens, irrespective of sex."[10] When her pleas were ignored, she started a Virginia woman suffrage committee in 1893.

Virginia was fallow ground for feminists. In a region impoverished by the Civil War both economically and politically, women found outlets for their desire to participate in public affairs by creating memorials for veterans, supporting the Woman's Christian Temperance Union, and preserving historic sites. The era saw the founding of the National Society Daughters of the American Revolution, the National Society of the Colonial Dames of America, the United Daughters of the Confederacy, and the Association for the Preservation of Virginia Antiquities. On one occasion, when Mary-Cooke Branch Munford injected a political topic into the meeting of the Woman's Club of Richmond, she was silenced by members who thumped their umbrellas on the floor. The cause of woman suffrage languished and it was the $2.50 remaining in Orra Langhorne's trust account to carry on her work posthumously that funded the suffragist revival in Virginia just one year before the woman's movement in the South "was moving out into the open."[11]

Ellen Glasgow and her sister Cary McCormack were enthusiastic suffragists when they returned to Richmond from a trip to England in 1909. Glasgow had marched with militant suffragettes like Emmeline Pankhurst and Lady Constance Lytton. She had met and talked with intellectual feminists like Beatrice Harraden and May Sinclair. She and McCormack planned to introduce the woman's vote in Virginia. Langhorne's trust was being held in Kentucky by Laura Clay "until a proper group got going in Virginia." Glasgow wrote and invited Clay to come to Richmond and help restart the suffragist movement. The Kentuckian was glad to accept.[12]

Lila Meade Valentine, an active suffrage leader

The Glasgow sisters invited Clay and their Richmond friends to a tea party in their elegant house at One West Main Street in November 1909, a few months after Glasgow had vacationed in Colorado where women had just gained the right to vote. Guests included childhood friends as well as reformer Lila Meade Valentine, novelist Mary Johnston, and others. They agreed to petition the General Assembly to grant women the vote. After the women had founded the Equal Suffrage League of Virginia at a second meeting that same month, the League agreed to affiliate with the National American Woman Suffrage Association (NAWSA), the more radical of the two national woman suffrage groups.

With Glasgow's support, Lila Meade Valentine was elected president of the new Equal Suffrage League. Although Mary Johnston said that both Glasgow and her sister Cary were "bound up heart and soul in Woman's Suffrage," Ellen Glasgow eschewed an active role.[13] She was more dedicated to her writing than was Johnston and she had vital family concerns that distracted her from civic responsibilities. Glasgow explained that "while sadly lacking in executive ability, I am none the less heartily in sympathy with the movement, which I look upon as an inevitable reform."[14] The choice of Valentine was a happy one. A courageous champion of the first kindergartens in Richmond, she was a dynamic crusader who achieved international eminence for her work on behalf of the woman's vote. Glasgow kept in touch with this old friend, offering her moral support and sending money for the suffragists' cause after she moved to New York City.

Many years later, in her autobiography, Glasgow wrote that the fight for suffrage came at "the wrong moment" in her life. Her heart was too "heavy with grief for Frank," her much-beloved older brother who had committed suicide in April 1910.[15] Her sister Cary's death, after a long illness, followed in August 1911, after which Glasgow left her home in Richmond and moved to New York City where she lived until 1915.

Unlike some other feminists both of her own time and later, Glasgow recognized the need for women to understand political processes and use them to achieve their goals. Unlike today's feminists who target *manifestations* of women's inequality like inadequate day care and sexual harassment, Glasgow focused on the basic causes for female oppression, women's political and economic inequality.

In 1916 Glasgow published a novel set in New York City about a single mother and aspiring entrepreneur, *Life and Gabriella*. Glasgow's biographer, Julius R. Raper, describes it as a "dedicated portrait of a liberated woman" comparable to Isabel Archer in Henry James's *Portrait of a Lady*.[16] In one scene, Gabriella's mother, Mrs. Carr from Virginia, deplores the diminishing number of perfect gentlemen she finds in her social circles. "And there'll be fewer than ever by the time you Suffragists get your rights," retorts Charley, her ne'er-do-well, wife-abusing son-in-law. Glasgow, with wicked irony, shows him hurling the term "suffragist" to insult his petulant mother-in-law.[17]

In another literary effort for the suffragists, Glasgow published a long poem, "The Call," a militant rallying cry to women to awaken to their sisters' needs. The poem was printed in several popular magazines, publicizing the feminist cause. In newspaper interviews Glasgow further pressed the cause of votes for women. She said she rejoiced "that at least we are shaking off our chains—many of them our own welding—and that we are receiving our just and honest privileges."[18] Glasgow's arguments were clear and logical as well as witty. When a reporter for the *New York Times* asked her if a majority of women would be unfit voters, Glasgow quickly rejoined: "Oh, yes. Probably the majority of them would be, but, for that matter, so now are the majority of men unfit to vote."[19]

Glasgow labeled herself a Democrat as well as a democrat, but she sometimes showed favoritism toward her own social class. An example was her invidious comparison of immigrants' voting rights with those of an upper-class New York matron, Helen Miller Gould Shepard, eldest daughter of railway magnate Jay Gould. While male immigrants routinely received the right to vote when they got their naturalization papers, Shepard was disenfranchised because of her gender. Glasgow noted indignantly that it was "a singular state of society which will withhold from such a woman a voice in matters vital to her interests, and at the same time grant to foreign immigrants naturalization papers and the privilege of the franchise."[20]

During her four-year sojourn in New York City (1911–1915), Glasgow published another feminist novel, *The Miller of Old Church,* and she marched with the suffragists in a parade. Her feminism and sympathies for woman suffrage never remained static, however, but reflected changes in her own personality and in the world she knew. Optimism about woman's future rights characterized Glasgow's public statements in the early years of her interest in woman suffrage. Her well-educated, rational self firmly believed that equality for women was logically "irrefutable and incontrovertible."[21] In 1913 she spelled out her suffrage views clearly, deploring the tendency "to foster sex antagonism." She was "convinced that when women have once made it plain to men that they all want the ballot … the men will promptly let them vote."[22]

The small coterie of remarkable Richmond women with whom Glasgow had started the suffragist movement in Virginia carried on, even after she had moved to New York. In addition to Mary Johnston and Lila Meade Valentine there were Adèle Clark, who worked closely with Valentine and succeeded her as head of the

League of Women Voters after Valentine's death, and Mary-Cooke Branch Munford. In 1917, however, after the United States had entered the war with the Allies, the Equal Suffrage League, in deference to the greater cause, suspended its operations and supported the war effort. The last suffragist demonstrations were held in 1914 and 1915: the first was a parade, the second was a picketing of the governor's office. But the Virginia suffrage movement

Richmond suffragist Mary-Cooke Branch Munford

Ellen Glasgow, 1909

never again recovered its momentum. Following the armistice in 1918, the national movement swept ahead in those states with likely prospects of ratification until the Nineteenth Amendment was added to the U.S. Constitution in 1920. In a note to Lila Meade Valentine after final ratification, Glasgow congratulated her on "the splendid work that you have at last brought to victory." She asked her old friend about "that day in the first *hope* even of the League when Cary and I came to ask you to start such a movement in Virginia? We were the first, I know, to suggest it to you."[23]

How important was Glasgow's influence in the achievement of feminists' and suffragists' goals? Her writings were more important than her political activism. Glasgow's eminent French biographer, Monique Parent Frazee, praised her efforts "for the emancipation of women's intelligence, spirit, self-accomplishments, self responsibility." Women, she added, are "preponderant" in Glasgow's novels, especially their evolution.[24] Glasgow's first published short story, "A Woman of Tomorrow," appeared in 1895 when she was just twenty-two years old. In the story, the heroine (transparently autobiographical) "cast her first vote, and from that day had been free—capable and free."[25] Later, the heroine, abjuring marriage and motherhood, attended college, studied law, and became the first female justice of the U.S. Supreme Court. Fifty years later, Glasgow wrote in her autobiography: "If women wanted a vote, I agreed that they had a right to vote, for I regarded the franchise in our Republic more as a right than as a privilege; and I was willing to do anything, except burn with heroic blaze, for the watchword of liberty."[26]

Intrinsic to Glasgow's novels are her early convictions that suffrage and other woman's rights were "grounded on irrefutable, incontrovertible logic." She grew to understand that this did not mean that men would "promptly let [women] vote." But she consistently believed that it was legitimate for women to be able to develop their potential regardless of their sex and to have free access to all activities open to men, including active participation in politics and government. Her final word on the subject in her posthumous autobiography was: "I was always a feminist, for I liked intellectual revolt as much as I disliked physical violence."[27]

SEVEN

What Ellen Glasgow Meant by "Average": Southern Masculinity and the Rise of the Common Hero

MARK A. GRAVES

Ellen Glasgow struggled to find a personal philosophy as a woman growing up in the South where traditional conceptions of class, gender, and aesthetics were in transition, but where the vestiges of the old order still adequately served as instruments of oppression. Of this period of transition, Glasgow wrote: "Although it was a time of change, it was also, perhaps because of this shifting surface, a time of opportunity. . . . The average man was at last in the saddle, and since average men compose so large a majority, democracy was already marching with banners."[1] Perhaps Glasgow was merely punning Virginia's equestrian past here—one of the vestiges of the aristocratic class she critiqued in most of her fiction—but what seems clear is Glasgow's awareness that concepts of Southern masculinity could no longer be defined by the class-based Cavalier mythology. Instead, Jeffersonian democracy and the rise of industrialism supplanted the "evasive idealism" of the planter class as the prevailing class and gender ideology of the New South. With characters such as Nicholas Burr in *The Voice of the People*, Ben Starr in *The Romance of a Plain Man*, and Abel Revercomb in *The Miller of Old Church*, Ellen Glasgow chronicled not only the shift in social class and economic dominance in the postbellum South, but also changes in the traditional locations of Southern masculine identity.

Glasgow certainly did not have to look far in defining the Southern Cavalier, whose demise she meticulously chronicled, since a legend surrounds his image in both the folklore and literature of her home state. Because Tidewater Virginia

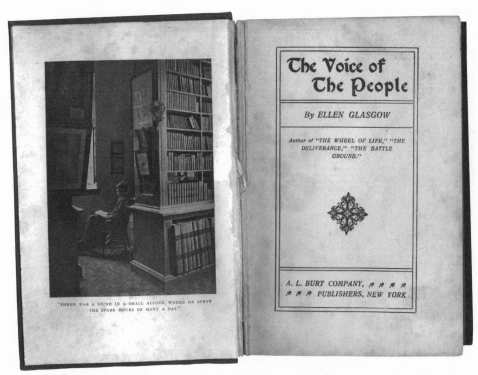

The Voice of
The People

By ELLEN GLASGOW

Author of "THE WHEEL OF LIFE," "THE
DELIVERANCE," "THE BATTLE
GROUND."

A. L. BURT COMPANY, ⚜ ⚜ ⚜
⚜ ⚜ ⚜ PUBLISHERS, NEW YORK

"THERE WAS A NICHE IN A SMALL ALCOVE, WHERE HE SPENT
THE SPARE HOURS OF MANY A DAY."

The Voice of the People is Glasgow's first work to challenge long-held romanticized conceptions of Southern masculinity.

society developed and thrived nearly one hundred and fifty years before the rest of the South, it is not surprising that the Southern Cavalier archetype was first modeled after the English or Scots-Irish plantation owners settling there.[2] Indeed, the image of the tall fair-haired gentleman dressed in a closely fitting waistcoat, high jacket, and boots standing beneath a Greek Revival facade with a riding crop in one hand, a mint julep in the other, and a crinolined woman clinging to his side became synonymous with the romantic and sentimentalized image of the South that Glasgow fought to dispel.

Clearly the popularization of this heightened image owes much to novelists such as Thomas Nelson Page, William Gilmore Simms, James Lane Allen, and even Margaret Mitchell, who quenched the thirst of both Southerners and Northerners alike for tales of the grandeur and graciousness of the Old South. Even though they may have based their portrayals of the Southland more on a fantasy that they wished to legitimize, and thus capitalize on, their (re)construction of this Southern masculine paradigm—no matter how fantastic—could not diminish the importance of personal honor to the Southern Gentleman. An exaggerated sense of honor dominated nearly every aspect of his life, both public and private, and attempted to reconcile the paradoxical relationship between the planter's self-concept and his public reputation, while at the same time controlling the darker side of Southern life: slavery, violence, and miscegenation. The Southern Gentleman held personal bravery in utmost esteem, to the degree that the Civil War became a "simple test of manhood" sure to prove the superiority of the Southern male and the code he lived by, rather than the culmination of a complex web of political and social interactions.[3] The forces that enabled the Southern Gentleman to develop a sense of grandeur and exaggerated honor— namely, leisure time and a comfortable financial situation—also encouraged a tendency toward romanticism and hedonism. Filled with bright colors, fragrant foliage, warm weather, and mist, the Southland assumed an idyllic cast that fit perfectly into the Cavalier's image of himself as a benevolent caretaker.

The Voice of the People (1900) contains Glasgow's first comment on these sentimental, class-based conceptions of Southern masculinity. From the beginning, Glasgow's distrust of the aristocratic sense of noblesse oblige is apparent. Impressed by Nick Burr's aspirations to the bench rather than to peanut farming like his father, Judge Bassett agrees to train Nick for the bar, treating him as a member of the family against the objections of the aristocratic social code. To Glasgow, Bassett represents the graciousness and chivalry of the code of the South, but he also represents the hypocrisy of the aristocrat's benevolent paternalism. While he actively mentors the young Nick to a point, the Judge assumes that Nick should "stick to the soil" of his fathers rather than become a judge and finds the boy's stubbornness offensive to his own gentlemanly Southern civility.[4] On his deathbed, and almost half out of his mind, the Judge responds to Nick, who has risen to become governor of the state, in a way that both surprises and wounds the younger. "'Yes, Nicholas,' repeated the judge doubtfully; 'yes, I remember, what does he want? Amos Burr's son—we must give him a chance.'"[5] Governor Burr comes seeking the advice of a fellow statesman, but finds only a senile paternalist. Bassett's reaction to Nick reflects the noblesse oblige of a privileged Southern aristocrat; the judge has no interest in affirming Nick and the New South values he represents.

If Glasgow's delineation of Judge Bassett presents a conflicting portrait of the aristocratic culture, her depiction of General Battle clearly embodies the outright prejudices, obsoleteness, and complacency of the cult of the Southern Gentleman. General Battle's reputation rests heavily on his devotion to the Lost Cause, which grants him the honorary title of general although he was actually only a colonel. More than happy to stay immersed in the past, he has grown too fat and too fond of bourbon to mount his own horse. His class-dictated attitudes toward women, poor whites, and former slaves remain firmly rooted in the past as well, making him appear indecisive and, at times, a buffoon. Although he has spent much of his life mourning his beloved wife's early death, his deference to

Southern women stems solely from a refusal to believe that any woman can look at anything as coolly as a man can.[6] Battle operates under similar assumptions when dealing with his former slaves who have returned to the security and familiarity of the plantation, vowing one moment to let them starve, and the next to divide his own meager supplies with them.

In her portrayal of these two aging Cavaliers, Glasgow presents an ambivalent portrait of the Southern Gentleman. While some of the virtues of the Old South tradition remain sacred and nostalgic to her, they also seem outmoded and static in the New South, and they possess little, if any, of the masculine vigor she believes the New South requires. In Glasgow's work, men steeped in Jeffersonian democracy provide an alternative. For example, the mold in which Glasgow casts Nick Burr is, ironically, Abraham Lincoln's, who, as commander in chief of the Union forces in the Civil War, struck a mighty blow to Southern gentility. Nick's wish to become "the voice of [his] people" attests to the yeoman class's worthiness to wrest class control from the plantation aristocracy. Marriage to an upper-class woman, Eugenia Battle, may have hastened this legacy, but as Glasgow reveals, class prejudices run too deep to be eradicated just yet. When Nick is unjustly accused of impregnating the daughter of his former employer, the Cavalier class all too readily assumes Nick's guilt, although one of their own actually fathered the child. When Eugenia breaks their engagement based on class assumptions, Nicholas reacts violently. While his anger is somewhat understandable, he hardly resembles the Lincolnesque hero described earlier. Instead, Glasgow seems herself to accept, unchallenged, stereotypes about nonaristocratic whites, because for Glasgow Nick's reaction is brutish, barbaric, and even animalistic, departing from the gentlemanly demeanor required by the status he has begun to assume.

Ultimately, Nicholas foregoes human passion and love altogether, finding happiness by restoring principles to Virginia politics even though it results in his death while defending a black man against a lynch mob. He dies for what he believes in because he cannot survive in the Virginia Glasgow creates. Not worthy to be an aristocrat or a gentleman according to the models Glasgow presents, but too noble and ambitious to sink back into "poor white" obscurity, Nick is caught somewhere in the middle, perhaps in the South of the future instead of the South of the present.

For Glasgow, the parallel courses of Nicholas Burr and Ben Starr in *The Romance of a Plain Man* (1909) exemplify the new democratic spirit blossoming in the New South. What spurs Nick Burr to succeed in politics also drives Ben to prevail in industry, namely to be thought of as something other than "common." Glasgow's Southern heroes must often battle against overwhelming social, political, and economic odds to rise above their circumstances, but seldom does the author place these struggles against a background of industrialization. Yet in the novel an interest in railroading unites aristocrats such as General Bolingbroke and rising-middle-class men like Ben Starr under the guise of mutual ambition. Bolingbroke, the son of a great planter and the failed savior of Joseph E. Johnston's army during the Civil War, breaks tradition by entering into business to redeem the honor of his home region. Unlike the majority of Glasgow's Southern Gentlemen, the General has adapted to the social change occurring at the time by outwitting the carpetbaggers financially, while at the same time maintaining his genteel status. As Ben Starr views it, Bolingbroke's gentlemanliness only enhances his authority in business, but Ben fails to realize that the General devotes himself to business solely for his own enjoyment of gain. The glory Bolingbroke amasses from contributing to the economy and the admiration he garners from beating the Yankees at their own game are secondary to the sheer ruthless pleasure and pride he experiences when succeeding in yet another commercial venture.[7]

Ben admires the General, one of the few aristocrats who combines the traits he hopes to develop himself, and adopts Bolingbroke as his personal model in business, putting his ambition to succeed before the needs of those around him. When his wife Sally inherits a $10,000 legacy after months of surviving on her laundering and baking skills alone, Ben squanders the money speculating on copper. Only after he loses the money and must tell his wife does he lament succumbing to ambition. From the beginning, then, Glasgow expresses an ambivalence about his new obsession with business, which replaced the morals and standards of the professions. While she admires the drive and ambition that allow the middle-class man to overthrow the stifling pretensions of the aristocracy and revitalize the Southland with new blood and vigor, she also mourns the loss of scruples and gentlemanly competition legendary in the Old South.

Of course, what ultimately compels Ben to amass a fortune by any means necessary is a desire for acceptance into the upper classes, and in turn, to prove his worthiness of Sally. His rivals from the most prestigious families in Richmond highly regard him in the business world, but in the social sphere they consider him an inferior. Even though the culture that nurtured them collapsed, the values and prejudices of the antebellum tradition are still revered and upheld by traditionalists such as Sally's aunts, the Misses Bland. Polite but condescending to him in her reserved manner, Miss Mitty expresses her reservations about Ben in a conversation recounted by General Bolingbroke: "'That wonderful boy of ours is the finest looking-fellow in the South to-day, Miss Mitty,' I burst out, 'and he stands six feet two in his stockings.' 'Ah, General,' she replied sadly, 'what are six feet two inches without a grandfather?'"[8] Even though self-made men like Ben Starr wrestle economic and political control from their aristocratic predecessors, the hereditary fibers of the aristocracy are still tightly woven.

Glasgow criticizes Ben for trying too hard to penetrate the upper ranks of the social order with its reverence for the past that he finds personally stifling, but that also represents his need to prove his worthiness to his wife. For Ben, this means, of course, becoming a slave to his ambition in providing Sally with a comfortable lifestyle and, ironically, it means neglecting her as well. Along the way, Glasgow suggests that he loses sight of his priorities until his aristocratic wife becomes dangerously ill. Through Ben's neglect of his wife in favor of the demands of business, Glasgow criticizes middle-class entrepeneurs, and the aristocrats who have joined their ranks, for their obsession with making money. But again, Glasgow reveals her ambivalence by questioning the tightly knit hereditary fibers of the aristocracy that exclude these entrepeneurs, igniting middle-class ambitions. Further developing the themes she introduced in *The Voice of the People*, Glasgow suggests through the marriage of Sally and Ben that the Southern social structure has been sufficiently disrupted to ensure that democratic virtues can prevail.

The Miller of Old Church[9] was Glasgow's most emphatic assertion to date of the ability of the rural hero to rise above his circumstances and become a power in the South, supplanting the aristocracy. Casting her protagonist in rural Southside Virginia in 1898–1902, Glasgow creates in the mold of Nicholas Burr and Ben Starr her most fully realized self-made hero yet. Though no more trained to become a leader of his people than her previous heroes, Abel Revercomb nonetheless has political power thrust on him, but, as Glasgow suggests, he seems capable of handling its responsibilities in the transitory South, for he does not aspire to a masculine identity based on aristocratic foundations.

As conventionally read, the novel portrays the exchange of power between two rival families, the Revercombs and the Gays, and in turn, two conflicting social factions. While aristocratic landowners like the Gays sit idly by, simple farmers and millers like the Revercombs work to improve their line and their legacy in the New South. When the novel opens, the elder Jonathan Gay's illegitimate daughter, Molly Merryweather, approaches her twenty-first birthday, at which time she will come into a sizable yearly legacy from her father's estate with the understanding that she agree to live with the Gay family. Abel has watched Molly grow up and he has always worked to be worthy of her love, but Molly initially refuses his marriage proposals because once she inherits her father's legacy, both familial and monetary, she all too easily adopts the postures and class attitudes of the aristocracy and realizes she cannot be the wife he needs. While she despises Abel's more rustic mannerisms, for Molly, and for Glasgow as well, Cavalier sophistication is equally problematic. In uncharacteristic fashion, Glasgow grants the aristocrats in the novel little of the sympathy or grudging admiration that typifies the author's previous portraits of the decaying upper

Glasgow continued her exploration of the South's notions of power, class, and masculinity in *The Miller of Old Church*.

The Miller of
Old Church

by Ellen Glasgow

Garden City, New York
Doubleday, Page & Company
1911

classes. Corrupt, tyrannical, and indolent, the aristocrats in the novel—young Jonathan Gay, his invalid mother, and his hideous Aunt Kesiah—are the residue left after the best of the antebellum tradition has been transformed into fond memories. In the novel, Jonathan Gay seems little more than the stereotypical aristocratic epicurean. Irresponsible and reckless like his uncle and namesake before him, Jonathan only returns to manage the family estate when duty to his mother or a lack of funds demands it. Perhaps the best that can be said of Gay, and for the aristocratic stereotype he represents, is that his intentions are always good even if they are never borne out in actions.

Glasgow contrasts the decadent aristocratic lifestyle that Jonathan Gay represents with the more industrious, uncomplicated existence that the middle-class Revercombs enjoy. Abel Revercomb rises above the limitations of his class and overcomes the aristocratic prejudices that Nicholas Burr and Ben Starr had not been able to dissolve. As an educated man of a good family, his mere ambition and his ability to articulate the democratic aspirations of the Southern yeoman catapult Abel into prominence as the foremost businessman and rising politician in the region around Bottom's Ordinary, and he challenges the aristocratic conception of the "poor white" as shiftless, immoral, and complacent. Though political responsibility is thrust on him as the best representative of Southern democratic principles put into action, Abel seems capable of shouldering the burden for his class.

While Glasgow's sympathies clearly lie with her rustic heroes in these three early novels, she quickly reminds us that the good fortune of these men is the exception and not the rule in the New South. Few, if any, of her contemporaries attempted to chart realistically the rise of the middle-class men and the decay of the Southern Gentleman ideal so largely mythologized in American culture.

Believing that she was creating a form of Southern Realism that departed from the sterile romantic glorification of the South and its Cavaliers, her early novels set in Virginia largely reflect a young writer's disillusionment with the stifling conventions of the Old South. These stale traditions not only suppressed independent thinking and discussion of political and social issues for nonaristocratic men and women alike, but also prevented the infusion of the masculine vigor— the "blood and irony"—she felt was so desperately needed in her home region at the dawn of the twentieth century. While the early Southern civilization that emerged from the frontier may have required the intricate social order that the Cavalier code offered, the New South rising like a phoenix from the ashes of the genteel age required the enterprise and energy obtainable only from a resource, a class, historically ignored by antebellum class and gender norms. Novels such as *The Voice of the People*, *The Romance of a Plain Man*, and *The Miller of Old Church*, then, not only reflect Glasgow's commitment to portray realistically the rise of the common man and to dispel the romanticized image of the Southern Cavalier, but also serve as Glasgow's call to action to a new generation of Southern men and women, a call to learn from the mistakes of their predecessors and to build a civilization and an identity of their own.

EIGHT

Without the Glory of God:
Ellen Glasgow and Calvinism

Susan Goodman

Two things, and two things only, were requisite to my identity both as a human being and as a writer—an intense immediate experience, and the opportunity to translate that experience into forms of creative imagination.[1]

Ellen Glasgow, *A Certain Measure*

Ellen Glasgow's struggle with Calvinism was predestined. In her autobiography, *The Woman Within* (1954), she recalls that her father, Francis Glasgow, "regarded every earthly affliction, from an invading army to the curdling of a pan of milk, as divinely appointed by God." A Scots-Presbyterian, he seemed to need neither comfort nor pleasure: "A God of terror, savoring the strong smoke of blood sacrifice, was the only deity awful enough to command his respect." Although he wept copiously—to his amazed family's scorn—over sentimental fiction recounting a prodigal daughter's return, his own daughter felt that he was patriarchal rather than paternal. "He gave his wife and children everything," Glasgow writes, but love, "the one thing they needed most." What virtues he did have—complete integrity and an abiding sense of responsibility—she thought alien to his dispassionate character and more "Roman" in their austere practice than Calvinistic. Because Glasgow was never able to dissociate her vision of her father's religion from her vision of him, she saw Calvinism as a punitive, authoritarian, and irrationally sentimental system.[2]

Glasgow believed that her father's unbending Presbyterianism made him one of the last men on earth her mother, Anne Gholson Glasgow, should have married. "A creature of light and ... a figure of tragedy," Anne Glasgow provided the model for Virginia Pendleton, the "perfect" (and doomed) "flower of Southern culture" in *Virginia* (1913). In her daughter's mind, she survived the occupation of Richmond, the financial reversals of Reconstruction, and the birth of ten children only to surrender to depression after learning of her husband's one secret pleasure, his affairs with mulatto women.[3]

Blaming her father for her mother's unhappiness and disliking him for his cruelty to dogs, Glasgow claimed: "Everything in me, mental or physical, I owe to my mother."[4] Yet she also associated his Scots-Irish ancestry with the fortitude or the "vein of iron" (later the title of her 1935 novel) she thought stoical and necessary for survival. The metaphor reflects not only the iron will Francis Glasgow passed on to his daughter, but also the source of his family's income, gained from his management of the Tredegar Iron Works, once the largest supplier of Confederate weapons.[5]

The Glasgow household, just blocks from Tredegar, flourished on two traditions, the myth of True Womanhood and the myth of the Old South. Glasgow's mother, eulogized by friends and family for her unselfish devotion to others, embodied the first; her father, remembered for keeping the Tredegar Iron Works operating with pig iron produced by slave labor, the second.[6] Glasgow saw these myths as cultural manifestations of a religion she found both sexist and racist. Satirizing True Womanhood in comedies of manners like *They Stooped to Folly* (1929) and offering a revisionary history of the South from the Civil War through the First World War in novels from *The Battle-Ground* (1902) to *In This Our Life* (1941), she bequeathed future writers another tradition: A brand of Modernism that redefines the oppressive Calvinism of her childhood to include the maternal and the aesthetic.

Above: Francis Thomas Glasgow. *Opposite:* Anne Jane Gholson Glasgow with her oldest daughter, Emily

A crucial text for understanding Glasgow's vision of both Calvinism and Modernism, *The Woman Within* is possibly no more autobiographical than *Barren Ground* (1925). Of herself and her heroine, Dorinda Oakley, she confirms: "We were connected, or so it seemed, by a living nerve."[7] Together, *Barren Ground* and *The Woman Within* illustrate part of Glasgow's fluid process of making and unmaking meaning. Although the novel predates the autobiography, it grows from the emotional and intellectual context the autobiography reveals. It fixes one stage in its author's development and partly determines another.

More than any other of her novels, *Barren Ground* (1925) represented a turning point for Glasgow. "I wrote *Barren Ground*," she recalls, "and immediately I knew I had found myself. . . . I was at last free." Most important, the novel allowed her to approach the unapproachable—her father's wartime employment of slave labor, for example. This "conversion . . . to [a] new creed in fiction" that privileged the world within over the one without gave Glasgow "a code of living . . . sufficient for life or for death." What she called "freedom" was an ambivalent reconciliation with the past, for after *Barren Ground* her social history encompasses a more complex and sympathetic attitude toward characters who have survived on the meager diet of faith. This shift toward a Modernism defined not by subjects that Glasgow thought shockingly unromantic, such as illegitimacy or free love, but by a psychological realism patterned on her response to Calvinism signaled a new phase of her career and—with the exception of *Virginia*—the beginning of her finest work.[8]

Part *Kunstlerroman*, part spiritual autobiography, *The Woman Within* articulates the personal myth that informed Glasgow's fiction and gave birth to *Barren Ground*. Both books show how she came to terms with the emotional legacy of her father's religion. If Glasgow believed that an autobiography's "truth" depended on its duplication of a state of mind, she also believed that a novel should have a planned, implicit philosophy. *Barren Ground*, the story of a betrayed woman who becomes the victor instead of the victim, illustrates how Glasgow altered the feelings explored in her autobiography into an argument for feminist self-determinism. In this interplay between fact and fiction, there is—to twist a phrase from Hemingway's *A Moveable Feast*—a chance of what has been written as fact throwing some light on what has been written as fiction.[9]

• • •

Glasgow worked on the manuscript of *The Woman Within*—kept in a locked black leather briefcase and labelled "Original Rough Draft"—for eight years, from 1935 to 1943. During this time, she also wrote the essays for *A Certain Measure* (1943), which contemporary reviewers compared favorably with Henry James's prefaces to the New York edition of his own works. Because the autobiographical and critical acts coincided, the books sometimes echo one another, suggesting—as *Barren Ground* and the autobiography illustrate—that the private and public sectors of existence are not so easily divided.[10]

The Woman Within integrates the worlds of father and daughter. Its content is fundamentally Calvinist; its circular, fragmented, and sometimes repetitive form is Modernist. "I have tried to leave the inward and the outward streams of experience free to flow in their own channels, and free, too, to construct their own special designs," she explains. "Analysis, if it comes at all, must come later." To borrow Glasgow's own metaphor from *Barren Ground*, the words of the covenant may have altered, but "the ancient mettle" still infuses the author's spirit.[11] Like a good Presbyterian, Glasgow struggles against the powers of evil and suffers for a purpose. Like a true modern, she finds the universal in the personal. The autobiographical act confirms her being, agency, and talent.

The autobiography's first section recounts Glasgow's awakening to self; the second to art; and the third to "God."[12] Successively focusing on the Calvinist beliefs of particular election, redemption, and irresistible grace, *The Woman Within* reflects her lifelong interest in the mutation and variation of self. It honors those whom her father scorned, including artists, skeptics, and scientists. Glasgow was drawn to the teachings of Charles Darwin and Herbert Spencer for professional as well as personal reasons. Knowing that her father hated anything to do with Darwinism, she read *The Origin of Species* when nearly twenty and assimilated an extended discussion of inherited characteristics and environmental influences into her first novel, *The Descendant* (1897). The "minor religious persecution" that Ellen Glasgow suffered at home for reading Darwin was more than offset by the temporary sense of identity and authority his theories afforded.[13] He became a kind of intellectual father, whose views on heredity vaguely echoed those of her own father on predestination. In a sense, Darwin's beliefs were to the body what Francis Glasgow's were to the soul. If *The Descendant* sides neither with nature nor nurture, later works like *Barren Ground* and *The Woman Within* present heredity and predestination as almost interchangeable concepts.

Near the end of her life, Glasgow felt that science had failed to cure her body in the same way that religion had failed to cure her soul. She rejected the cate-

Glasgow at seven. "In my seventh summer I became a writer," Glasgow recorded in *The Woman Within*, and entered "that strange exile to which all writers who are born and not made are condemned."

gories of science when writing *The Woman Within* because they seemed to simplify or exclude what she had come to see as unclassifiable: her own "dubious identity." "I am concerned, now," she writes, "only with the raw substance and the spontaneous movement of life, not with the explicit categories of science." Glasgow's assumption that intellect and sensation are so closely intertwined that it is impossible to "tell where one began in pure feeling, and the other ended in pure speculation" would have shocked her father as heresy.[14]

Following a pattern more commonly associated with British and American male autobiographers, Glasgow presents her "self" on a grandly dramatic, or even epic, scale worthy of Milton. Her soul becomes a battleground where opposing and hostile forces—the "stalwart, unbending, rock-ribbed" Calvinism of her father and the radiant sympathy of her High Church Episcopalian mother—contend. Feeling like "the last unwilling scapegoat of Predestination," she is torn between mother and father, nature and civilization; she belongs everywhere and nowhere.[15]

Although Glasgow claimed that she was never a disciple and disliked "the current patter of Freudian theory," *The Woman Within* favors a world in which a densely knit cluster of emotions, memories, and perceptions dominate, even predetermine, the historical course of life.[16] Glasgow identifies this amorphous state—described in terms that suggest she never fully rejected scientific categories or ever disowned Darwin—with her mother and nature.

The first moment of consciousness thrusts Glasgow from womblike comfort into a terrifying void. "Moving forward and backward, as contented and as mindless as an amoeba, submerged in that vast fog of existence," she recalls:

> I open my eyes and . . . beyond the top windowpanes, in the midst of a red glow, I see a face without a body staring in at me, a vacant face, round, pallid, grotesque, malevolent. Terror—or was it merely sensation?—stabbed me into consciousness. . . . One minute, I was not; the next minute, I was. I

felt. I was separate. I could be hurt. I had discovered myself. And I had discovered, too, the universe apart from myself.[17]

In the child's vision, the setting sun, which seems symbolic of the father, eclipses the female sphere of love and ritual where Mother and Mammy Lizzie benignly reign. The world, now inexplicable, menacing, and revelatory, houses gods less indifferent than pernicious. The face at the window may as well anticipate Jacques Lacan, for the passage re-creates the subjugation of the amoeba-like self to an emerging and increasingly insistent "I." The appearance of the "face without a body" marks the child's fall into a symbolically ordered world of the father, who "had little compassion for the inarticulate, and as his Calvinistic faith taught him, the soulless." As a writer, Glasgow internalized her father's Calvinist equation of speech and being; however, she never forgot the child who could not put her fear into words. Her empathy for all the abused, helpless, and mute victims of life grows from her experience of being voiceless when first faced with what her Calvinist ancestors might also have called "the cold implacable inhumanity of the universe."[18]

Glasgow's apparition owes its shape to "the late revenge of that [paternal] Calvinist conscience."[19] It curiously resembles the Satan of James Hogg's early-nineteenth-century text, *The Private Memoirs and Confessions of a Justified Sinner* (1824):

> delineated in the cloud [were] the shoulders, arms, and features of a human being of the most dreadful aspect. The face was the face of his [the hero's] brother, but dilated to twenty times the natural size. Its dark eyes gleamed on him through the mist, while every furrow of its hideous brow frowned deep as the ravines on the brow of the hill.[20]

Both writers see no end to the "eternal conflict between human beings and human nature." For Glasgow no less than for Hogg, the conflict is predetermined and therefore Calvinistic; yet, even in Hogg's book, it is also modern in the sense that the apparitions, which impress themselves on the landscape, function like mirrors to reveal "the bloated face of evil"[21] as one's own.

When framing her life story, Glasgow did not shun the religious myths she thought represented a form of "evasive idealism"—defined as a "whimsical, sentimental and maudlinly optimistic philosophy." The "strange transference of identity" that heralds her waking to consciousness also distinguishes her as an artist. Feeling chosen for a life of suffering made bearable only by her sense of anointment, she testifies: "I, alone, saw the apparition . . . I saw it hanging there once, and forever." This sign, which reinforces Glasgow's inherited sense of estrange-

Annie and Emily Glasgow with a family slave, ca. 1858. The Glasgow children formed close bonds with their female house servants.

ment and recalls the crucifiction, also fixes, like Hester Prynne's scarlet letter, her moral superiority: "A sensitive mind," she concludes, "would always remain an exile on earth." What Puritan typology would have revealed as part of a universal history of providential significance she individualizes.[22]

Instead of asking, "How can I best prepare myself for what is to come?" Glasgow, in effect, asks: "How can an oversensitive nature defend itself against the malice of life?"[23] The answer lies in art. The muse is her angel of annunciation. Writing becomes a way "to break through" or "push back into nothingness" the old wall of silence Glasgow first associated with the face at the window. Consciously or unconsciously, she is driven by an "old antagonist, a past from which [she is] running away." Trying to lessen the gap between the writer and the word, Glasgow approximates reality with "a prose style so pure and flexible she hopes it c[an] bend without breaking."[24] Art, which in some way allows her to relive or revise the past, also allows her to transcend it by creating a current self in language. That self, introduced initially in the present tense, is modern in its continual becoming.

The style of the memoir reflects what Glasgow defines as the "modernity" of its structure. "For the modern process," she explains in her interpretation of prose fiction, *A Certain Measure*, "means a breaking up on the surface of facts, and a fearless exploration into the secret labyrinths of the mind and heart." The enigmatic repetitions and interrupted chronology parallel the "tunnelling process" of Virginia Woolf (1882–1941), a writer whom Glasgow admired. They also serve to obscure meaning. She mentions her brother Frank's death three times, for example, before the reader can confidently guess suicide as its cause. Reverting perhaps to the genteel tradition in which she was raised, she rationalizes the waste: "In a last effort to spare us as far as it was possible, he went, alone, from the house, and, alone, into a future where we could not follow him."[25] The false starts and hesitations underscore the ways in which Glasgow makes meaning, while her recurrent memory of Frank, and particularly of the setting sun, highlights how she alters meaning.

The image of the setting sun accrues meaning each time it occurs. Glasgow first associates her unchildlike, brooding sense of exile with the "half-forgotten presence of the evil face without a body."[26] Later, she agonizes over God's indifferent gaze and Judas's despairing face. These "hallucinations" are far less frightening than their prototype (the evil face), for imagination can "convert" Christ's grimace on the cross to a guardian angel's smile. When Glasgow feels betrayed by her fiancé, Henry Anderson (called "Harold S." in the text), the image, unutterably hideous and malignant, appears again. In despair, she takes an overdose of sleeping pills. Dreaming of her mother, sisters, and Mammy Lizzie, she returns to the comforting maternal world of love and ritual the apparition cast in shadow.

Instead of the horrifying surrender or extinction of identity originally associated with the vision, Glasgow now experiences an "enlargement and complete illumination of being" with "the Unknown Everything or with Nothing . . . or with God."[27] The once-malevolent apparition, having been feminized, now wears a countenance inclusive of all humanity. No longer fearful, she surrenders to process, welcoming the dissolution of boundaries between self and other that forms, in her mind, the "universal" or "catholic" basis of art: the path "to greatness leads beyond manner, beyond method, beyond movement, to some ultimate dominion of spirit." In this way, Glasgow redefines the terms of the epigram, "Calvinism is Catholicism without the glory of God." Her version of Calvinism is a kind of secularized humanism that "rememories" (to borrow Toni Morrison's word from her 1987 *Beloved*) the face at the window. Janus-like, its features reflect the androgynous ideal that Virginia Woolf called man-womanly or woman-manly.[28]

Glasgow's account of her life story—one of victimization, conflict, and isolation—paradoxically ends, as do so many Puritan spiritual autobiographies, with a communion or symbolic bonding between reader and writer. This conclusion, however, does not exclude the modernist assumption that solitude nurtures creativity.[29] Perhaps in no age would Glasgow have felt anything other than a stranger and an exile; nevertheless, she finds beyond the constraints of time and place a home in art where the grace achieved comes from doing the work she wished to do "for the sake of that work alone."[30] Unlike her father or her Presbyterian forebears, Glasgow lives in a world of her own, not God's making.

The Woman Within and the woman herself are Modernist mosaics. The child who saw the face at the window becomes the artist who calls her coherent and assimilable self-portrait into question. Warning the reader to question her earliest memory, to which meaning is "attached, long afterwards," she ironically asks, "Doesn't all experience crumble in the end to mere literary material?" The reader, having seen Francis Glasgow's "rock-ribbed" Calvinism transformed into a literary conceit, might answer, "Yes."[31]

• • •

In *A Certain Measure*, Ellen Glasgow, the theorist, argued that all living books contain "the essence, or the extension, of a distinct identity," yet Glasgow, the "biographer of life," knew that she did her best work once emotion had passed. Only then could the untiring critic winnow, reassess, and dispose of idiosyncratic material. *Barren Ground* illustrates how the personal becomes political in its message and scope. The novel's heroine is as alone and besieged as Glasgow in *The Woman Within*. Seduced and abandoned, Dorinda Oakley plows her hatred of her former lover into the land, finding in the process the philosophy of humane stoicism Glasgow thought sufficient for life and for death. Dorinda's story exists within the larger one Glasgow associated with Calvinism and the beginning and the end of American democracy. Just two generations of the Oakleys encompass the change, their pioneering spirit of adventure having disintegrated into a philosophy of either heroic defeat or moral inertia. From this "dying culture" Glasgow hopes to extract the "raw stuff of American civilization." The novel's title comments on Dorinda Oakley's literal and spiritual inheritance. Writing about a region and a people bound by a rigid caste system, Glasgow emphasizes a moral, not a mannered, order.[32]

Like her author, Dorinda has always lived with Calvinism, either as an ethical principle represented by her grandfather, John Calvin Abernethy, or as a nervous malady personified in her mother. Fashioned after Francis Glasgow, Abernethy is a retired missionary who embodies what Max Weber called "the Protestant ethic and the spirit of capitalism." The same uneasy alliance that fueled the Tredegar Iron Works during the Civil War allows him to view slavery—one of "the strange gestures of divine grace"—as a preordained form of submission to legitimate authority. The doctrines of election and predestination absolve the individual of personal responsibility. As Hogg's antihero argues, we *must* do whatever is preordained, "and none of these things will be laid to our charge." The fifty slaves, on which Abernethy founds his fortune if not his estate, constitute "a nice point in theology." His conscience finds ease in the material success that indicates probable election. Later he sees no irony in selling "black flesh" to redeem "black souls in the Congo."[33]

The doctrine of social, cultural, and sexual predestination entitles Abernethy, in his roles of patriarch and minister, to colonize natives in Africa and women at home. Glasgow's equation of slavery and marriage condemns Calvinism's not-so-benevolent paternalism. Dorinda has as little place in this tradition as Glasgow had in that of Southern plantation novels or, for that matter, legendary Southern belles. The face that Glasgow first saw at the window now wears Abernethy's specific features. In the memoir, Glasgow found refuge from the unknown in self-irony; in the novel, she directs the deflating irony at an express power—Calvinist patriarchy.

Mrs. Oakley's uncongenial marriage with its resulting neurasthenia recalls that of Glasgow's mother, Anne. She too inherits an adventurous and romantic spirit but no agency. With the death of her missionary fiancé, Mrs. Oakley transfers her visions of the Congo and exotic heathens to center on Joshua Oakley, a born failure with the profile of John the Baptist. He is as much her other as the natives she longed to save: "The gulf between the dominant Scotch-Irish stock of the Valley and the mongrel breed of 'poor white' which produced Joshua was as wide as the abyss between alien races"—or between Francis and Anne Gholson Glasgow.[34]

Mrs. Oakley's thwarted ambition finds shape in neurotic dreams of "blue skies and golden sands, of palm trees on a river's bank, and of black babies thrown to crocodiles."[35] Her dream, both sexual and maternal, is in truth little different from her father's reality in foreign countries, or for that matter, Pedlar's Mill, Virginia, where he peddled black flesh. Obsessed with the threat of eternal damnation, she madly perpetuates a system injurious to all women. Mrs. Oakley would like Dorinda to worship a Calvinist God and practice a domestic ideal that Glasgow sees as ancient antagonists. In Glasgow's analysis, romance is another kind of religion that subjugates women.

Glasgow finds little difference between a Calvinism nurtured on moral principle and a nervous malady. Extrapolating from her father's example, she had decided that religion and sentimentality made people cruelly "blind to what happened." She does, however, have more sympathy for Mrs. Oakley's religious mania because it allows her, however poorly, to survive an unsatisfactory reality. Glasgow connects "this dark and secret river of her dream [flowing] silently beneath the commonplace crust of experience,"[36] with creativity. The artist, as she writes in *The Woman Within*, is also immersed in "some dark stream of identity, stronger and deeper and more relentless than the external movement of living."[37] Mrs. Oakley's recurrent bouts of madness, which emanate from her frustrated creativity, seem to comment—as does Charlotte Perkins Gilman's story "The Yellow Wallpaper" (1892)—on the imprisoned female imagination. She cannot mother more babies or, like her author, give birth to books because she cannot violate or revise traditions, such as Calvinism or paternalism, which Glasgow knew to be damaging, even insane.

Although Dorinda realizes that religion, sex, and duty have—to paraphrase Calvin—despoiled her mother of freedom and subjected her to miserable slavery, she still dreams the same quixotic dream. The Oakleys "might as well be living in the house, she sometimes thought with the doctrine of predestination; and like the doctrine of predestination, there was nothing to be done about it."[38] Her dream centers on Jason Greylock, a weak young doctor, whose submission to his father's "iron will" evokes the memory of Glasgow's suicidal brother Frank. Jason wants to convert the "natives" to modern methods of farming, but they unrepentently continue to deplete the land.

Barren Ground details what Glasgow called the "blissful tranquillity" of falling out of love. The outline of Dorinda's plot—an awakening to self, nature, and artistry (landscaping the wilderness)—parallels that of *The Woman Within* and effects in fiction what Glasgow, who took twenty-one years to recover from her experience with Harold S., found more difficult in life. Glasgow purposefully conflates and then condemns the dreams of mother and daughter. Jason's image, which Dorinda imagines on millions and millions of "prickly purple thistles,"

Glasgow's older brother Frank was her "idol, after my mother and my mammy."

represents the last vestiges of her faith in romantic/sexual love. Her tie to Jason has always been a form of egotism, a kind of pride stronger than love or even happiness, and with the symbolic marriage of her farm and his, bought at auction, it eventually lessens. Glasgow compares Dorinda's faith in love to her mother's belief in the Calvinism that "sprang up and blossomed like a Scotch thistle in Barren Ground." Whether religious or romantic, each woman's faith thrives on the evasive idealism that Glasgow held responsible for the corruption of American art, politics, and character. Both women's dreams prove "barren": Dorinda loses her baby, and Mrs. Oakley sacrifices her eternal soul by providing an alibi for a son guilty of manslaughter.[39]

Lacking a sense of original sin or outraged virtue, Dorinda stands as Glasgow's critique of mid-Victorian heroines, whose minds "resemble a page of the more depressing theology."[40] She refuses to take what God wills. By choosing celibacy, she ensures a future free from any form of social-sexual predestination. Her instinct for survival owes, like Glasgow's own, "less to the attribute of courage than . . . to an innate capacity to exist without living, to endure without enjoying." Glasgow presents Dorinda's choice as necessary, admirable, and, to the extent that it is a form of repression, abnormal. Nothing shields her from the realization that she is ultimately alone. The terrible knowledge that Dorinda attains is not of evil but of the void, "that unconquerable vastness in which nothing is everything." Call the snake in the garden "god" or "love" or "evasive idealism," it thrives on self-illusion. There may be no meaning, as Dorinda suspects, in "coral strands and palm trees and naked black babies" though the very question—"What was the meaning of it?"—prompts speculation.[41]

Trying to fill the void, Dorinda finds meaning in work. Her affinity for nature and the female world it represents most distinguishes the plot of *Barren Ground* from that of *The Woman Within* and the teachings of Calvin. Torn, like Glasgow, between the law of the father, represented by Abernethy, and the natural world of the mother, represented by Aunt Mehitable Green (a black midwife and conjurer modeled after Mammy Lizzie), she clearly chooses the maternal. Aunt Mehitable's ministering to babies, the lovesick, and the infirm ties her to the cycles of nature. With Aunt Mehitable and her granddaughter Fluvanna, Dorinda shares an affection "as strong and elastic as the bond that holds relatives together."[42] The women's collaborative effort to restore Old Farm highlights the exploitative and hierarchal quality of Grandfather Abernethy's Calvinist system financed by the selling of human flesh and sustained by the endless drudgery of Dorinda's mother.

Dorinda sculpts the land that in turn nourishes a series of her evolving selves. Unlike her Calvinist forefathers, she neither eroticizes the wilderness of Old Farm nor sees it as a psychic territory that must be crossed to reach the promised land.[43] Her relationship with Nature is as personal and self-reflective as Alexandra Bergson's in *O Pioneers!* (1913): Kinship with the land was filtering through her blood into her brain; and she knew that this transfigured instinct was blended of pity, memory, and passion. Dimly she felt that only through this emotion could she attain permanent liberation of spirit. This mysterious unity with the land becomes the guiding principle of the novel. Through the labors of her surrogate son, John Abner, Dorinda will achieve a form of immanence in "the immutable landscape." Glasgow isolated the dominant elements of *Barren Ground* as space and time and made her heroine part of the "eternal sequence,"[44] captured for her in Thomas Hardy's *Dynasts* (1904–1908). When she visited Hardy in 1914, he was moved by her recitation of his own lines: "O Immanence, that reasonest not / In putting forth all things begot, / Thou build'st Thy house in space—for what?" Eleven years later, Dorinda gives the existential answer: " 'I think, I feel, I am.' The only thing that mattered was her triumph over circumstances."[45]

Dorinda's state of mind and her responses to circumstances are analogous to Glasgow's after her mother's death. In the first draft of *The Woman Within*, Glasgow notes that she prevailed by turning "with an almost physical aversion from the material symbols of the sacrificial lamb and of the redemption through blood" to the writings of Marcus Aurelius.[46] Having adopted a version of Aurelius's "humane stoicism," she felt that she could bear what she had to bear, but she "could not pretend it away." "I will not be broken," Dorinda similarly vows: "The vein of iron which had supported her through adversity was merely the instinct older than herself, stronger than circumstances, deeper than the shifting surface of emotion."[47] The passage anticipates Glasgow's more conciliatory attitude toward Calvinism, embodied in the motherly figure of Grandmother Fincastle in *Vein of Iron* (1935) or the enduring ones of Asa and Roy Timberlake in both *In This Our Life* (1941) and *Beyond Defeat* (1966).

Embracing her grandfather's personal tenets (divorced from their religious context) of "integrity, firmness, and frugality," Dorinda grows to resemble Glasgow in *The Woman Within* and foreshadows John

Anne Glasgow. "It was as if the world rocked suddenly, and fell to pieces," Glasgow wrote of her mother's death in 1893.

Fincastle, the protagonist of *Vein of Iron*, whose "inner life alone . . . was vital and intimate and secure." Discovering "the secret ecstacy at the heart of experience" also makes him an exile, separated forever from those he most loves. Like an artist who inherits the religious habit of mind without the religious heart, Dorinda creates an interior space that is remote, inviolate, and self-sufficient; nothing disturbs it: "Not joy, not pain, not love, not passion, not sorrow, not loss, not life at its sharpest edge"—nothing. Ironically, her perseverance leads, as Calvinism teaches and *The Woman Within* elucidates, to a kind of election. Dorinda's "deep instinct for survival" becomes "a dynamic force"—indicated by the section titles "Broomsedge," "Pine," and "Life-Everlasting"—that transforms, like art itself, barren ground into Elysian fields. She comes to grace or experiences, in secular terms, what Calvin termed a "quickening." By recovering herself, she begins the journey that ends for Glasgow in a vision of Everything or Nothing or God.[48]

• • •

Barren Ground and *The Woman Within* insist that the life of the mind contains "an antidote to experience," that work can give one what Henry James called "a standpoint in the universe," the something that "holds one in one's place."[49] Paired, they illustrate how much Glasgow lived both inside and outside history and myth, in selected realities and the "Reality" she thought "profounder than the depths of experience."[50] The Reality that Dorinda finds in Nature was not an option for her creator, who believed that the artist, almost by definition, mediates between the worlds of father and mother, between realities and Reality.

Authorizing the personal, Glasgow found her own versions of the universal and Modernism. Someone as anomalous as Glasgow—woman, writer, feminist, and animal rights activist—had perhaps no other place she could turn but to herself. It is not surprising that an author who came to believe that all creative writing was, in some manner, autobiographical might have wondered, "How can one tell where memory ends and imagination begins?"[51] Neither is it surprising that her version of her career changed as she aged, the first Realist in the South becoming in retrospect the first Modernist. Glasgow's valuation of subjectivity and historicity set her apart from poets, such as Pound or Eliot, who exalted the word as language rather than symbol above all else. Offering herself as both text and archetype, Glasgow revised Calvin's plot to accommodate, even favor, her highly self-referential and lettered world. In her fiction, Calvinism becomes, historically and psychologically, marker, measure, and foil. Glasgow's work bridges two worlds: the Calvinist world, whose diarist tradition she continues in *The Woman Within*, and the modern world, whose past and present she traces in her social history. Her belief in a recoverable and transferable history—along with her belief in words like loyalty and honor—may distinguish her from the so-called Lost Generation, but it also makes her a foremother of Southern Agrarians, such as Robert Penn Warren and Stark Young, who wanted to reclaim the native humanism they saw rooted in the rural life of their particular region. Despite Glasgow's feeling that it was "easier to break with tradition"—whether that of True Womanhood or the sentimental histories her father enjoyed—than to endure it, *The Woman Within* and *Barren Ground* suggest, in their representations of Calvinism, not only how much the inherited realities comprise Reality, but also how arbitrary such distinctions are.[52] Only in the imagination, perhaps, can Calvin and Darwin sustain a kind of unholy and empowering alliance that grants a feeling of spiritual luxury.

NINE

The Invisible Stigma in
Ellen Glasgow's *The Descendant*

Linda Kornasky

Generally, literary criticism about Ellen Glasgow's work at least briefly addresses her hearing impairment, the condition that Blair Rouse aptly terms "a hampering affliction."[1] However, most of this commentary is all too brief and limited to Glasgow's personal, rather than her literary, experience. These approaches range from Linda Wagner's excellent 1982 book, commending Glasgow for transcending her hearing loss, to Marcelle Thiebaux's study, published in the same year, emphasizing the supposedly comical manifestations of Glasgow's condition.[2] Other critics even play down Glasgow's hearing impairment, while nevertheless dismissing her descriptions of emotional difficulties as petty displays of maudlin or morbid "victimization." For instance, Monique Parent Frazee claims that "today, Ellen Glasgow would *not* publish *The Woman Within*" because, according to Frazee, if Glasgow had lived in our postfeminist age, she could have found "more sensible and positive means of psychological liberation."[3] Yet, Frazee never mentions Glasgow's hearing impairment, and so one can only wonder how feminism might liberate women from this particular difficulty.

Overall, these critical responses to Glasgow's hearing impairment do not adequately indicate the influence her hearing loss had on her art. Being hearing impaired myself and familiar with recent research on the complex nature of hearing loss, I would argue that the significance of Glasgow's hearing impairment for her art is more positive than her critics and literary biographers suppose. All the same, these scholars are not to be blamed out of hand. As a review of audiological research demonstrates, the assumptions reflected in the critical commentary about her hearing loss have been reasonable according to accepted attitudes toward acquired adult hearing loss, attitudes that appear even in Glasgow's own personal documents. These attitudes persist because of the lack of thorough scientific research on acquired adult hearing loss. Although audiologists have studied extensively the effects of prelingual deafness in children, until recently they have given surprisingly little attention to the separate issue of hearing loss in postvocational adulthood, especially in the vocationally productive period between the ages of eighteen and sixty-five.[4] Only since the mid-1980s has the entire spectrum of hearing loss in adulthood been investigated by the scientific community.

In the past, audiological researchers, presupposing an inherent pathology connected with hearing loss, simply compiled lists of emotional and behavioral disorders from which the hearing impaired were assumed to suffer.[5] The hearing world concludes from this that adjustment to acquired hearing loss means achieving a vaguely defined, but preferably passive "acceptance" of one's condition and a subsequent "progress" beyond maladjusted behaviors. Likewise, hearing people often place all responsibility for overcoming such "maladjustment" on afflicted individuals, and to a lesser degree on their families.

Noting the lack of specific guidelines establishing what constitutes "adequate adjustment," a team of British researchers, James G. Kyle, Lesley G. Jones, and Peter L. Wood, conducted a study and in 1985 published a model of adjustment to acquired hearing loss.[6] Their report attempts to evaluate the level of actual maladjustment among hearing-impaired people, to account for the positive function served by so-called maladjusted strategies of coping with hearing loss, and to identify other positive coping strategies. Throughout their report, Kyle, Jones, and Wood emphasize the need for the hearing impaired to feel fully informed and capable of controlling access to information both privately as well as in social situations. This model identifies three phases of adjustment to hearing loss and, most important, stresses the positive adjustment strategies developed throughout.

The first of the three phases occurs prior to the formal acknowledgment of hearing loss. Unfortunately, researchers have little definite knowledge of this phase because they cannot accurately identify this population. Yet, according to the British team, this stage may be especially crucial in the process of adjustment to hearing loss for two reasons: first, it can last many years (indeed, some hearing-impaired people never acknowledge their hearing loss); and second, it can include much of the most effective and affirmative, though unconscious, development of adjustment strategies. The relatively brief second phase comprises a medical diagnosis of hearing loss, followed, if feasible, by the prescription of a hearing aid.

Glasgow braved a visit to novelist Joseph Conrad (*far right*) and his family in Kent, England, in the summer of 1914, by which time she was using an "electric device" to aid her hearing.

Usually, this phase is more emotionally disturbing than the first because at this point hearing-impaired people are compelled formally to acknowledge their hearing loss. Furthermore, in this second phase, psychological trauma is exacerbated because audiologists can offer the hearing impaired medical help only in the form of hearing aids.

After medical confirmation of hearing loss, the third phase is the "subsequent accommodation" by the individual to the exigencies of hearing impairment. This final phase is the focus of most of the research on the alleged "maladjustment" of the hearing impaired. As Kyle, Jones, and Wood explain, at this point preconceptions about acceptance of hearing loss begin to cause conflicts between hearing-impaired people and their families and friends. In many respects, hearing-impaired people feel as if this phase were the first and thus that they can legitimately be expected to take some time to adjust to what is for them recent news. On the other hand, those around hearing-impaired people at this stage have sometimes been cognizant of hearing impairment for a longer time than the hearing impaired themselves, and many feel that adjustment ought to be almost complete by this time. Mutual resentment can cause hearing-impaired individuals to withdraw defensively after those closest to them become convinced that they have willfully avoided acceptance. This conflict partly explains the reason for the medical overemphasis on the pathological emotions and behaviors of the hearing impaired. More positively, the third phase also features the development of further adjustment strategies for controlling access to information. For many intelligent and energetic individuals, adjustment progresses well during this period along the same path as the more unconscious adjustment of the first phase.

This three-part model prompts the reexamination of the artistically important aspects of Glasgow's adjustment to hearing loss, especially during the first phase, when hearing impairment was a positive force in the birth of her artistic ambition. Significantly, in Glasgow's case, the first phase of adjustment was not only of considerable duration but also occurred simultaneously with the beginning of her vocational plans and culminated in her first novel, *The Descendant*.

In 1889, at the age of only sixteen, Ellen Glasgow began to detect the loss of her hearing, but because for several years she did not receive medical confirmation that her hearing loss would worsen and become a case of serious hearing impairment, she, like many other hearing-impaired people, did not move quickly out of the first phase of adjustment. In fact, in 1891, both in Richmond and in New York City, doctors mistakenly told Glasgow that the difficulty she was experiencing with her hearing would not likely increase. Glasgow recounts in her autobiography that during the period between 1891 and 1895, when she was writing *The Descendant*, she continued to detect increasing hearing loss, particularly after the death of her mother in 1893 when debilitating grief and influenza markedly damaged her hearing. Still, just after the joyful completion and editorial praise of her first novel, Glasgow recounts that hearing loss, and the fear and shame of the prospect of deafness, "was only beginning to afflict me."[7] She would not become extremely distressed by hearing loss until the summer of 1896, during and immediately following her first trip abroad, when her hearing deteriorated even more frighteningly.[8]

The timing of *The Descendant*'s composition, during the less emotionally tormenting years of initial adjustment, suggests that the creation of this novel was at least partly a consequence of the first phase described by Kyle, Jones, and Wood. Glasgow believed while writing this novel that a vocation as a novelist was the only way "to survive in the struggle" of coping with the deaths of her mother and brother-in-law, her own frequent illnesses, and the possibility of further hearing loss.[9] At this point, also in reference to her hearing loss, she asserts to herself, "If only I can have my work and adequate recognition . . . I shall be satisfied to give up everything else."[10]

The telling aspect of this statement with regard to the adjustment to the hearing-loss model is that Glasgow conceptually links artistic creation and critical recognition; in other words, Glasgow conceived of her art both as a means to communicate and to control the movement of information in her surroundings.[11] In adjusting to her hearing loss, Glasgow hoped that a career as a novelist would meet her needs for sharing and receiving information, a process that for her is embodied in the dual ideal of "my work and adequate recognition."[12]

Linda Wagner takes a different approach to Glasgow's concern for critical recognition, which she cleverly phrases "the favor-currying of which [Glasgow] is sometimes accused." Wagner theorizes that Glasgow's concern for and personal investment in the critical reception of her work in part signify the feelings of inferiority Glasgow was made to suffer because she was a woman. Wagner considers Glasgow subject to something like the difficulties of British women writers described by Elaine Showalter in *A Literature of Their Own* (1977). Showalter claims that women writers, facing the "doublebind" of disappointment with the lack of serious or fair commentary on their work and the fear of seeming unfeminine to the public eye, pursued several personal "strategies" for assuaging this psychological stress. Of various strategies, Glasgow, according to Wagner, was especially guilty of "coy assurance-seeking" but also occasionally of excessive humility.[13] While Wagner's argument is certainly correct in part, one should remember that Glasgow's efforts to get positive critical reception and her often-angry response to negative critical commentary were not always coy, but rather frequently demanding in tone. Thus, Glasgow's desire for "adequate recognition," integral to her ambition as a writer, can also be seen as stemming from a need to exert control and authority in, what were to her, primary acts of communication (that is, to initiate a "discussion" of sorts between herself and critics in which she was a dominant or equal participant). Thus, her instinct to perceive an interpersonal or communicative dimension in professional, critical dialogue, and to react accordingly, can be viewed as a positive strategy of adjustment to hearing loss.

Glasgow's conception of her art as a two-way channel of information has both general and particular implications for understanding *The Descendant*. Generally, the creation of this novel, coupled with the substantial reading campaign Glasgow undertook with her sister Cary at the same time, reflects Glasgow's increasing need to procure and produce information. As Kyle, Jones, and Wood indicate, the hearing-impaired population, including all socioeconomic classes and educational levels, practice literacy skills more frequently than those with normal hearing, for these skills provide optimum reception of information.[14] With her own unique vigor and intelligence, through reading and writing, Glasgow pursued a course of adjustment common to the hearing impaired.

More particularly, Glasgow's experience with the first phase of adjustment to hearing loss shapes what critics recognize as both the weak and strong elements of *The Descendant*. In long, discursive passages about radical, turn-of-the-century social philosophy and biology, Glasgow awkwardly exhibits her extensive reading knowledge and her over-enthusiastic desire to contribute to the exchange of contemporaneous ideas. As virtually all critics observe, these tedious passages constitute a weakness in the novel. But the two redeeming elements of this novel— Glasgow's contribution to the emerging genre of American literary naturalism by exploring Darwinian concepts about human intelligence and morality, as well as her ability to conceive and render the deeply felt emotions of her central characters, the outcasts Michael Akershem and Rachel Gavin—also may stem from Glasgow's drive to communicate ideas derived from her own difficult experience. Specifically, Glasgow in her first novel transforms her own invisible stigma of partial hearing loss into emotionally powerful and well-executed themes about social responsibility and the psychological stress of invisible stigmata for characters in conflict with social ideology.

Throughout her life, yet particularly in the first phase of adjustment, Glasgow, like most hearing-impaired people, struggled painfully with the fear of exposing her hearing loss. In *The Woman Within*, she observes that during the years around the turn of the century she was tormented by "the intolerable effort of pretending to hear," that is, of trying to keep an invisible difficulty from becoming visible in her conduct. Glasgow stresses that her fear of hearing loss was particularly prompted by "its effect upon others," as they became aware of it. She recounts that her fear of exposing her hearing loss caused her to avoid informal meetings with strangers or even friends. Candidly, she asserts that "the hardest part of such an affliction, I think, is the wasted nervous effort of trying to pretend it away." As Kyle, Jones, and Wood suggest, and I have known from my own experience, people with partial hearing loss, like Glasgow, are especially prone to the stress of such "nervous effort." Since they are frequently successful in concealing hearing

Glasgow (*second from left*) dining with James Branch Cabell (*center*) and others at his Richmond home in 1928. She once commented that despite her hearing loss, "like so many Southerners, I had been born with the gift of talk, and enjoyed mingling with people."

THE INVISIBLE STIGMA IN ELLEN GLASGOW'S *THE DESCENDANT*

loss, those with partial loss often feel that occasional lack of success in hiding their stigma signifies personal failure. In *The Descendant*, Glasgow creatively weaves conflicts similar to her own into the novel's naturalistic plot.[15]

A central theme in *The Descendant* is the predetermined self-defeat of the two main characters as they struggle to hide stigmata that inevitably become visible. As Julius Rowan Raper explains, the novel's somewhat vague biological determinism is accompanied by a more developed analysis of the determining and significantly invisible force of Michael's Calvinistic "conceptual environment." The psychologically warping force of his environment persists until, combined with the ineluctable power of biological determinism, it leads Michael to murder. Raper accurately considers Glasgow's handling of this ambiguity clumsy, but, as he also points out, this ambiguity contributes to the novel's critique of the social stigmatization of poor white males in the South.[16]

The finest aspect of this early novel is the rendering of the psychological stress leading to the main characters' self-defeat. Michael, the illegitimate son of an uneducated farm woman and a mysterious, no-good transient, has been mistreated by a hypocritically religious small Southern community. Michael seeks in advanced education both a possible escape from social injustice and a way to take revenge on his persecutors. After first succeeding as a student, he moves to New York City and becomes a writer for the radical, leftist newspaper, the *Iconoclast*. There he begins a systematic attack against social conventions. While still young, he becomes editor and initiates a sexual affair with bohemian artist Rachel Gavin, to whom he unashamedly, yet bitterly, confides the secret of his stigmatized origin. But as successful as he is in his personal and professional battle against righteous conventionality, he never stops fearing that his stigma will become visible to the society he claims to despise. This paradox is one of the well-conceived aspects of Michael's characterization and Glasgow creates several of the best scenes in the novel to highlight the tension in Michael caused by this paradox.

For example, at a society dinner early in his newspaper career, Michael is humiliated when he commits a "breach of etiquette" by allowing his wine to be poured into his champagne glass. Although afterward he mocks social rituals, he still feels anguished knowing that this mistake reveals his disadvantaged childhood, and Glasgow elicits a sympathetic response for Michael from readers at this moment. But not until later, in his visit with the virtuous philanthropist, Anna Allard, does Michael become deeply concerned that his stigma might become truly visible to others around him. Anna tells him first that she is "so sorry" to know of his connection with the *Iconoclast*, and at their next visit she informs him that his angry political message is socially dangerous because its violence is contagious to impressionable poor youth and the morally weak. These conversations force him to realize that his facade of moral idealism is no more than an unconvincing veil covering his hatred toward those who rejected him. He must therefore recognize that his hard work has amounted only to a marker, for anyone like Anna perceptive enough to read it, of his poorly concealed social stigma. At the end of this discussion, he almost involuntarily reveals his background to Anna when responding defensively to her regret that the truth should hurt him. Tellingly, as if his whole past were under scrutiny, he cries, "It is little to me what people say of my" and then he stops without finishing his sentence and bids her good-bye.[17]

Walking the streets after parting from Anna, Michael ponders how his fear of stigmatization has thwarted his life's work. He "despised himself that he had fought for the sake of fighting, not for the sake of the cause; for what men might say of him he had wrestled for the things that were. . . . For a name he had given his salvation." After this revelation, Michael begins to fantasize about leaving the *Iconoclast* and fashioning a new social ambition on Anna's principles, but even this seemingly moral idea is problematic in his current situation. His nervous apprehension of others' judgment of him, either for his already-published views or for the hypocrisy of his intended rehabilitation and marriage to Anna, leads to his murdering Kyle, one of his political acolytes. His uncivilized act is in part a biologically determined expression of his inheritance, but it is also the result of Michael's resentment against Driscoll's and then Kyle's condemnation. Calling Michael a "damned scoundrel" and a "blackguard," both men use the terminology of Michael's boyhood persecutors, and he is overcome with angry shame that the stigma he has tried so desperately to conceal has become visible.[18]

Michael's obsession with visible stigmata also appears in his evaluation of Anna and Rachel. He judges them based on what he believes are visible representations of their respective "goodness" and "moral laxity." Despite the awkwardness of the narrator's prose in this passage, Glasgow's depiction of Michael's attraction to the neat and trim Anna is crucial:

> A Mulberry Street missionary, possessing a withered profile and a shrinking manner, might have been doubly virtuous with but slight success [in attracting Michael]. And, after all, there are few of us capable of dissociating the attraction of virtue from the attraction of the earthly habiliments which it chooses to adopt.[19]

Conversely, Michael immediately thereafter is repulsed by what he considers to be the visible signs of Rachel's sexual stigma, that is, her willingness to succumb to her sexual passion for him without any regard for her own feminine "honor." After seeing Anna, he goes to Rachel's apartment and there he notices Rachel's less trim appearance, comparing it to Anna's neatness. Though self-consciously aware of his own cowardliness, he nevertheless thinks "at that moment the fall of her gown seemed careless, the loosened coil of her hair a trifle unkempt."[20] Thereafter, Michael becomes convinced that Rachel's perceived stigma makes her unworthy as a potential wife. Michael's judgment of her unworthiness stems from his own fear of revealed stigmata and thus contributes to the psychological plausibility of his character.

Rachel's characterization, however, has often troubled feminist readers, who find her impurity and the role of biological determinism in her professional decline as a painter weak points in the novel. In their view, the novel confusingly portrays Rachel both as a clinging lover blinded by misplaced passion for an undeserving man and as an independent woman who bravely and proudly faces losing a lover toward whom she is still drawn. Yet, despite the flaws in Rachel's characterization, her stance against Michael's attempt to make her sexual passion for him a stigma, by treating her as a mere pitiable victim, is convincing. Interestingly, she detests Michael's duplicitous attempt to conceal her "stigma" more than she fears its exposure. Thus, when he covers his changed feelings for her with an improbable tenderness, she refuses to be fooled and seeks out signs of his indifference. Equally interesting, unlike Michael's mother, Rachel does not become pregnant from her premarital sexual contact; thus, without such a visible manifestation of sexuality, her stigmatization by Michael and a hypocritical society is based only on rumor.

As their relationship disintegrates, Rachel refuses to accept the stigma Michael thrusts on her, breaking with him as if she could easily forget their affair and return to art as well as other lovers. That she in part acts bravely here only for Michael's sake is troubling. During the sleepless night before she renounces him, she is tormented by fears that perhaps she actually is stigmatized and unworthy. She thinks with scorn, "'I hate myself! Oh, how I could curse and spit upon myself! What am I—I, a target for the stones of the world—what am I that I should chain him to me?'" She imagines that "a shadow upon the wall . . . took the shape of the devil's face, mocking her with its grotesqueness . . . always seeming to draw a little nearer." Here, Rachel fears that the previously invisible stigma of alleged sexual depravity, made visible in her imagination, has marked her.[21]

Of course, a modern reader cannot help feeling a distaste for the novel's tendency to uphold the convention that Rachel's sincere sexual affection for Michael "taints" her. Nonetheless, these psychological passages do profoundly treat the effect of a woman's fear of sexual stigma. As this scene and those in which Michael suffers over a similar fear demonstrate, Glasgow somewhat successfully constructs her first novel's plot around a central psychological conflict, a conflict derived from what she called the "transfigured experience" of her own life.[22]

Although this novel is not one of Glasgow's major works, it reveals the potential of a writer whose strongest attribute is the ability to communicate emotional experience powerfully, and to use this experience as means to energize ideological debate. In *The Woman Within*, Glasgow ends her discussion about her partial deafness with an unanswered question about "how much [her] horror of deafness had to do with [her art]."[23] If it were possible, I would answer her that she may have turned to fiction not only as an outlet for her intellect, but also because her hearing loss gave her a unique insight into certain aspects of the nature of experience and, most important, the need to communicate this insight to her readers in a manner that demands their personal involvement.

TEN

Living without Joy:
Dorinda's Rejection of Love

Benita Huffman Muth

According to her later preface to *Barren Ground* (1925), Ellen Glasgow intended Dorinda to be a universal heroine who triumphs over cravings for happiness and feelings of futility: "She exists wherever a human being has learned to live without joy, wherever the spirit of fortitude has triumphed over the sense of futility."[1] Indeed, Dorinda does triumph over some seemingly hopeless situations. Instead of taking her place as a "fallen woman," Dorinda leaves for a new life in the city and, as in a heroic quest, returns bringing new information to revivify the barren land of her home. Yet in achieving her success, she shows her kinship with the logic of her great-grandfather, who sold his slaves down the river to finance missionaries to save the souls of Africans. In following her self-imposed mission to live without romantic love, she suppresses her sexuality, thus denying her femininity and her potential fertility, becoming as barren as the soil ever was. Her determination to restore fertility to the land masks her mission to control and contain her passions and to attain dominance over her own threatening femininity.

At the beginning of the novel, Dorinda strives to bring fertility to her inner life. She has a "starved craving" for happiness; and here, as elsewhere, happiness can be translated as love. Her father, with his low self-esteem, offered his daughter affection only once, never holding her again after she cried, and her mother smiles only at very young things such as babies, puppies, and chicks, not at Dorinda. When she meets Jason Greylock, she is ready for love, and the love she finds makes the emotional waste of her life newly fertile. After they meet, it is "as if an April flush had passed over the waste places," and "her inner life . . . was suddenly rich with bloom." Even though the object of Dorinda's love is mainly a creation of her own imagination and the real Jason proves unworthy of her devotion, the vivifying effects of her love on her own life are real, and her desire to recapture those effects continues to resurface throughout her life.[2]

Dorinda's expression of passion, however, makes her vulnerable, and when Jason abandons her, her hopes and budding emotions are crushed by the pain of rejection. She feels caught by the life that she had appeared to run toward.[3] In shock over the failure of her attempt at love, she begins to run in the opposite direction:

> Nothing was alive except the burning sore of her memory. . . . Every other emotion—affection, tenderness, sympathy, sentiment—all these natural approaches to experience had shrivelled up like nerves that are dead.[4]

So when emotion does reawaken in her at the concert, she views this emotion as an enemy that has returned to conquer her:

> Something that she had buried out of sight under the earth, was pushing upward in anguish. Something that she had defeated was marching as a conqueror over her life.[5]

Rebirth of passion and, thus, of potential fertility become linked with danger and loss of freedom; and strong emotion becomes an inner invader that must be resisted.

Rather than allow this reborn emotion to find an object in Dr. Burch, who more closely resembles her imaginary lover than Jason ever did, Dorinda channels this passion into memories of and plans for her farm. Passion betrayed her once, and her undemonstrative family has not provided her with a model for allowing her love a second attempt at expression. She responds to her crisis therefore by following the only example she knows. Like her father, Dorinda does not recover from her first rejection to try again; and she compensates, like her mother, by sublimating her romantic feelings into her work and repressing them into her dreams. Between her pain and her childhood lessons, she has no incentive to believe that a new expression of her sexuality or of romantic feelings would lead to anything other than further rejection.

Yet having been awakened, her passion must now be redirected. It becomes "transfigured, recoiling from the personal to the impersonal object," the land, which cannot hurt or betray her. As she states later, "the farm isn't human and it

Ellen Glasgow, ca. 1925

won't make you suffer. Only human things break your heart," showing that avoiding suffering and a broken heart, not simply a desire for economic success or community standing, underlies her furious efforts with the farm.[6]

Dorinda's desire to find in the farm a safe substitute for a human object mixes with her anger toward Jason and toward her own lingering, unacceptable passion for him. After the reawakening of her emotions, she dreams of plowing under thistles bearing Jason's face. When she tells Dr. Burch of her aversion to intimacy, she rises to leave him "because the thought of Jason had come to her out of the vision of Old Farm." Even though she feels the farm calls to her for help, helping the farm becomes inextricably tied to ridding herself of the desire for the love that has hurt her. Yet, like her passions, the farm, too, has been associated in her mind with forces that catch women and eat their lives away. "Poor Ma," she says, "[the farm] caught her when she was young, and she was never able to get free."[7] While functioning as an acceptable outlet for her repressed femininity, the farm also becomes a symbol of the danger inherent in those female impulses toward love and fertility that she lavishes on it. She can closely control and manipulate the extent of her involvement with the land in a way that she could not completely control the depth of her involvement in a human relationship.[8] Controlling the farm and forcing it to submit to her will become expressions of her determination to compel the forces of life that trap women—their physical desires, their cravings for love and affection—to submit to her will.

Since all of these impulses are part of herself and her femininity, her drive is as much to control a part of herself as it is to make the farm profitable or to avenge herself on Jason. Her dangerous craving to bring fertility to her inner life is projected outward as a drive to bring fertility to the exterior world. Her continuing desire to possess Jason sexually becomes a desire to possess his farm. Instead of dwelling on her own weakness, she concentrates on Jason's weaknesses. To avoid her own desire for passion, she avoids Jason, hardly ever leaving her farm. Those parts of herself she wishes to suppress and refuses to acknowledge are projected onto others and onto the land.[9]

That Dorinda can easily project her femininity onto the farm is not unusual, because the land's metaphorical femininity has been used to express human interaction with the American continent since its discovery. In choosing to direct her passions toward the land, Dorinda reacts to what Annette Kolodny calls "the uniquely American 'pastoral impulse,' " an impulse that has at its core "a yearning to know and to respond to the landscape as feminine" and to find in it the "total female principle of gratification." In literary terms, this pastoral impulse has been expressed both in the form of white Southern womanhood taken to represent an unspoiled aristocratic Eden, as seen in William Gilmore Simms's work, and later in the form of an earth mother, especially William Faulkner's Lena Grove, who is needed to redeem a corrupted Southern landscape. Yet, as Beth Harrison notes, both of these versions create a problem for women writers who wish an unsymbolic, active female character.[10]

Glasgow responds to this problem by having a woman, not a man, actively project her own femininity onto the earth. The earth, not the woman, thus becomes symbolic. In this instance, however, a projection that had indicated desire becomes transformed into self-denial. Having abandoned the roles of both belle and earth mother, Dorinda adopts a dominating "male" attitude toward the earth to which she transfers her disowned fruitfulness. While the role of farmer (especially that of a dairy farmer) need not be a masculine one, Dorinda clearly does not wish any longer to relate to her world and her community as a woman. Besides taking a traditionally male profession and wearing male clothing, she feels triumphant when Bob Ellgood stops seeing her as a woman and looks at her "just as if she had been a man." Taking what she sees as the biologically dominant position of the male to a submissive, feminized earth acts as another mechanism that she uses to feel in control of the unruly feminine passion that unsettles her.[11]

When Dorinda, after thirteen years, still will not reclaim her sexuality and insists on a platonic marriage with Nathan Pedlar, this appropriation of maleness proves more than simply an understandable wish to be considered a social equal. This marriage does not, as Harrison suggests, attempt to create a new male-female relationship based on equality; Dorinda definitely puts herself in the dominant position. Her husband remains little more than a hired hand on the farm, and Dorinda consciously uses her "incalculable advantage" of simply liking Nathan, who loves her, to keep him from having a vital part in her life.[12]

The cycles of work on the farm have long since become an antidote for feeling, because they possess a kind of stability that feeling has not demonstrated in her relationship with Jason. Because the cows must be milked no matter what happens, she can use work in the cow barn to soothe her nerves and to avoid her wedding night. Her mother's decline after lying for Rufus reinforces Dorinda's tendency to consider woman's love a weakness that puts her at a disadvantage, just as the contentment of her days of sexual passion when she "ceased longing, ceased striving" later seems a passive surrender to her biology. Being "done with all that" and choosing a sexually sterile marriage in which *she* has the power to inflict any hurt but is invulnerable herself allows her the tight control over her sexual drive and its attendant emotions that an intimate marriage would not.[13] In order to overcome what she would see as a weakness of female fate, Dorinda maintains total control of herself and her marriage and resolves to remain self-determined and autonomous, a resolve for which she denies her female sexuality.[14]

Likewise, Dorinda never allows herself involvement in any relationship over which she does not ultimately maintain some form of control. Her closest friend, Fluvanna, is an employee and black; by virtue of her racial status, Dorinda, whose friendship was always tinged with "an inherited feeling of condescension," can maintain a feeling of superiority. John Abner alone receives tenderness from her, but her attitude toward him is more that of a benefactor than a substitute mother. The farm evokes her deepest responses, but the "fierce sense of protection" she feels toward it is aroused by the knowledge that the farm is her possession. By virtue of its inanimate status, the farm remains the thing over which she has the greatest control and receives "the deepest obligation that her nature could feel." In this impersonal relationship, as in all the others, she is firmly in control.[15]

Yet her impulse for self-control and autonomy wars with deterministic notions that have held over from her Calvinistic upbringing. Even as she strives to remake her life after Jason's abandonment, she claims, "Life makes and breaks us. We don't make life. The best we can do is bear it."

The dust jacket for the first edition of *Barren Ground* was adapted from this woodcut design by Virginia artist Julius John Lankes.

Shortly before she criticizes her mother's death as an "unconditional surrender to decay," as though blaming her mother for not fighting a defeatable foe, Dorinda herself has already decided that this end is fixed: "Nothing endured. Everything perished of its own inner decay." Although she does not tolerate imperfection in herself, she cannot maintain her anger at Rufus, for "after all, who was to blame? Who was ever to blame in life?"[16] Despite her agreement with her mother's advice not to let a man ruin her life and her unending work both to remake her existence and to control her emotions, she repeatedly claims that Jason has irrevocably ruined her life and blighted her youth. While seeming to contradict her earlier assertion that no one is ever to blame in life, blaming Jason performs the same function on a grander level, by taking the responsibility of her own actions and any imperfect consequences of them away from herself.[17]

Despite all efforts to contain it, dissatisfaction with the life Dorinda has made for herself revives periodically. At times, she feels the loss of her emotional realm intensely: "She longed with all her soul to suffer acutely; yet she could feel nothing within this colourless void in which she was imprisoned." As she looks back on her life, she sees a moment of closeness with Nathan as the single "fertile valley in the arid monotony of her life" that she has allowed herself.[18]

Her occasional, seemingly contradictory assertions of determinism become her means of coping with the regrets that her chosen life produces. Regrets, after all, could be dangerous to her control, because they indicate her desire for the emotion she has suppressed. That Dorinda, with all her determination to re-create the world around her, should maintain a contradictory sense that life must be borne, not changed, that all work in the end is futile, and that Jason's action can irrevocably ruin her whole youth demonstrates that she does not want to take responsibility for the dissatisfaction she feels with the loveless life that she has chosen.[19]

Jason's death brings her dissatisfaction most strongly into her consciousness and highlights the insufficiency of her deterministic philosophy. Neither her attempt at revenge nor her years of self-denying work have filled the void that suppressing the passions has left in her life. In her desire to live the past over again and live it differently and in her recognition in dreams of the life that might have been hers, she has the insight that might spur her toward claiming personal responsibility for her loveless existence, possibly inspiring her to try romance again with Bob Ellgood.[20]

But the morning, which seemingly could fulfill the promise of the night, does not. When she awakes, she is "caught again in the tide of material things," the same material world of cows and milking times that has allowed her to avoid thinking of love and participating in human relationships. Just as she found consolation in the unending cycle of farmwork, she now finds consolation in the stability of the repetitions of the seasons. By linking herself to the earth's archetypal cycle of growth, harvest, death, and rebirth, Dorinda finds a model for the personal strength and fortitude that she has practiced in order to bring the barren ground of the farm back to life.[21]

The pastoral model of a single year as representative of an individual life allows her, again, to refuse responsibility for the fact that her life has been transformed into an emotional winter. By accepting the metaphor that the ages of a person's life correspond to the seasons of a year, her ending in the cold, futile, lifeless winter that she has created in her life becomes natural, inevitable, and acceptable. Her loveless life again simply becomes a fact, not something that she could have controlled or changed.

Thus, the revelation of the morning is not a change for Dorinda, but a stronger continuation of her past ideals, a continuation that is not as clear-sighted as she would wish to think. Although she claims to face the future without "romantic glamour," she tells herself that the best of life is ahead of her, forgetting perhaps that she is growing old and that death is also ahead. As she thinks of the future autumns, summers, and springs from which she will draw her strength, she fails to describe accurately the cold barrenness of winter, mentioning it only as a "red afterglow" of harvest.[22]

Likewise, as Julius Raper notes, the novel's structure does not support Dorinda's faith in the return of spring and summer. Since the dry summer of her affair, the only seasons shown of Dorinda's life have been autumn and winter. Even though her final assertion that she has "finished with all that" (a claim she makes before her marriage to Nathan) carries an ambiguous message that might suggest the possibility of marriage with the bull-like Bob Ellgood, her earlier words to John Abner, reminding him that she controls his inheritance, show that she is not ready to relinquish the dominant role in relationships. If she is not ready to relinquish the dominant role in her relationship with John Abner, she would probably be equally unwilling to enter a marriage that she did not control.[23]

As Glasgow says, fortitude does triumph over futility. Dorinda has endured. She has not responded to her troubles by suicide (like Geneva), alcoholism (like Jason), or heroics (like Nathan), and she has made a profitable farm. Nevertheless, the price she has paid for her success has been heavy, and the contentment she finds to ease her regrets will probably prove temporary as well.

ELEVEN

From Jordan's End to Frenchman's Bend: Ellen Glasgow's Short Stories

Edgar MacDonald

One of the best things to happen to Ellen Glasgow was Henry Anderson.[1] In her earlier fiction she had juxtaposed the virile self-made man and the effete aristocrat, her heroines usually giving their hearts to the former but marrying the latter. Now here under her minute scrutiny was an exemplar of both fictional males, a well-born man who had not gone to seed but had risen from the ashes of Reconstruction and like a good Virginian had reverted to being an "Englishman," very much as her brother Arthur Glasgow had done. She had fixed her romantic imagination on other males earlier, notably on her brother-in-law, the idealistic Walter McCormack, and on a married man, "Gerald B." She had tried very hard to feel something for the Reverend Mr. Paradise, liking his name. Now on this most auspicious day, Easter of 1916, she was studying a man she knew she would not like; she noted every detail about him, "his skin was burned like his hair, to a deep sand color." She was close to forty-three, no longer young, not yet old. He was not quite three years older.

The two met on equal ground. Recently returned to Richmond from New York, she had won respectable literary recognition as the author of ten serious novels. Early in her career, fatherly Walter Hines Page had warned her away from the lesser genre of the short story, a vehicle for local colorists. Her meeting with a healthy male egotist coincided with her emergence from an artistic malaise. It had to do with reality. Psychiatrists were teaching her there was no one universal perception, *the truth*, and as she had come to realize in her writing, a cataloging of external details constituted nothing more than a surface realism in a work of fiction. It bothered her that *Virginia* (1913), a work from deep within her psyche, had not received the popular recognition of *Life and Gabriella* (1916), her current best-seller but one that did not contain her heart. She had labored over the style of the former, and its early pages capture Virginia's ecstasy, but the later pages of the novel drifted into the earnest, flat realism of earlier work, not conveying the passion the writer had felt as an artist. Unknown to both the lawyer and the lady who met that fateful Easter Sunday, he would become a part of a regeneration of her work, indeed, enter into its fabric. If he was good for her, she was good for

him. He liked strong women, she liked strong men. "When I met him, however, he was drifting in purpose, unsatisfied by his hard-won success in his profession; and much of his sudden interest in public affairs was directly owing to me."[2]

In her confessions, Glasgow observed that she had emerged from a "dark Wood," quoting Dante ("for I had lost the way") early in the spring of 1916. Arthur Glasgow had handsomely modernized One West Main, installing bathrooms and central heat, but with parents dead along with four siblings, and with the suicides of brother Frank and brother-in-law Walter McCormack, Ellen Glasgow saw their ghosts everywhere. As for herself, she was convinced that for the past twenty years she had played in a "comedy of errors." Though also convinced that she and pompous Henry Anderson shared nothing in common, "the kind of person I had always avoided," he might set her "free from remembrance." Thus the two began their comedy. He became "Harold," she became "Vardah." They began collaborat-

Colonel Henry Anderson in Red Cross Commission military dress glittering with regalia, 1917

ing on a novel. She polished his speeches. As befitted their years, their courtship was courtly, intellectual. "For seventeen months out of twenty-one years, we were happy together."[3] A remarkably good record, especially considering the contributions Henry Anderson unconsciously made to Ellen Glasgow's maturing artistry.

Another unintentional collaborator had entered the artist's life shortly before her spiritual regenesis. Anne Virginia Bennett, a trained nurse, had cared for Cary, Emily, and Francis Glasgow in their final illnesses. She had been retained to stay on at One West Main as Glasgow's secretary-housekeeper. Devoid of any interest in literary matters, she too was to make her contributions to the writer's perceptions of reality. Although Glasgow enjoyed the income of a small trust set up by Francis Glasgow for his daughters and another set up by her brother Arthur, who wanted "no poor relations," she felt financially restricted. Miss Bennett as keeper of accounts suggested she write and sell a short story. She had published none since 1899 when "A Point in Morals" and "Between Two Shores" had appeared. The genre had returned to respectability, and having proved she was no miniaturist, Glasgow set to work; she could think of it as a literary exercise. When "The Shadowy Third" was sent off to her agent, she demanded at least $1,000 for it. She took from Anne Virginia Bennett details of her profession; from the ghosts of One West Main their psychic presence; from herself the allusions to a writer's excitable imagination; and from Henry Anderson character traits bestowed on the male antagonist. In addition, we know that sometime before 8 March 1916, the writer was discussing her work and perhaps collaborating with a noted New York psychiatrist. Dr. Pearce Bailey, trained in Germany, "her suitor, probably her lover and doctor combined," according to Julius Rowan Raper, enters the "The Shadowy Third" as Dr. Maradick. This story was published in the December 1916 *Scribner's Magazine.*

It appears obvious that Glasgow had read Henry James's "The Turn of the Screw" before writing a story that parallels it in so many ways. In her safari to meet literary lions in England in 1914, she had encountered "slightly foppish" James. In the Glasgow clone, Margaret Randolph, an inexperienced twenty-two-year-old nurse, travels from Richmond to New York to care for neurotic Mrs. Maradick. Telling her story in the first person and somewhat in the fevered style of the governess in the James story, Margaret too has a girlish crush on her employer. She admits to having a novelist's imagination and wanting to write. Simple Mrs. Gross in "The Turn" has her counterpart in another old housekeeper; housekeepers have no imaginations, being paid to attend to practical matters. Through psychic sympathy with her patient, Margaret sees the ghost child that the mother sees and that the physicians and the insensitive do not. Glasgow deftly leaves the reader in doubt whether Margaret is indeed the passive teller of the tale she claims to be. Just as James's governess becomes the active agent who

brings about Miles's death, Margaret Randolph, having fallen out of love with Dr. Maradick ("His vanity was incredible in so great a man"), becomes the avenging force that precipitates his fall. In the Greek dramatic tradition, we see things that protagonists blinded by vanity do not.

Finding she had a newly discovered facility to depict the introspective female consciousness, surely the result of her psychological counseling, she followed the success of "The Shadowy Third" with another ghost story, "Dare's Gift." It was published in *Harper's Magazine* in two parts in February and March 1917. The first of three stories bearing names of places, "Dare's Gift" borrows architectural and ownership details from Westover, the home of the Byrds. It is a house imbued with betrayal, and like her other House-of-Usher stories, owes its conception to Edgar Allan Poe. Writing Van Wyck Brooks the year before she died, Glasgow observed:

> Of the South you write as if the beauty and the tragedy were in your nerves and in your blood, without that vein of cruelty which seems to me to run through the beauty of all things Southern, wherever that South may be. As for Poe, you might have looked on the shabby splendour of his genius. For the splendour was his own, the shabby cloak was the outward form of his destiny.[4]

Strangely, this story of Cavaliers who settle on the James River will conclude with *Beyond Defeat* (1966), her very last, flawed effort to impose vision on reality. Prefiguring in miniature the epic canvas of William Faulkner, "Dare's Gift" encapsulates several generations, incorporating the Civil War (the Yankee soldier betrayed by the Southern Belle), and, as Raper points out, it conveys a "Southern 'sense of place,' especially the excessive loyalty and evasive idealism of the region."[5]

Also in this experimental period based on her analysis, what Raper terms a *homeostasis* (of seeing where she had been and what she had accomplished, counterbalanced with a projection of who she would like to be both as woman and as artist), she wrote "Thinking Makes It So." It falls into the seventeen-month period of happiness in the company of Anderson, and it reflects that fact significantly. It appeared in *Good Housekeeping* in February 1917, and it gave birth to

Frank Glasgow (*opposite*) and Walter McCormack (*right*) were important men in Ellen Glasgow's life and continued to influence her writing after their deaths.

other works. Glasgow was clearly working with materials and in a state of psychic immersion that could have been only partially apparent to her at the time. Richard Meeker dismissed "Thinking Makes It So" as "unquestionably the weakest of the Glasgow stories, made up of leftovers from *Life and Gabriella*. Its only interest is biographical."[6] Although Glasgow herself did not include it in the 1923 collection of her stories, it is certainly of biographical interest, but it points forward rather than backward. Its secondary characters reappear in the "comedies," those novels of manners presumably marking Glasgow's new phase. Raper is kinder to "Thinking," seeing more than simple wish fulfillment. Phantasy (as opposed to fantasy) "is transformed into a reality, not because Glasgow has ceased to be critical of evasive idealism, but because she has begun to see that, if imagination is rooted in psychic need, surface reality has no right to tyrannize phantasy." Raper also liked the happy, self-ironic tone. That tone marks a growing objectivity on the part of the artist in treating a character that is essentially the artist herself.[7]

Margaret French is the name for her central consciousness in this story, clearly Glasgow herself. She uses the name Margaret in three of her stories from this period; a fourth story has a Miss Wrenn who is clearly a Margaret. Glasgow was given to reciting poetry aloud, she tells us, in the hope that its musical qualities would infuse her style. She, like many of her generation, was fond of Matthew Arnold's elegiac verses. She too felt suspended, "Wandering between two worlds, one dead, / The other powerless to be born." She empathized with the forsaken merman as he called for his Margaret who had grown a soul and moved into the society of humankind. Margaret, sea-pearl, a woman with a hidden treasure, will be juxtaposed to an alter ego clothed in rose-colored silk, an alter ego *named* Rose in "The Difference." A rose breathes out its fragrance in a single, transitory night. But in "Thinking Makes It So," Glasgow combines the two into a single character, suggesting that most women combine both traits. We are reminded that in her confessions she wrote, "At last I recognize my dream for a buried reality"—the pearl within.[8]

Margaret French lives on Franklin Street, Glasgow moving One West Main to One West Franklin, the Branch house. She is a tired forty-three, precisely Glasgow's age. She has given up writing unremunerative poetry to write "silly stories," denying herself to provide luxuries for a neurotic sister-in-law and pretty, selfish nieces. Neglecting herself, she dresses in gray. Then the letter arrives, a device Glasgow employed with some frequency. A lonely, middle-aged bachelor out west writes "My poet," envisioning her as "rare and pale and all in rose-colored silk." She replies to "Dear lover of my poems." Their letters give them a sense of renewed youth. Margaret blossoms into a rose, just as in real life Henry Anderson had blossomed into a poet for Glasgow, who is now writing the silly stories. Margaret buys the rose-colored silk dress, just as Dorinda in *Barren Ground* will buy the blue to match her eyes. When John Brown, the distant lover, arrives unannounced, a niece sees him as "awfully dry and uninteresting," but as Margaret, in the rose silk, crosses the room, John Brown smiles at her. "It is all, she thought to herself afterward, in the way one happens to look at a person."

Early in 1917 Glasgow began writing the novel she and Anderson projected, *The Builders*. If she was intent on repairing "the hole in reality" while living in a ghost-haunted house, Anderson was intent on self-improvement, a matter for her mingled mirth and admiration. In a sense, he was larger than life, a character destined for an exterior drama. Intellectual interest, as she had illustrated in "Thinking Makes It So," can stimulate the hormones. Ellen wrote in her journal on the evening of Thursday, 19 July 1917, "engaged." On 3 August, Harold, with the courtesy title of "Colonel" as head of a relief commission to the Balkans, sailed from Seattle on *The Empress of Russia* for Japan. The commission was composed

of a number of prominent Richmonders, including Arthur Glasgow. They crossed Asia via the Trans-Siberian Railroad to Russia. Feted there, they turned south to Romania, isolated from the Allies, where a glamorous queen gave them a palace for their mission. Childe Harold's letters became shorter and fewer. In March 1918 Anne Virginia Bennett left to play in the larger drama of world the-

Anne Virginia Bennett (with Jeremy and Billy) informed Glasgow's character Margaret Randolph in "The Shadowy Third."

ater. Carrie Coleman, a friend, stayed nights at One West Main to help ward away the ghosts, but during the day Ellen was alone in the theater of her mind. With her collaborator away and with ambivalence in her heart, *The Builders* went badly.

As the Germans encroached on Romania, the Red Cross Commission left for home in October, but Henry Anderson lingered. On 1 January 1918, he was in Rome, May in London, June in New York, and finally home in July. The first night in Richmond he came to see "Vardah" in his resplendent uniform, glittering with decorations.

> "I thought you would like to see me as I looked abroad," he said, with innocent vanity. But at my first glance I saw only the difference; I saw only that nothing would ever be again as it was before he had gone to the Balkans. Something had intervened. I could not give this something a name, nor even a habitation.[9]

"The Difference" will be the title of a new short story, "this something" will be described in another short story, "The Past." Harold's unheroic welcome home from Vardah placed a powerful chill on their relationship. Ellen Glasgow had not yet become Medea, but neither was she Penelope, nor any other waiting woman of romance. Harold and Vardah quarreled on the evening of 3 July 1918, and the ghosts crowded around. Glasgow would write that she attempted suicide, but as Monique Parent Frazee observed, Ellen was too desensitized to barbiturates for a few extra pills to be lethal. She had a few bad dreams and awoke again to a nebulous reality.

Anne Virginia Bennett also returned home from France later that month, commendably exhausted in spirit and with a touch of tuberculosis. She had also suffered from an unrequited crush on one of Richmond's society physicians while in service. The Allies had liberated Romania, and early in November Childe Harold was on his way back to succor the welfare of the Circe of the Balkans. With the war over, she was the only enemy Vardah had to fear. Technically still engaged, an uneasy Glasgow felt another story welling to the surface. When she and Anderson had dined, she had felt another presence enter the room and seat herself between them. "He could talk of nothing but the Queen." The evil queen was a shadowy third.

In "The Past" the Southern girl in New York is a secretary to the second Mrs. Vanderbridge, another Southerner. The secretary is called "Miss Wrenn" throughout, but surely her name is *Margaret*. Through her sympathetic nature she too sees the ghost of the evil first wife that Mrs. Vanderbridge sees. Through the latter's moral force, Miss Wrenn will help banish the intruder from the past. Ellen was still trying to be patient Penelope, not vengeful Medea. Again the first-person narrator speaking in the voice of a character close to Glasgow's own allowed her to achieve a higher degree of artistic control, superior to that of *The Builders*. She can allow herself to exclaim, "Oh, I realize that I am telling my story badly!—that I am slurring over the significant interludes! My mind has dealt so long with external details that I have almost forgotten the words that express invisible things." Meeker links this story with Poe's "Ligea" and notes that the doomed poet might have preferred the ghostly wife. "The Past" appeared in the October 1920 *Good Housekeeping*. And Harold returned to Richmond that month. Vardah presented him an inscribed copy of *The Builders* acknowledging his contribution. Harold continued to bring the favored yellow roses when he came to dinner; Vardah provided the favored deep-dish apple pie.

As Anderson became more interested in politics on a local level, the evil queen intruded less frequently, although his house was full of her autographed photographs and her portrait had been commissioned. Glasgow began a new novel. She had treated Virginia politics in *The Voice of the People* (1900), her first truly impressive achievement. When Henry Anderson became the Republican candidate for governor of Virginia on 14 July 1921, it was almost as if he had decided to be a character in a Glasgow novel. They were both challengers of the conventional mores, the status quo, the past. She wrote and delivered a speech entitled "The Dynamic Past." The new novel would not succeed as literature, but it would depict the shifting political scene of its time. *One Man in His Time* was published in May 1922, and while Anderson did not take part in its actual writing, biographical details are everywhere apparent. Widely reviewed, not unfavorably, the consensus was that "Miss Glasgow has it in her to do better work." Raper sees it as an improvement over *The Builders*, its failure owing to a loss of focus or nerve; "propaganda is still not one of the higher literary arts."[10]

While no short stories from Glasgow's pen were published during 1921 and 1922, she must have been working on one or more at this time; 1923 saw the publication of four. "Whispering Leaves" appeared in the January and February issues of *Harper's*. It is another of Glasgow's House-of-Usher stories, all bearing names of places. "I have always felt a curious (because improbable) kinship with Poe."[11] Just as E. M. Forster's *Howard's End* (1910) is a metaphor for England and its fate, so too are Glasgow's place stories delphic commentaries. She had rebelled against her father's Calvinism; now she led the way for others to denounce the sins of Southern patriarchs. In "Whispering Leaves," she delves deeper into her psyche, into her childhood at Jerdone Castle. It reveals a repressed maternal instinct in the writer; oddly the repressed Pell, the birdlike boy, is another alter ego, the Little Willie of her awakening artistic consciousness. The symbolic sunken garden in the story has gone untended by the unworthy inheritors of Whispering Leaves, and the neglected house will end in flames, as will Sutpen's Hundred in Faulkner's *Absalom, Absalom!* (1936).

Henry Anderson is nowhere apparent in "Whispering Leaves," but he is very much present in "The Difference," which appeared in the June issue of *Harper's*. Six years after writing the happy "Thinking Makes It So," Glasgow saw there was a better story to be extracted from the materials of the earlier effort. Vardah and Harold had really been a companionable study team, "a marriage of true minds" rather than a dalliance in the garden. "The Difference" is perfectly plotted, a series of scenes in which the central character learns something about herself, a novel in miniature.[12] A cataloging of external details is limited to a few poetic images carrying psychological significance. The central intelligence is again named Margaret. "But the real Margaret, the vital part of her, was hidden far away in that deep place where the seeds of mysterious impulses and formless desires lie buried." In this study of the "Margaret" psyche, Glasgow separates the external "rose" alter ego of "Thinking" into a separate entity named Rose. George, described in Henry Anderson terms and an early sketch for George Birdsong in *The Sheltered Life*, is a faithful-faithless husband, loving Margaret but dallying with Rose. Meeker sees Glasgow returning to "man's moral inferiority to woman," but surely the story illustrates a more telling truth: the doubleness of male adultery is the counterpart of female ambivalence, the Margaret-Rose syndrome. As one of the secondary characters observes, "When a man and a woman talk of love they speak two different languages. They can never understand each other because women love with their imaginations and men with their senses."

The dramatic structure suggests drawing-room comedy, similar in feeling to one by Henry James, "The Beast in the Jungle." The series of carefully set scenes are the "outside" of the interior drama, the discovery of multiple selves. "Outside, in the autumn rain, the leaves were falling," undoubtedly revealing outlines of bare trees. As a tragicomedy, living is a series of improvisations. A letter from the other woman arrives. George enters briefly with domestic requests while the letter burns in Margaret's bosom. A visitor intrudes, chatting about a domestic crisis in another household, a parallel that makes Margaret determine to confront the other woman. She leaves the ordered comfort of her city home to venture by streetcar to an unfashionable suburban villa. Here Miss Glasgow describes accurately a trip from central Richmond, through the northern suburbs, to Lakeside, but it is also a symbolic trip, from past security to contemporary transience. Modern, red-haired Rose Morrison is an artist. "Only an artist," Margaret decides, "could be at once so arrogant with destiny and so ignorant of life." Margaret, as a beautiful Victorian, will give up her husband. She clings to "the law of sacrifice, the ideal of self-surrender." On the ride home in the lurching streetcar, she charitably envisions a "remorseful" George. "What agony of mind he must have endured in these past months, these months they had worked so quietly side by side on his book!" Returned home, Margaret is met by a concerned husband.

Jerdone Castle, the Glasgow summer home in Louisa County, had a profound comforting and healing effect on Glasgow, inspiring her story "Jordan's End."

Glasgow handles superbly George's bewilderment over Margaret's taking his little fling so seriously. Raper misses the happily ironic tone of "Thinking Makes It So" in "The Difference," but nothing could be more delicious than Margaret swept up in George's protective arms and his telling her she's upset because she's hungry. As Edmonia would shortly make clear in *The Romantic Comedians*, a good appetite is the best remedy for disillusionment; living on duty upsets the digestion. Glasgow is accused of being unfair to males, but her treatment of George, while comic, is not devoid of amused comprehension. Like most males he may have romantic fantasies about other women, but he is realistic enough to admit he is only one of a series for the Roses of the world and that his basic comforts lie at home with Margaret. As a type George will reappear like a popular film star in later comedies. In this seriocomic curtain-raiser, brief images of leaves, fires, rain, flowers, mirrors are used tellingly, suggesting the four elements and the humors they engender.

"The Artless Age" expands the threesome to a foursome—the perfect lady, the flapper, the fatuous young male, and the fatuous older male. It appeared in the *Saturday Evening Post* on 25 August 1923. Termed by Meeker Glasgow's most frivolous story, it can be seen as a continuation of the author's analysis of her own divided anima and as a sketch for *The Romantic Comedians*, explaining why she was able to follow up *Barren Ground* so quickly with a sparkling comedy. Glasgow's irony had evinced itself early, notably in *The Deliverance* (1904) with blind Mrs. Blake as the unreconstructed South, as well as in secondary chorus characters such as Old Adam and Matthew Fairlamb. Like Shakespeare, Glasgow had put her telling truths into the mouths of clowns. By the time she wrote "The Artless Age," however, she was ready to let her protagonists play the fools. Soon, in "Romance and Sally Byrd," she would laugh at herself. Surely Henry Anderson helped her to peer more deeply into the mirror out of which the Lady of One West Main spun her fantasies.

> I am wondering if it ever occurred to you that your judgment might be wrong. You judge me so freely and with such apparent sureness that your conclusions are right that it makes me strong in my belief that no human being is or can be capable of judging another. Your judgments seek not only to cover the present but to sweep back over the past.[13]

The happy seventeen months with Harold had sustained Vardah's illusions of romance, but the rest of their nearly thirty-year friendship helped to shape her perceptions of reality.

When *The Shadowy Third and Other Stories* appeared in October 1923, reviewers were unanimous in their praise. Richmond's own perceptive Hunter Stagg, writing in the *New York Tribune*, averred that it contained some of the best "writing Miss Glasgow has ever done."[14] To six stories previously published in periodicals, she added a seventh, "Jordan's End." With this work Glasgow achieved an exemplum that stands with the best of any age. Antigone will bury the dead at Jur'dn's End, just as a cemetery is all that marks the site of Frenchman's Bend. Poe was the seer who foretold the Fall, but the Emily Dickinson of One West Main had looked deep into the soul of her South before she had looked into her own. Following the early death of her grandmother, her maternal grandfather, William Yates Gholson, had moved to Mississippi and sired a second family. Later he freed his slaves and moved to Ohio where he became a justice of the State Supreme Court. He had children on both sides in the Civil War; William Yates Gholson Jr., first lieutenant, Ohio Volunteer Infantry, was killed in Tennessee at the age of twenty. In failing health, Ellen's mother went to Mississippi to visit her brother Samuel Creed Gholson. Glasgow praised Stark Young's *So Red the Rose* (1934) and called him "Cousin." Like a Renaissance Pope, she could have called William Faulkner "Nephew." He too was a seer, a *poietes*, one with an apocalyptic vision of the Cavalier South. Her vision had its genesis in her earliest memories.

At Jerdone Castle, the Glasgow summer retreat in Louisa County, Ellen had known happiness as a child. There she discovered the healing power of nature. Roaming the fields and woods, alone or with her sympathetic siblings Frank and Rebe, she discovered sights, sounds, and smells that whispered of myriad forms of life. There she felt the first tentative impulses to record her states of ecstasy. Later, an old spiritual would echo in her consciousness: "Deep River, My home is over Jordan" (JUR'dn). A deep river separated the woman in middle life from the happy child, from the life forces that had given her an artistic mission. Her studies in Jungian psychology, however, were building a bridge. She knew with increasing conviction that her spiritual home was on the North Anna River, back at Jerdone Castle. Just as nature had healed the child, psychiatry was healing the woman. She was learning to accept human nature for what it was, not necessarily to forgive, but to accept. Laughter was better than tears. In the summer of 1922, Henry Anderson helped her select a new therapist. The psychiatrist is an intimate prober, like a lover. His presence is felt in all her stories of this period, whether "ghost" or character analysis. At the center of everyone is the ghost of self. From the self, one probes into other selves, into society, into the past. "Jordan's End" represents Ellen Glasgow's deepest understanding of the forces that shaped her as a personality and as an artist.

In *The Battle-Ground* (1902) she had attempted an honest, realistic depiction of the Civil War. *The Deliverance* (1904) offered an analysis of the period that followed. While hinting at causes, she was primarily concerned with results, yeomen replacing Cavaliers, new codes replacing older orders, the homely face of democracy replacing patrician privilege. And always she was concerned to depict how the changes affected women. But with the psychological studies she began to look beyond events to causes, and she was finding the lost words, the symbols, the poetry to convey causes in literature rather than in tracts. As Meeker aptly observes of Poe, he had been too close to causes to see, as Glasgow had been as a child. "The families that go to seed are those that refuse to believe in the intangible. They love material comfort more than beauty; they love tradition more than progress."[15] Still later Glasgow would come to distrust "progress" in its commercialized forms. She saw that World War II had destroyed society as she knew it. In her very last statement, *Beyond Defeat* (1966), she envisions a synthesized family, based on love and need. This utopian society will be returned to the lower James where the concept of Cavalier Virginia, the New World garden, had its beginning. E. M. Forster envisioned a similar future for Howard's End wherein Mrs. Wilcox, a nature deity, totally unlike her materialistic offspring, leaves the symbolic house to Margaret Schlegel, another protective spirit.

In "Jordan's End" and in the next story, "Romance and Sally Byrd," Glasgow says farewell to two aspects of her earlier psyche. Can one doubt that the shawl that slips from the shoulders of Judith Jordan as she reenters the house at the end represents a dead past, or that the narrator has passed through a tunnel of dreams and, as Raper observes, "made contact with his vital center"? Glasgow exorcises the ghosts at One West Main and those within, but it takes a ritual "murder." At

Jur'dn's End Judith kills her insane lover. "He had gone from life, not old, enfeebled and repulsive, but enveloped still in the romantic illusion of their passion." One last cry of despair escapes Judith: " 'He was my life, and I must go on!' So full of agony was the sound that it seemed to pass like a gust of wind over the broomsedge." In relinquishing, she will enshrine. Eva Birdsong in *The Sheltered Life* kills poor George, living up to her marriage vow "Til death do us part." In earlier works, Glasgow's irony frequently undercut her characters; now it was Greek, a medium for universal truths. In a distant past there had been a garden, Jur'dn Castle. In the end all gardens are lost—except in literature. Dorinda-Glasgow will, with Nathan Pedlar's help, make Five Oaks flourish anew, in the novel to follow.[16]

Ellen Glasgow published one more biographical short story after the appearance of *The Shadowy Third and Other Stories*. "Romance and Sally Byrd" appeared in *Woman's Home Companion* in December 1924, just before *Barren Ground* brought her the recognition she felt was hers by right. A bittersweet sketch of Dorinda in another guise, "Sally Byrd" (of Westover?) is another farewell to the illusions of romance. "Never again!" Sally vows at beginning, middle, and end. But if Glasgow cannot believe Sally, can we believe Dorinda when she says she is through with "all that"? That note of ambivalence can be felt in all the works that follow. Sally Byrd echoes George Bernard Shaw's consummate romantic, Marchbanks in *Candida*, "As long as you have something beautiful to think about, you can't be a beggar." Do we detect James Branch Cabell in this spoof of the romantic attitude? Its pervasive irony is disguised by an undertone of lightness. When Sally, ready to nurse the errant, romantic male, visits the neglected wife, the latter is darning a sock, filling in another hole in reality.

Henry Anderson had not been everything Glasgow had half hoped but knew he would not be that Easter Sunday ten years before; he had, however, helped fill in the hole in reality. Their uneasy friendship lasted till death did them part, and his vibrant personality informed her best works, *Barren Ground, The Romantic Comedians, They Stooped to Folly, The Sheltered Life*, giving them a vitality that endures to the present. By the age of fifty-two, Ellen Glasgow was living proof that she had almost come around to Cassius's viewpoint. Perhaps the fault was not in one's stars: it could, just possibly, lie within.

In *Phases of an Inferior Planet* (1898), Glasgow's heroine had gone to New York to study voice.[17] In the short stories she wrote in midcareer, Ellen Glasgow discovered her own voice. In addition she learned that everyone projected his needs, desires, on another, and therefore everyone was a creation in someone else's drama. "Your reality is not my reality—except for brief shared moments." For a while, seventeen months, she had shared a mirror with Henry Anderson. With understanding came psychic release, artistic control, firmness of purpose. With the achievement of "Jordan's End," not sullied with prior periodical publication, she stands with the best, with James, whom she met, with Joseph Conrad, whom she met, with Faulkner, who may have met her. We can regret with Meeker that Scribner's did not elect to include the short stories in the *Virginia Edition* (1938) of her works, for then we would have her commentary concerning their composition. We know she liked them, preferring the English edition because she had been able to correct it more thoroughly. She did, however, express a thought for us to keep in mind.

> I have tried to leave the inward and the outward streams of experience free to flow in their own channels, and free, too, to construct their own special designs. Analysis, if it comes at all, must come later.[18]

TWELVE

Ellen Glasgow's *In This Our Life:*
The Novel and the Film

DAVID W. COFFEY

In *This Our Life*, Ellen Glasgow's last novel, while not generally considered by literary critics to be among her best, was the recipient of the greatest immediate recognition of any of her works.[1] In 1942, a year after its publication, *In This Our Life* was awarded the Pulitzer Prize for fiction, and a few weeks later a movie version opened throughout the nation. *In This Our Life* remains the only work by Glasgow to have been presented on the silver screen; it is, moreover, one of the few Hollywood productions with a recognizable Virginia setting.

Glasgow, who was by 1942 in declining health, took pleasure in the honor paid her by the Pulitzer committee (which, in fact, was more for the general body of her work than for this particular novel), but she was not pleased with the movie version. In fact, she boycotted the film. "No, I did not see the movie of *I.T.O.L.*," she wrote to her friend Bessie Zaban Jones. "The advertisements were enough to make me understand that Hollywood had filmed a different book, not mine at all, and had entirely missed the point of my novel. I hated the whole thing, but there were practical reasons why I had to let it be done."[2] The practical reasons most certainly included the $40,000 that Warner Brothers had been willing to pay for the movie rights.[3]

This essay delineates the major differences between the literary and film versions of *In This Our Life* and offers some suggestions as to why the film version strayed from its literary source. Of particular interest is the depiction of the

African American characters in Glasgow's original and in the subsequent motion picture.[4]

Ellen Glasgow was born in Richmond in 1873, the eighth of ten children, to what she might have called "mixed" parentage. Her father, who was the manager of the Tredegar Iron Works, a job obtained through family connections, was a native of the Valley of Virginia and of Scots-Irish stock; Glasgow's mother was a descendant of a moderately aristocratic Tidewater family. When Ellen was fourteen, the family moved to a distinguished residence at One West Main Street in Richmond, where Glasgow was to live the remainder of her life. From her vantage point at One West Main, Glasgow recorded in twenty novels the changing life of her native city and state. Her contemporary James Branch Cabell, a fellow author, commented in the 1920s that Ellen Glasgow had produced in her novels a "social and economic" history of Virginia from the Civil War to the present day.[5] Glasgow (and her publisher) took note of Cabell's statement and reissued her entire collection of novels as the *Virginia Edition,* arranging them in a chronological order based not on their original dates of publication, but on the historical periods they covered.

To her contemporaries (and much to the horror of her father), Glasgow was known as a feminist, a progressive, and an independent spirit. Denied a formal education due to her presumed "nervous disposition" and the absence in Virginia of a state-supported university open to white women (her more fortunate brothers were able to attend the University of Virginia and the Virginia Military Institute), Glasgow nevertheless acquired an education through extensive reading.[6] The author she credited with having been most influential in shaping her thinking was Charles Darwin (an attraction that met with great disfavor from her staunchly Calvinist father).[7] Like many of the progressive-minded people of her generation, she was a Social Darwinist, she supported woman suffrage, and she decried with William Jennings Bryan the "cross of gold" on which Americans were presumably being crucified. As a white Southerner *and* a Social Darwinist, Glasgow was particularly troubled by miscegenation—her own father's sexual dalliance in the black quarters of Richmond was probably a trigger for her lifelong concern.[8] Along the way, Ellen Glasgow managed to develop a long-term relationship, initially romantic, with one of Richmond's few prominent Republicans, Henry Anderson, who as an organizer of relief to the Balkans during World War I humiliated Glasgow by engaging in a much publicized affair with Queen Marie of Romania.

From this less-than-complete biographical sketch, a few relevant conclusions can be drawn that a more detailed accounting of Glasgow's life would affirm with greater certainty. First, Ellen Glasgow was a genetic determinist in the nature versus nurture controversy, and she could be expected to side with those

118   ELLEN GLASGOW'S *IN THIS OUR LIFE*

Bette Davis as Stanley and Olivia de Haviland as Roy in the film *In This Our Life*

who argued that the determining factor in shaping a person was inheritance rather than environment. (In this, she differed from many of the reformers of the Progressive Era.) Second, Glasgow believed that love and romance were much overrated and often led to the deterioration of the best qualities of otherwise promising women. Thirdly, while denouncing interracial sexual relationships, Glasgow was inclined to credit the achievements of the issue of such liaisons to their "white blood."

In This Our Life (the novel) has as its backdrop the late 1930s and early 1940s. As the last installment in her Virginia chronicle, it was designed to bring her social history of Virginia forward to the outbreak of World War II. The story Glasgow tells is of two families, the Timberlakes and the Fitzroys, who had once been partners in a tobacco business. Through chicanery on the part of the Fitzroys, a family of robber barons on the make, the Timberlakes had been squeezed out of ownership of the tobacco enterprise, which the Fitzroys had later sold to a Northern conglomerate. The Fitzroys thus were rich, the Timberlakes poor. The present generation of Timberlakes consisted of Asa, who had been accorded a relatively unimportant and minimally remunerative position in what had once been his family's business; his sickly wife, the niece of the current mogul of the Fitzroy family; a son (who figures little in the story); and two daughters rather incongruously named Roy (short perhaps for Fitzroy?) and Stanley.

The film character Roy showed much less independence than Glasgow's original heroine, relying instead on the strength of her husband.

Glasgow's favorite among all the characters is Roy, an independent woman who shows signs of possessing that "vein of iron" (an inner strength and determination verging on stoicism) that is shared by all Glasgow heroines. Stanley, on the other hand, lives for the moment, and in the course of the novel, elopes with Roy's husband, drives him to suicide, and then returns to the family fold to disrupt a budding relationship between Roy and Craig Fleming. Once Stanley's fiancé and an idealistic lawyer, Fleming, as it turns out, is not as firmly rooted in his principles as one would have assumed at first glance. The penultimate crisis in the novel ensues when Stanley's car strikes and kills a young pedestrian in a hit-and-run accident. An attempt is made by family members supportive of Stanley to pin the accident on Parry Clay, the light-skinned son of the Timberlakes' maid. Roy and her father know Stanley, however, and they instinctively surmise the truth about the accident. Parry is released from jail and Stanley, being the daughter of a "good family," is given a mere slap on the wrist. Roy has by now had enough both of her strikingly dysfunctional family and of Craig, who has been tried and found wanting in his reaction to Stanley's culpability. Roy leaves home and has a one-night-stand with a mysterious and hideously disfigured English-man. As *In This Our Life* concludes, Roy, with her inner strength motivating her to break free and determine her own destiny, is contrasted with her father, who lacks the will to leave his wife and spend his remaining years in peace and tran-quility on a farm owned by a widow with whom he has long been friendly.

Having spent $40,000 for the movie rights to *In This Our Life*, Warner Broth-ers studio turned over the Glasgow project to an impressive team: screenwriter Howard Koch (soon to gain renown for his script for *Casablanca*) and director John Huston (then currently at work on *The Maltese Falcon*). The cast of the film was equally first-rate. Bette Davis was assigned the role of Stanley, a logical choice given her previous appearances as Jezebel in the film of that name and as Regina in *The Little Foxes*. At that time, Davis seemingly had a patent on such roles; only the ultimate prize, the part of Scarlett in *Gone With the Wind*, had eluded her. Olivia de Haviland was selected for the role of the nobly suffering Roy, an assign-ment more than reminiscent of her turn as Melanie in *Gone With the Wind*. As if to strengthen further the connection with the 1939 MGM blockbuster, Hattie McDaniel was chosen to play the role of the Timberlakes' domestic and Parry's mother. Other leading roles were filled by Billie Burke, Charles Coburn, and George Brent. Significantly, the part of Asa Timberlake, a pivotal character in the novel, was deemphasized and given to a lesser-known actor, Frank Craven.

The casting choices are a sure indication that the film was intended to be a star vehicle for Davis and de Haviland, and consequently the novel's plot was streamlined to focus on the conflict between the two Timberlake sisters, a "minor theme" in Glasgow's estimation.[9] This is the film's first significant deviation from the novel—but there are others. More harmful to her original intentions was a major change in the ending of the story. The hit-and-run accident is elevated in importance to become the pivotal event in the film. Craig Fleming's role is expanded to make him, rather than Roy or her father, the prime defender of Parry Clay's innocence. In the novel, Stanley survives to muck up other lives; in the film, her life is snuffed out just before the final credits. In the movie version, as Stanley's guilt is proved beyond any doubt, she panics and attempts to flee in her sports car, giving rise to a melodramatic pursuit by police cars with sirens roaring. Stanley's end is not a pleasant one; she plunges over a cliff to a fiery demise. With Stanley's well-deserved death, Roy and Craig are free to live happily ever after. Evil is thus punished and virtue rewarded.

Left out of the picture (literally) is the ambiguity of Glasgow's novel. It was the simplification of her story into one of bad sister versus good sister (as made obvi-ous in the newspaper ads for the film) that so deeply horrified her. Furthermore, Roy and Craig's reward, an enduring love, was a much overrated commodity and perhaps nonexistent in Glasgow's opinion. Although glimmers of Roy's

independent spirit, her "vein of iron," survive in the film, she is depicted as relying primarily on Craig's manliness rather than her own inner strength. For this reason, among others, the role Craig plays in the film had to be modified and expanded; he becomes a quasi-ACLU activist in the movie version. Asa Timberlake is left at the end of the film as he was at its beginning—a rather befuddled and pathetic character. No hint of the extramarital relationship (which grants him sustenance) is given in the Huston film.

Why these changes? Obviously, Warner Brothers wanted a film that would make appropriate use of the talents and (perhaps more important) the perceived personae of their two female leads. Moreover, one can assume they wanted to create a film that would attract satisfied customers in large numbers. Equally obvious, if unstated at the time, was a desire to replicate the success of other Southern genre films about dysfunctional familes, most notably *The Little Foxes*. Given the liberal political views of Huston and Koch (which created considerable difficulties for them both during the anticommunist fervor of the 1950s), it is not difficult to understand why a Craig-like character, nobly defending the underclass against the evils of the system, would be an appealing and logical role for them to create, even if it required a substantial divergence from the literary material that they had received from Ellen Glasgow. Notably, the takeover of the Timberlake business by the aggressive Fitzroys, which in Glasgow's novel had occurred in the late nineteenth century at the height of boosteristic "New South" greed, is

Bette Davis's Stanley lacks the ambiguity of character that Glasgow had given her. In the film she is unmistakably the evil sister, who meets her just end.

moved forward in time to the late 1920s in the film, a more relevant period of capitalist excess for the filmmakers (and probably their audience as well).

Further differences between Glasgow's novel and the film are obvious in the treatment of the African Americans characters. Ellen Glasgow exhibits more cognizance of Parry's plight as he deals with the workings of Virginia justice than one might anticipate from a white Southerner of her generation. Nevertheless, her concern with Parry's situation can as easily be seen as her interest in the dilemma faced by an aspiring law student (whom she repeatedly describes as having the capability of passing for white) suddenly faced with a realization of the consequences of his racial identity. Parry's experiences in jail create within him a sense of hopelessness and despair, which strip him of his Caucasian characteristics. His speech patterns, his demeanor, even his physical features as Glasgow tells it, lose their Caucasian qualities, revealing his underlying African heritage. Parry's crisis gives the lie to his seemingly white characteristics and he "reverts" to what the laws of Virginia then said his black ancestry, however limited, made him, a member of a lower racial order. Most tellingly, perhaps, once Stanley owns up to her guilt and Parry is released from jail, he disappears from Glasgow's story. What

becomes of him would appear to be of no further interest to the author—he has served as a convenient plot device that, while revealing something of the inequities of the Southern racial situation, does not interest Glasgow sufficently to pursue any further.

Like almost all Virginia's progressives and suffragists, Glasgow was unable to break with the prevalent attitudes on race of her time and place. John Huston and Howard Koch saw things differently, and their efforts to temper the racist overtones in *In This Our Life* gave rise to perhaps the most interesting aspects of their cinematic creation. The role of Parry Clay was assigned to Ernest Anderson, a recent graduate of Northwestern University and a newcomer to Hollywood. Light-skinned like Parry, Anderson was described by the *Richmond Afro-American* as "the sepia dramatic find of 1942."[10] The revisions in the novel's plot, of course, made his role more central, and Anderson rejected the stereotypical norms assumed appropriate for black actors. A battle with the film's dialogue coach ensued as Anderson refused to conform to "black speech patterns" as he spoke his lines (which had not been written in dialect). There are two moments in the film when Parry Clay is allowed to speak his mind. One is the scene that screenwriter Koch created for him in which Clay explains to Roy his motivation for aspiring to become a lawyer. A law degree, Parry states, will grant him independence and relieve him of the necessity of being dependent on white patrons for his liveli-

The film's African American actors, Hattie McDaniel (*above*) and Ernest Anderson (*opposite*), appeared in scenes that were deleted from the reels shown at some black theaters.

hood. Second, in the jailhouse confrontation with Bette Davis, Anderson was allowed to exhibit (visually, if not in words) a rage and a contempt for his white oppressors that varied markedly from the resigned and submissive nature of Glasgow's original Parry. One of the scenes in the movie, Anderson said years later with pride, had literally stopped the show when the film was shown in the segregated army camps of the Second World War. The African American soldiers cheered loudly, Anderson recalls, and demanded that the film be rewound so the scene could be savored a second time.[11] Although it is not clear from Anderson's reminiscence which of the actor's scenes produced this response, it seems likely that it was the conversation between Roy and Parry rather than the prison sequence that had the potential to electrify an audience of black enlisted men.

In This Our Life played Richmond twice in the spring and summer of 1942. In mid-May it opened to a white audience at the Colonial Theatre and was reviewed favorably in the *Richmond Times-Dispatch* and the *Richmond News Leader*. While recognizing the film's divergences from the literary material on which it was based, both papers gave it a good review, while noting that highballs were not available in Richmond taverns as Hollywood had carelessly assumed.[12] Meanwhile, ironically, another Bette Davis film, *The Man Who Came to Dinner*, was

making a second-run appearance at Richmond's Walker Theatre, one of its leading black cinema houses.[13] Seven weeks later, *In This Our Life* premiered at the
Walker for an unusual two-week run. For the first time the film was advertised
and reviewed in the *Richmond Afro-American*. Notably, the advertisements in the
black newspaper, while basically identical to those appearing in the *Times-
Dispatch* and the *News Leader*, listed Hattie McDaniel and Ernest Anderson as
among the film's stars; those in the white papers had instead given pride of place
to Dennis Morgan and the other white supporting actors. Surprisingly, the
reviewer for the *Afro-American* did not comment on the roles played by
McDaniel or Anderson, or the manner in which they portrayed them.[14] Possibly,
the version shown at the Walker was also the one shown in Harlem, a version
that excised the few scenes showing the black characters taking a stand against
white bigotry. Interestingly, while thought safe for white audiences, these scenes
were deleted from the reels circulated to black movie houses, even if they had
been inadvertently retained in the version shown to servicemen.[15] Although John
Huston never much cared for *In This Our Life* as a film, he nevertheless took
pride in the modeling of the Parry and Minerva Clay characters as portrayed by
Anderson and McDaniel. In his memoirs he writes, "It was the first time, I
believe, that a black character was presented as anything other than a good and
faithful servant or comic relief."[16]

Offended by the cinematic version of the Timberlake saga that she feared
would further the confusion about her intentions in writing the novel, Glasgow,
though nearly bedridden, set about to write a sequel to *In This Our Life*, an
undertaking unique in her literary career. Though never finished and published
only posthumously, this sequel, which Glasgow called *Beyond Defeat*, told of her
heroine Roy's life as a single mother to a child born of her brief affair with the
Englishman she had met the night she escaped from the Timberlake household.
Interestingly, in *Beyond Defeat* Parry Clay is not mentioned; in fact, no black characters appear at all.[17] Ellen Glasgow's concern that her message had been ruined
by Hollywood's treatment of Roy led her to struggle in the sequel to restore
Roy's image and to rescue her from the uncomprehending treatment given her
by Huston and Koch. As Glasgow saw it, they had failed to grasp the reasons why
she had assigned Roy the central place in her story.

Had Glasgow seen their film, she might also have noticed that Parry Clay had
transcended the purpose for which *he* had been created. For Huston, Koch, and
Ernest Anderson, Parry Clay was more than a contrivance to advance the plot.
Given by them the kind of inner strength with which Glasgow had endowed
Roy, Parry became a heroic figure for Huston, Koch, Anderson, and those black
audiences not denied by censors the right to see his sense of self-worth triumph
over the defeat that had been *his* fate in Glasgow's novel.

THIRTEEN

Ellen Glasgow: Gaps in the Record

Julius Rowan Raper

Imagine American fiction as a great big house. Imagine Ellen Glasgow and her collected works as an elephant on the back veranda of that house. Her twenty novels and single volumes of poems, short stories, prefaces, miscellaneous essays, and autobiography are still worth too much to throw out. They prove difficult, however, to fit into the standard literary categories. So they have been quietly moved to the back veranda. Every time we enter the house from that particular side—whether to read about American women, poor American whites, African Americans, genteel America, the South, the Southern Renaissance, the rise of realism, naturalism, modernism, the evolution of American thought and fiction, and so on—we walk directly by them. We do not know what to do with them, they are so earnest, so accurate, so grimly honest in what they present. So we try to ignore them—we omit the stories from anthologies, fail to reprint most of her novels in usable editions.[1] But an elephant on the veranda is difficult to deny forever, and Glasgow does not quite go away. Dorothy Scura's gathering of the contemporary reviews of Glasgow's works gives us an opportunity to survey more efficiently than ever the way informed readers responded to each of her volumes as they appeared and to identify major gaps in our understanding of the woman and her work.[2] Two such gaps involve her dramatizations of black characters and our lack of knowledge about her mysterious lover, Gerald B.

The importance of Glasgow in American and Southern literary history has seldom been in question. As early as 1904, John R. Ormond, writing in the

Ellen Glasgow, by Richmond's
W. W. Foster studio

South Atlantic Quarterly, recognized that she, "of all the living Southern novelists, [had] perhaps the strongest grasp on actual life." In the same year, Archibald Henderson, in the *Sewanee Review*, agreed that Glasgow was preeminent among novelists of the New South for her blend of art, story, charm, introspection, and rigid self-examination. In 1941, W. J. Cash in *The Mind of the South* pointed out that since 1900 Glasgow had been dealing realistically, not romantically, with the region and that in 1925 with *Barren Ground* she had produced "the first real novel . . . the South had brought forth; . . . the first wholly genuine picture of the people [the simple or common whites] who make up and always have made up the body of the South." A decade later, the historian C. Vann Woodward, in *Origins of the New South, 1877–1913* (1951), called Glasgow the forerunner of all literature of the New South and accounted her rebellion against the traditions of the South the most unexplainable "of all the strange mutations in this age of the South's transition." To the extent that Glasgow's social history in fiction influenced Cash and Woodward, she both furnished part of the blueprint for the writing of Southern history and secured her position in that history.[3]

What has been questioned often, and is still in doubt, is Glasgow's contemporary significance—that is, how effectively she speaks to, about, and for readers in a given period. Here Scura's book does much to end the deep denial that surrounds Glasgow's looming presence on the veranda. For it was this enigmatic woman who cleared the ground for the South's literary rebirth, destined to occur at the end of the 1920s. Even those who know her works well will be surprised to discover the extent and intensity of the acclaim she earned between 1897 and 1943. Experiencing, for example, the almost universal recognition in 1932 of *The Sheltered Life* as a masterpiece, contemporary readers will find themselves perplexed about the reasons this fine novel (like the vast majority of the others) was until recently out of print.[4]

When we search the reviews for the commodities that our own age, the post-modern South, values—class, gender, and race—we discover that, for the most part, Glasgow's contemporary readers found sufficient supply of these staples in her novels to satisfy their appetites. From *The Descendant*, her first novel, with its illegitimate poor-white protagonist, reviewers responded positively to her revolt against the region's class system, even when they could not avoid euphemisms—Ishmaelite, swineherd, child of shame, postbellum man of very humble origin, and so on—in designating such characters.[5] Although none of the original commentators in 1902 recognized the newness of Betty Ambler, the take-control heroine of *The Battle-Ground*, reviewers eventually gave Glasgow the credit she deserves for her pioneering work with liberated women. Scura's introduction to the reviews uses the emergence of Glasgow's recognition as a feminist writer as a helpful thread to guide us through the novelist's long career.

When it comes to the third commodity of contemporary cultural interest, race, the situation is more complex, and the reviews contemporaneous with Glasgow herself provide no help. On this issue, Glasgow is restrained, compared to writers of the next generation such as Thomas Wolfe or William Faulkner; and the reviewers let this restraint pass with little comment. In contrast, our contemporary reader-response critics, especially Wolfgang Iser, have taught readers to *look* for the blanks or gaps in works of literature, and feminist critics have alerted readers to the resounding silences in texts dealing with characters the culture regards as marginal. Thus, this gap in Glasgow's novels and the reviews of her work merit our attention.

From the death of Nicholas Burr as he attempts to stop a lynching in *The Voice of the People* in 1900 through the last novel published in her lifetime, Glasgow's silences regarding race were brilliant. Among her most powerful and efficiently sketched minor figures, we have to include Mandy in *Virginia* (1913), Memoria in *The Sheltered Life*, and Parry Clay in *In This Our Life* (1941). It is through these three and the elder Dr. Greylock in *Barren Ground* that Glasgow deftly dramatizes the existence and effects of miscegenation in Southern culture. So restrained is her presentation that none of the reviews reprinted in Scura's volume even mention Mandy or the death of Virginia's father while trying (like Nicholas Burr) to halt a lynching. In 1925, only one review, in *Time*, alludes to the miscegenation in *Barren Ground*. By 1932, four reviewers are willing to refer, usually unsympathetically, to Memoria's relationship with George Birdsong, an essential connection that leads to Jenny Blair's discovering George in Memoria's house, surely one of the most subtle discoveries in Southern writing. By 1941, six of the reviewers felt comfortable focusing modest attention on the central role Parry Clay plays as the scapegoat of *In This Our Life*.

When Glasgow exercises restraint in her presentation of Southern race relations, she is following the conventions of realistic fiction; that is, she is mirroring
the denial of her characters. When so many reviewers neglect such important
matters, they perpetuate the conspiracy of silence that formerly surrounded sexual relations between races in the South, whether those relationships involved
exploitation, as in Mandy's case, or arose from mutual consent, as seems to be the
case with Memoria and George Birdsong. The charitable view of reviewers'
omission of these characters would be to recognize that in an essay of 1,000 to
1,500 words reviewers could not cover everything, so they followed Glasgow's
own emphases, thereby neglecting the emphasis of her silences.

A second gap Glasgow willed to her readers, this one in her autobiography,
provides an intriguing parallel to her restrained treatment of African Americans.
Here I have in mind her reluctance to give us the real name of the lover that *The
Woman Within* calls "Gerald B." Gerald B. was the married man and father of two
sons whom Glasgow says she met during the winter of 1899–1900 in the drawing room of a mutual friend living in New York. The attraction was immediate.
The relationship transformed Glasgow, she writes, from a woman still in her
twenties who had known years of bitterness, into one determined to hold to her
chance at love and, in the process, make herself well, happy, beautiful. The
romance, which spread itself from Manhattan to the Swiss Alps and transformed
her fiction as completely as her life, ended in the summer of 1905 when Gerald
B., according to the autobiography, died while Glasgow was vacationing in
Switzerland.

While critics have not done very much with the large blanks in her novels
regarding black characters, biographers have known exactly what to do with the
gaping blanks in her account of Gerald B. These gaps have become a major stim-
ulus—and barrier—to every writer who has tried, or even wanted, to create a
biography of Glasgow. Gerald B. generates the central excitement the would-be
biographer feels when he or she takes up Glasgow as a subject, rushing into this
gap as though it were a gold mine. All of us end up filling the gap with whatever
evidence—or fool's gold—we manage to lay our hands on.

As a result, Gerald B. has been variously identified as a figment of Glasgow's
imagination; as another woman; as a middle-aged New York aurist, H. Holbrook
Curtis (1856–1920); as an important New York neurologist, Pearce Bailey
(1865–1922); and as the fiction editor of Bobbs-Merrill, Hewitt Hanson
Howland (1863–1944). Other suggestions continue to emerge. While some of
these possibilities need not exclude one another—that is, Gerald B. could be a
composite figure—the variety of identities that biographers have produced supports one of my favorite bits of traditional wisdom—that "we don't see things as
they are; we see them as *we* are."

When I started my work on Glasgow about 1963, I had good luck early on pinning down what happened to Glasgow's favorite brother-in-law, George Walter McCormack, who died under sordid circumstances during an 1894 trip to New York. I was able to discover that McCormack had registered, at the Lower West Side hotel where he was later found shot, under an assumed name; that his body was claimed by a "pretty and stylishly dressed" young woman as that of the man she had refused to marry; and that this woman said he had passed himself off to her under yet a third identity.

Because of my success with McCormack, I naively assumed it was only a matter of time before the past would also cough up the true identity of Gerald B. I spent a good part of several years pursuing him. The best I could do was to suggest the neurologist Pearce Bailey. The evidence for and against Bailey appears in *Without Shelter: The Early Career of Ellen Glasgow*, published in 1971, as does the story of George Walter McCormack.

As Glasgow's mysterious Gerald B., Pearce Bailey satisfied the demands of my portrait of Glasgow especially well, for I was intent on painting Glasgow as an intellectual novelist, a woman steeped in the juices of the late-nineteenth-century biological sciences, the more psychological those sciences the better. Bailey had exactly the psychological flavor I was anticipating. Born in 1865, Bailey became a distinguished New York neurologist, one of the founders, in 1909, of the Neurological Institute of New York, and among the earliest defenders in this country of psychosomatic medicine.

In 1899, however, as a former student of the Universities of Heidelberg, Paris, Vienna, and Munich, Bailey was establishing his medical reputation with publications on general analgesia, epilepsy, and nervous disorders following accidents. His major book, *Accident and Injury: Their Relations to Diseases of the Nervous System*, had appeared in 1898.[6] In addition to his scientific studies, Bailey possessed a strong interest in literature, publishing a psychological study of Gustave Flaubert in 1908 and assisting Glasgow in 1916 with writing at least one of her short stories, "The Professional Instinct." The latter dramatizes the dilemma an analytical (Jungian) psychologist encounters when he tries to leave his authoritarian and estranged wife in order to marry, or live with, a more intelligent younger woman. Beyond his intellectual interests, Bailey moved in a social milieu that Glasgow might have found intriguing, for his family also had a home at fashionable Bailey's Beach in Newport, Rhode Island.

There were important difficulties with my suggestion that Pearce Bailey was Glasgow's secret lover. The first was that Bailey himself married Edith Lawrence Black of New York in November 1899, the exact period when Glasgow says she met Gerald B. The second was that Bailey died in 1922, not in 1905 when Glasgow reports that Gerald B. died. The third is that I could find no physical evidence to connect Glasgow and Bailey before 1908. This absence in itself does not argue either against or for Bailey, as Glasgow admitted having destroyed her most highly prized letters in order to escape the "tragedy of the past." Further, Carrington Tutwiler has described the trip he took with his mother, Glasgow's sister Rebe, immediately after Ellen died, to remove any papers that might prove embarrassing. Because I could not solve these difficulties, I offered Pearce Bailey as a useful hypothesis to work with until concrete evidence for another Gerald B. turned up.[7]

Then, in "An Essay in Bibliography," which appeared in the 1976 collection, *Ellen Glasgow: Centennial Essays*, Edgar MacDonald quoted electrifying excerpts from a letter that journalist Burton Rascoe wrote to James Branch Cabell. In his letter, Rascoe claimed that he once heard Irita van Doren, one of Glasgow's literary executors, tell a group gathered in the *New York Herald-Tribune* offices that "Ellen had been deeply in love with Hewitt Howland" and that she "had been Howland's mistress, since Howland was married and not free to marry her."[8] Howland was the Bobbs-Merrill fiction editor.

I talked with MacDonald, as I recall, by telephone. The Howland lead seemed a likely one so I spent a very cold and lonely Christmas holiday sometime in the later 1970s hopping planes from Raleigh-Durham to Chicago to Indianapolis to Bloomington and back, following up this clue. In Bloomington, where I combed the Bobbs-Merrill files and afterward in Indianapolis I came up with nothing except the legal record that showed that Howland's wife of fifteen years had sued him for a divorce in 1903 on grounds that he had failed to provide financial support. The year of the divorce was roughly in the middle of the period Glasgow reports that she had her relationship with Gerald B. So the Howland clue was still alive, though all the evidence remained hearsay or circumstantial. I could find nothing beyond what MacDonald offered to tie Howland to Glasgow. There the mystery lay until the summer of 1989 when a biographer reported to me the outlines of a new identification for Gerald B. Once again all of the evidence was circumstantial and more research in New York, Switzerland, and Richmond would be necessary before the new name could be revealed. Nevertheless, the biographer hoped eventually to publish a solution to the mystery in the *Ellen Glasgow Newsletter*.

In October 1993, the new theory regarding Gerald B. appeared, as predicted, in the *Glasgow Newsletter*. In three pages, Frances W. Saunders performed an important service for readers who take Ellen Glasgow and her writing seriously. As a side product of biographies she has written on women whose lives overlapped Glasgow's, Saunders uncovered an individual who matches up well with "Gerald B.," the man with whom Glasgow's autobiography, *The Woman Within* (1954), reports she conducted an illicit relationship between 1899 and 1905 and to whom she assigns the pseudonym, Gerald B. While a number of critics, most recently Pamela R. Matthews, have suggested that it is "at least possible that there was no Gerald,"[9] Saunders's evidence is apt and, if correct, so important that future scholars must surely give it their attention.

Rebe, Ellen Glasgow's younger sister. After Glasgow's death in 1945, Rebe Glasgow Tutwiler retrieved some of her sister's personal papers to protect the author's privacy.

Admittedly, Saunders's evidence that Gerald B. was, in fact, William Riggin Travers, a wealthy New York financier, is indeed all circumstantial. Saunders followed Glasgow's clue "that she read [Gerald B.'s] obituary in the Paris edition of the *New York Herald* just before she sailed home from Europe in the autumn of 1905."[10] This remark led Saunders to the international edition of the *Herald* for 30 September 1905, where a front-page article provides a "lengthy treatment of the death by suicide of an affluent New Yorker," William Riggin Travers.[11] The date, 6 October 1905, accords well with Glasgow's sailing on the *Deutschsland* back to the United States, a detail mentioned in one of Glasgow's letters. For more information of Travers and his suicide, Saunders turned to the *New York Times* of 30 September and a New York gossip publication *Town Topics* for 13 July 1905.[12] In none of these publications does Glasgow's name appear. Saunders's arguments always read backward from our knowledge of Glasgow's life to published facts about Travers. Unlike the other models scholars have considered for Gerald B., Travers thus far has no direct connection to Glasgow. On the other hand, the circumstances Saunders has uncovered fit Gerald better than the details we know about the other candidates.

Saunders has herself laid out some of the avenues that researchers might follow in their efforts to tie Travers directly to Glasgow and thus build concrete support for her hypothesis. Such lines of investigation include searches of divorce records, ships' passenger lists, hotel records in Switzerland where Glasgow reports she and Gerald B. were together, and the medical records of Dr. Hermanus L. Baer, Travers's attending physician at the time of his suicide. Saunders has pursued several of these avenues, for she has dealt with the Travers possibility for some time, from before 1989 when she first showed me her documents. To date, her efforts along these lines (clearly not the most important of her own research projects) have not produced the documents needed to turn a strong possibility into an established fact.

Two other angles of investigation occur to me. Lily Harriman Travers, who married Travers in 1889 and who was divorcing him at the time of his death, was the sister of Mrs. William Kissam Vanderbilt, whom *Town Topics* called "the real silent power in the best New York society." She was also a first cousin to the father of Averill Harriman. The strong possibility exists that gossip about the divorce could turn up in papers of the Vanderbilt or Harriman families of that generation. In addition, Travers's "impossible behavior" as a husband had, as Saunders reports, become a topic of social gossip at Newport, Rhode Island, where Travers inherited a summer home from his father. If his conduct proved so public, the relationship between Glasgow and Travers likely left traces in letters, journals, and other personal records written by the good folk of Newport, especially between 1903 and late in 1905. Running down leads like these takes a great deal of time but could prove rewarding for scholars with access to such records. It may be that solutions to these mysteries will require the collaboration of numerous scholars, some working in New York, Newport, and Richmond, and others following up clues in France, Switzerland, and Austria. Collaboration among generations of scholars has characterized past contributions to our knowledge of Glasgow, for, like Faulkner's Thomas Sutpen, she turns out to be a little larger than any of us has yet been able to sum up in a single article or book.

Pamela R. Matthews's earnest doubt regarding the very existence of Gerald B. remains an important challenge, as does her contention that "if he existed, certainly his importance has been over-emphasized."[13] Matthews thinks that those of us who have tried to match Gerald B. with a series of flesh-and-blood men, including Curtis, Howland, and Bailey, have been looking for Glasgow's lover in all the wrong places. Matthews points out that such investigations suffer from a "certain blindness to the emotionally satisfying female friendships evident at this time" in Glasgow's life, friendships marked by a type of "spirituality" easier for women to experience with one another than with men.[14] Matthews's argument is a point well taken.

Is it necessary, however, in these matters to stake out an either/or position? Can we not recognize the ties Glasgow felt to women and still accept her account of Gerald B.? Do friendships not coexist with love relationships? As examples of Glasgow's new female friends, Matthews offers two writers, Mary Johnston (1870–1936) and Louise Chandler Moulton (1835–1908). With her contemporary and fellow Virginian Mary Johnston, Glasgow shared literary and philosophical interests, a certain amount of literary schmoozing, at which

Glasgow was always adept, but chiefly a concern for Glasgow's ailing sister, Cary McCormack, who was Johnston's companion before Glasgow herself became Johnston's friend.[15] With Moulton, who was almost forty years older, Glasgow also shared the profession of writer but, in addition, a feeling of "dear friends who meet again after a long absence," a "sweet familiar recognition" that, as Glasgow writes in her 5 October 1905 letter quoted by Matthews, "was the loveliest thing I have felt for a long time."[16] The language Glasgow uses here solidly echoes a book she was reading at roughly the same time, Edward Carpenter's *Art of Creation* (1904). Carpenter traces the "strange psychology of passion" to Plato's theory that certain events and individuals in our current life have an inordinate fascination for us because we half-remember them from a prior existence.[17] Although the echoes of Carpenter suggest a possible homosexual allusion in Glasgow's letter to Moulton (an allusion Matthews does not underscore), it is equally possible that Glasgow's reason for seeming to remember the much older woman after "a long absence" arises from the amnesia and pain that surround the primal loss of one's mother, a physical loss Glasgow sustained a dozen years before the death of Gerald B. and her letter to Moulton.[18] Admittedly, the quest for a dead, absent, or abandoning mother may lead in individual cases to lesbian ties. In Glasgow's case, however, the connections to Johnston and Moulton, as Matthews notes, took on an aura of mysticism and spirituality.

No matter what passions fueled such sublimations, they apparently did not lead to sufficiently vivid expressions that both Glasgow and her younger sister, Rebe Tutwiler, felt compelled, as they did with Gerald, to expunge the record and erase the better part of Glasgow's life prior to her literary success in the 1920s. For Glasgow's exchanges with Johnston and Moulton have in part survived, and with them the fundamental reason that we keep seeking the real Gerald B., the hope that discovering his identity will lead to letters, journals, other documents that help fill in the largely missing decades of her life.

In our culture, the private traditions of women have, as Matthews suggests in regard to Glasgow, suffered sufficient suppression to take on a partially underground existence. As a consequence, recovering access to them, as Glasgow did with Johnston, Moulton, and other women, might lead to the explosion of energy and creativity that frequently accompanies the recovery of whatever one has repressed. It is also possible, however, as analyst Ann Belford Ulanov suggests, that the attraction of the *opposite* sex activates the *strongest* pull of the unconscious on the conscious self; that such attraction "stretch[es] consciousness to make space for all that arrives from the unconscious"; that it "galvanize[s] the deepest issues of individuation—that process of differentiating out of unconsciousness one's individual personality in relation to other persons."[19] Ulanov's language regarding maturation parallels that Glasgow used to describe her own transformation from a gloomy intellectual hardened and brittle beyond her years into an adaptable woman aware of the new possibilities available simply by yielding a bit to the impulses of life.[20] This is a change that readers and critics frequently detect in Glasgow's novels and that she herself ascribes to the way Gerald B. recentered her sensibilities.

Thus, Glasgow's autobiography, her novels, and sound psychological theory—one interested in the wholeness of the individual—point to the existence of a flesh-and-blood model or models for Gerald B. While her new relationships with Johnston and Moulton are important, they come too late to have influenced her move in *The Deliverance* (1904) away from strict determinism. Although the loss of one's mother (especially the imagined mother of infancy) may be, as Julia Kristeva contends, the most severe absence one ever suffers, it remains both logically and intuitively probable that the *contrasexual* encounter opens the most profound access to the great reservoir of unconscious possibilities. Compared to such powerful energies, those released by like-sex encounters generally arrive with a sense of underlying sameness, even narcissistic familiarity, attached to them. There is no reason, it finally seems to me, to question for long the gender Glasgow assigns to Gerald B.

Susan Goodman, Glasgow's most recent biographer, takes a different approach. Solid evidence for the claims of any of these candidates to be the original of Gerald B. remains slight, she declares, and investigations to date "have all led to dead-ends." Obituaries of other possible candidates besides Travers appeared in the Paris edition of the *New York Herald* during that period, Goodman points out. Thus, she concludes that "the question of his identity matters far less than Glasgow's sense of the relationship's meaning and its import for her fiction."[21]

For the present, William Riggin Travers remains the leading contender for the ambiguous honor of having been Glasgow's most influential lover. Travers is a possibility that future scholars must pursue. The major test of the truth of this possibility will be whether it leads to new documents that help us comprehend the whole of Glasgow's life. Prior to that breakthrough, Travers as Gerald B. helps in several specific ways. Travers's economic standing and his marriage to Lily Harriman lend validity to the focus that Glasgow's novel *The Wheel of Life* (1906) directs at New York social life, for it increases our trust in the novelist's knowledge of the milieu. Along the same line, Glasgow's expanded knowledge of New York society would help explain why the Queenborough of her later novels sometimes seems a composite of Richmond and New York. In a different direction, the probable trauma for Glasgow of Travers's suicide—a pistol in his mouth, the bullet through his brain—would open old wounds for her, especially those left by the violent death of Cary's husband, George Walter McCormack,[22] and provide a context for the mysticism that Roger Adams and Laura Wilde experience in *The Wheel of Life*, the hallucinations, even dissociations, that Daniel Ordway suffers in *The Ancient Law* (1908), and the ghosts of a guilty past that visit characters in several short stories Glasgow collected in *The Shadowy Third and Other Stories* (1923).

The ultimate value, however, of pursuing Gerald B. remains the chance that a particular model for Gerald may lead to a store of documents or other information about Glasgow and through that new knowledge to a fuller comprehension of the literary work to which she devoted her life. For the time being, William Riggin Travers appears the best hypothesis to explore, one that is, like the story Quentin and Shreve invent in Faulkner's *Absalom, Absalom!,* "probably true enough"—at least to set a fire under the coming generation of biographical critics.

Other mysteries will surely emerge in the coming years. Perhaps one of them will be the issue of race as handled in Glasgow's novels and its relationship to her ambivalent attitude toward her father. Better yet, the new challenge may be the continuing mystery of Glasgow's art. It is, one hopes, this dimension of her life and work that will transcend both the biographical teasers and Glasgow's historical importance, great as the latter is, and endure when the commodities we now value have faded into history. If so, we will decide, at last, to invite this remarkable elephant back into the library, perhaps into the living room, of American literature. We may even discover that her crusty old volumes make up not a white elephant after all but a tiger with rippling grace and small, bright teeth.

FOURTEEN

Ellen Glasgow's Richmond

Tricia Pearsall

If you have lived in Virginia's capital, Richmond, Virginia, it will not surprise you that this southern metropolitan crossroad, which provided the setting and ambience for Queenborough in the novels of Ellen Glasgow, is for all intents and purposes the same Richmond, Virginia, experienced today. This is a city held holy by longtime residents, and prized by visitors and tourists for its historical significance, architectural gems, and homogeneous neighborhoods—yet a city that beats to its own ambivalent pulse, which harks back to former greatness while craving an incongruous future of modernity without change. Richmond will never be mistaken for Saint Louis, Dallas, San Francisco, or even Charleston or New Orleans. This city, its streets, exteriors, and interiors were probably never more knowingly or sagaciously observed, particularly in relation to its inhabitants, than by Ellen Glasgow. And yet, the same neighborhoods and dwellings portrayed with such vivid acuity by Glasgow are the very elements that make Richmond such a unique treasure at the dawning of the twenty-first century.[1]

A presentation of Glasgow's Richmond, either fictional or nonfictional, includes many sites still covered in the tours that residents and city promoters give daily to show off the city. Yet Richmond changed dramatically in Glasgow's own lifetime, and she employed her observations of the old and new Richmond in her novels to comment on the social conventions of the old Virginia elite, the rise of a new, aggressive upper-middle class, and the aspirations of working

One West Main, Glasgow's "old gray house"

people and of women. Blands and Carringtons[2] peered from the windows of Greek Revival mansions as their neighborhoods sank into genteel decline; stonecutters and clerks populated the once-grand neigh-borhoods of Church Hill and Gamble's Hill; and the brownstone mansions of the nouveau riche spread ostentatiously into the West End. Glasgow described a city obsessed with the past, yet unable to prevent the encroachment of the modern.[3]

Glasgow's Richmond begins with the house where she lived for almost sixty years: One West Main, "the old gray house" built in 1841 by David Branch, a tobacconist, and occupied for more than forty years by Isaac Davenport and his family.[4] In 1887, it was purchased by Ellen Glasgow's father, Francis Thomas Glasgow.[5] He may have bought the house because its size accommodated his large family, or because the house was near the homes of his uncle Joseph Reid Anderson and other family members. It was also within walking distance of the Tredegar Iron Works, where Francis Glasgow managed the foundry with noted skill and meticulous efficiency.[6] One West Main was not located in the newest or finest neighborhood of the late 1880s; that real estate was out Franklin Street west of Belvidere Street. But this house was gracious living nonetheless, near the shops on Broad Street, on a streetcar line, and near churches and some presti-gious, though probably older, neighbors. Ellen Glasgow was fourteen when her family moved into the house and elected to remain at One West Main after her father's death in 1916, continuing to write, entertain, and use its rooms and gar-dens for inspiration and setting until her death in 1945. In her novel *The Voice of the People* (1900), Glasgow described the house.

Presently the carriage turned into Main Street, halting abruptly while a trolley car shot past.

"Please be very careful," called Miss Chris nervously, gathering herself together as they stopped before a big gray house that faced a gray church on the opposite corner. A flight of stone steps ran from the doorway to a short tessellated entrance leading to the street, where two scraggy poplars still held aloft the withered skeletons of last year's tulips.[7]

Alas only one scraggly poplar remains and the house is no longer painted gray, but a warm tan.[8] Originally built of brick, the exterior walls were covered with stucco, and then scored to look like a facade of massive stone blocks. This treatment was typical of Greek Revival residences of the 1840s. The stucco, an almost café au lait shade of brown, was made from indigenous sand and other elements, such as iron filings. The white scoring, much of which has been found still in place, was applied to resemble mortar. The original stucco was a brown–gray, color, typical of the period. Given Virginia's climate of sudden temperature extremes, stucco may begin to crack after twenty-five years or so. The Davenports probably painted the house gray when cracks first appeared, a fashionable and less expensive alternative to restuccoing during tough economic times. It was, therefore, into a gray house that the Glasgows moved in 1887.

One West Main Street was constructed in a neighborhood known as Rutherfoord's Addition, an area annexed by the city in 1810. Thomas Rutherfoord, a

Glasgow's study housed many of the author's decorative pieces and part of her extensive library.

Scots merchant, had arrived in Richmond in 1785 and bought a farm just west of Foushee Street in 1794 from the brother of the beloved Episcopal clergyman, Parson John Buchanan. Rutherfoord built his house in 1795 on property now diagonally across the street from the Jefferson Hotel. As early as 1803, he started selling lots to his friends, thus building a neighborhood of compatriots. Most of these early lots faced Franklin Street, with dwellings such as the Cole Diggs house still standing in the 200 block of West Franklin Street, and the Wilson-Bayly house, built between 1805 and 1809 at 203 West Franklin Street.[9]

The earliest structures erected on the Main Street section of Rutherfoord's land were the Greek Revival double houses at 4 and 6 East Main, built in 1836 by William C. Allen. After many years of dereliction and total disrepair, they were recently renovated to house the headquarters of the Historic Richmond Foundation. Across the street at 1 East Main Street stood the Quarles house built in 1839, just two years prior to the construction of One West Main.[10] Mrs. Sarah Quarles lived there until 1887 when it passed to her nephew, Charles Phillips. It remained in the family until 1925, and was subsequently demolished in 1958.[11] So it appears that while the neighborhood was changing rapidly to commercial, retail, and office use, One West Main was not totally isolated as a residential structure during Glasgow's lifetime. In *The Sheltered Life*, General Archbald's home, standing in for the Glasgow house, "looked over the diminished grandeur of Washington Street to the recent industrial conquest of Queenborough."[12] The house is now an island in a lake of asphalt parking lots.

During the 1850s an urban Greek Revival–style house, built of brick with door and hallway along one exterior, blossomed throughout the city's established neighborhoods. Many examples can still be found in Church Hill, north of Broad Street, in the Court End, and along Franklin Street. Next door to the Glasgow home on the west side, Griffin Davenport, the son of Isaac Davenport, built a three-story Greek Revival house in 1853. Here Judah P. Benjamin, the famed Confederate secretary of state, resided during the Civil War years. On the opposite corner, at 11 West Main, lived Louis D. Crenshaw. He built this dwelling in 1862, having

Louis D. Crenshaw's house stood at 11 West Main Street.

Glasgow's lovely garden at One West Main appears as the Archbalds' enchanting retreat in *The Sheltered Life*.

sold his previous residence at the corner of Twelfth and Clay Streets to the city for the use of Confederate president Jefferson Davis and his family as their home and headquarters during the war. The Crenshaw house could very well have been the Birdsong house in *The Sheltered Life*. (The Birdsong house was at the other end of the block from the Archbald home and not as pretentious.)[13]

As referenced above, One West Main was the setting for the home of General Archbald. The garden behind the house, which was a well-kept and cherished oasis for Glasgow, is accurately described in the novel:

This was a magic spell to make the world more surprising; and enchantment worked immediately upon the sky, the sycamore, and the rich bloom of the walled garden. In the garden, which was reached by stone steps from the back porch, splendour flickered over the tall purple iris that fringed the bird bath, and rippled like a bright veil over the grass walks and flowerbeds. A small place, but it held beauty. Beauty, and that deep stillness through which time seems to flow with a perpetual rhythm and pause.[14]

Across the street from the Crenshaw house stood the Jenkins house, 14 West Main at Adams Street. This lovely tree-draped, pseudo-Italian villa later became the home of the Scott-Talcott kindergarten and primary school, fondly remembered by many for their founding education.[15]

Ellen Glasgow's neighborhood was not entirely residential in the antebellum era. Grace Church, built in 1858, stood on the corner across the street from One

West Main. This Romanesque-style Episcopal church, designed by Richmond architect Joseph F. Powell, served former parishioners of Saint Paul's Church who had moved westward from the center of the city. The continued migration of the congregation some years later, and the resulting change in the neighborhood from residential to commercial mentioned in Glasgow's later novels, signaled the demise of this church. It merged with Holy Trinity, located on the western border of Monroe Park, in 1924. The Grace Church building was then used by "the People's Church" before becoming Saint Constantine Greek Orthodox Church in 1930. When the Greek Orthodox church moved to Malvern Avenue this structure was torn down.[16]

The Glasgows' neighborhood was naturally associated with the renowned Tredegar Iron Works, which stood along the James River to the south, down the hill from these stately houses. A number of proprietors and managers of the ironworks lived along Franklin and Main, including the company's owner Joseph Reid Anderson, and his son and successor, Colonel Archer Anderson. For example, the residence of Carter Page, built in 1816 at 103 West Franklin, was purchased in 1853 by Charles Y. Morriss, a partner in the Tredegar Rolling Mills, and in the 1880s greatly Victorianized by architect Marion Dimmock for Archer Anderson.[17] Tredegar Iron Works had manufactured armaments for the federal government before the Civil War and became the largest single producer of cannons for the Confederacy. Tredegar's rolling mills provided armor plates for the famed ironclad CSS *Virginia* (known in the North as the *Merrimack*). Its elaborate operations prior to and during the Civil War gave it national prominence, and its resilience following the economically devastating war inspired unusual devotion by its employees to the Works and beloved company leader, General Joseph Reid Anderson.[18]

General Anderson and his family, so much a part of the Glasgows' life, lived at 113 West Franklin Street. Built in 1845 by Henry Ludlam, this classical temple–style house was sold two years later to Anderson. He lived there until his death in 1892. The property was then sold by his family to Major Lewis Ginter in 1893 and the house torn down for construction of the Jefferson Hotel, no doubt signaling to the residents of Franklin Street the beginning of a new era. Across the street from the elegant Jefferson stands the Mayo Memorial Church House. Originally the home of William F. Taylor, the house had also been constructed in 1845, similar in style to the Anderson residence. Tobacconist Peter Mayo expanded the house to its present proportions in 1884, complete with extensive mahogany paneling. In 1923, the Mayo family left the residence to the Episcopal Diocese of Virginia, which continues to use the house as its headquarters.[19] Anne Virginia Bennett, Ellen Glasgow's longtime secretary and companion, identified the Mayo house as the Bland house in *Vein of Iron*. John Fincastle, the father of the novel's heroine, Ada Fincastle, took a daily stroll past the home of his wife's prominent kinfolk.

> Every afternoon, rain or sun, he walked several blocks out of his way for the sake of passing the Bland house in Washington Street. It was there that he had first seen Mary Evelyn, as she came down the steps between the white columns and paused for an instant under the elms on the terrace. Sometimes, toward sunset, Ada and he would stroll up the street, with Ranny running between them, and for a little while they would watch from the opposite pavement to see the Bland family come in or go out. It was the one romantic image now left in their lives—the old yellow house, with the Doric columns, the grassy terrace, and the look of ancient nobility that had fallen on vulgar times.[20]

The Mayo house has Ionic, not Doric, columns, but regardless of attention to classical order, Glasgow conveys the refinement of Franklin Street, whose remaining mansions along this corridor only hint at the sophistication of yesteryear. By the time the fictional Fincastle clan moved to Queenborough from western Virginia during World War I, the street had already "fallen on vulgar times."

It is the "old" Franklin Street, the one Ellen Glasgow knew and observed in transformation from a fashionable address to an allée of decaying gentility, that is the Franklin or Washington Street setting in so many of her novels. On the site of

The home of Joseph Reid Anderson, located where the Jefferson Hotel was later constructed

the Second Baptist Church, for example, now located on the corner due east of the Jefferson Hotel, stood the Garret F. Watson house, built in 1857 and pulled down in 1904 to make room for the Neoclassical Revival church, a more exact replica of the Maison Carrée than the Virginia State Capitol.[21] On the site of the present Downtown YMCA was the Rutherfoord-Hobson house, built in 1842–1843 by Alexander Rutherfoord, one of Thomas's sons and bought by Joseph Reid Anderson in 1872 for his daughter Fannie A., the wife of Edwin L. Hobson. It was then enlarged and the mansard roof added, as Anderson's daughter had a large family with ten children living in 1938. She died there in 1939 at the age of ninety-two.[22]

The Mayo house was the model for the Bland residence in Glasgow's *Vein of Iron*. In 1923, the Mayo family left the house to the Episcopal Diocese of Virginia.

The expansion and modification of the older houses of Virginia patricians into more modern brownstones by Richmond's merchant class did not go unnoticed by Glasgow. She subtly signaled her disapproval of these changes, noting the pretentiousness and ugliness of the newer architectural styles. Across the street from the Rutherfoord-Hobson house, on the southwest corner of Foushee and Franklin, stood the former residence of the Petersburg merchant-banker Thomas Branch. Branch bought the residence from lawyer George Wythe Munford, a former secretary of the commonwealth and prominent antebellum politician, who had built it in 1840. Thomas Branch's son, John P. Branch, altered the house so drastically that no visible trace of the 1840 dwelling remained,[23] but it is this new imposing structure that is Judge Honeywell's house in *The Romantic Comedians*:

A few blocks away stood his house, of which he was inoffensively proud; a collection of brownstone deformities assembled, by some diligent architect of the early 'eighties, under the liberal protection of Queen Anne. In front of the stone steps, as they flowed down from a baptismal font of a porch, he recognized the heavily built figure of his twin sister, who was engaged in a dramatic monologue for the benefit of two restless listeners.[24]

Franklin Street had been extended west of Belvidere Street after 1867, and with the prosperity of the late nineteenth century had witnessed the construction of many handsome and elaborate brownstone and brick houses. Between 1889 and 1892 Major Lewis Ginter had reinforced the trend, building a mammoth Richardsonian Romanesque Revival structure at 901 West Franklin. This house, now part of the Virginia Commonwealth University campus, was apparently the new home to which newlyweds Ben Starr and Sally Mickelborough return in *The Romance of a Plain Man.*

It was a bright December evening when we returned to Richmond, and drove through the frost air to our new home. The house was large and modern, with a hideous brown stone front, and at the top of the brown stone steps several girl friends of Sally's were waiting to receive us.[25]

Franklin Street continued its westward growth during the turn of this century with the layout, development, and construction of the "Grand European

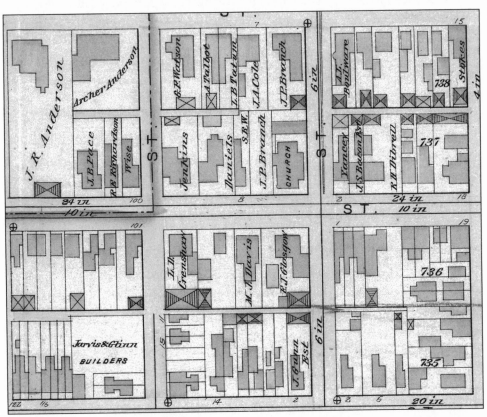

A portion of Glasgow's neighborhood, from an 1889 Richmond atlas. Many residents are noted, including the Glasgows, Andersons, Crenshaws, and Jenkinses.

Boulevard" and its giant equestrian and monolithic pedestals to the fallen heroes of the Confederacy: Monument Avenue. It seems fair to say that Glasgow regarded this continuation of Franklin Street with disdain, as nouveau riche and as a great symbol of ostentation. She refers to it as the "Granite Boulevard" in *The Romantic Comedians:*

> The Age of Pretence, The Age of Hypocrisy, The Age of Asphalt, Judge Honeywell reflected, while his car skirted a plebeian park, where the best taste of politicians was commemorated in concrete walks and triangular beds of canna. What, he wondered gloomily, was the peculiar merit in the middle-class mind? In what particular was the tyranny of the inferior an advance upon the tyranny of the superior? Beyond the few ancient elms, which had been threatened but not destroyed by the political axe, he could see the once aristocratic and now diminished length of Washington Street merging into the ostentatious democracy of Granite Boulevard.[26]

Just as Ellen Glasgow's Main and Franklin Streets environs were left behind by the westward march of progress, so too was the nearby neighborhood of Gamble's Hill, once a "prosperous quarter of Queenborough, but that was before the tide of fashion and business alike had turned toward the West End and the new Granite Boulevard."[27] Yet the promontory still offers visitors a commanding view of Belle Isle, the rapids, the James River and Kanawha Canal, and the famous Tredegar Iron Works. Gamble's Hill was the setting of Juniper Hill in *They Stooped to Folly,* where Virginius Curle Littlepage, "threading his way through noisy streams of children . . . passed rows of dilapidated houses, until at last the odours of boiled cabbage and decaying fruits were dispelled by the lighter air of the river, and the street emerged upon the brow of a terraced hill, which presided over an ochre-coloured canal, a group of empty smokestacks, and the smothered fires of the sunset."[28]

Ellen Glasgow liked to walk and frequently visited Gamble's Hill. She and Anne Virginia Bennett would often take off, dogs in tow, down Franklin Street to Monroe Park, then sometimes over to Leigh, Clay, and Marshall Streets in Jackson Ward, and most often down Third Street to Gamble's Hill.[29] Third Street was undoubtedly Mulberry Street in *Vein of Iron,* and the house at 217 South Third Street, the Pulliam house, was the home of Ada Fincastle, the courageous heroine of the novel. This house, built in 1856 by Charles Campbell, then foreman of the Tredegar Iron Works, had an ornate and imposing cast-iron porch and fence. It was given to the Association for the Preservation of Virginia Antiquities in 1938 by Mrs. Ione Crutchfield Pulliam. Unfortunately, it stood in the way of the Richmond Downtown Expressway and in 1969 was moved to Church Hill, where it was rebuilt at 2701 East Franklin Street.[30] Glasgow related that "there were two stories to the house, with three rooms on each floor, and an additional bedroom under the red tin roof over the kitchen and laundry. The living-room, which opened on a balcony of wrought iron above Mulberry Street, looked, even when it was bare . . . as if it had been lived in not by nomads, but by civilized people."[31]

Her description of Mulberry Street mirrored the actual fate of Third Street and Gamble's Hill generally, where "a few of the more spacious houses had been turned into flats. . . . A few others had become boarding-houses for the clerks and stenographers in the near factories and the saleswomen in shops."[32] Glasgow charted this decline in neighborhood fortunes through her characters. Ada Fincastle's mother, Mary Evelyn, had belonged to the aristocratic Bland family of Washington Street, but she now struggled to support her own family in the once-fashionable-but-decaying house on Mulberry Street. Ada, like many of her neighbors, worked as a salesclerk, walking from her home on Gamble's Hill to Shadwell's department store on Broad Street.

Unfortunately, the entire Gamble's Hill neighborhood was razed when it became part of the grounds of the Ethyl Corporation, although a portion of Third Street remains. One survivor that Glasgow passed on her walks was the Henry Coalter Cabell house at 116 South Third Street. Built in 1847, this is an unusually extravagant and massive house, now painted red, and the headquarters of the Virginia Education Association. Perhaps its most unusual feature is its

Pratt's Castle was a well-known Gamble's Hill landmark.

Egyptian-inspired columns.[33] Ruth Jones Wilkins suggests that this house was the site of the Culpepers' home in *One Man in His Time,* the "gray and white mansion with its Doric Columns."[34] As Glasgow continued walking toward Gamble's Hill Park, she would have passed rows of beautiful mansard-roofed large dwellings before reaching Pratt's Castle, an iron-front oddity built in 1853 by engineer and photographer William A. Pratt. The structure's turrets provided the English-born Pratt with an excellent bird's-eye view of the city and the James River.[35] Like most of its Gamble's Hill neighbors, Pratt's Castle fell to the wrecking ball after years of neglect.

Gamble's Hill was not the only neighborhood in Richmond that had fallen on hard times during Glasgow's lifetime. The popular Richmond tourist mecca, Church Hill, is chronicled authentically by the author in *The Romance of a Plain Man.* The novel's protagonist, Ben Starr, described the Hill and its environs:

> Across the street, and on either side of us, there were rows of small boxlike frame houses built with narrow door-ways, which opened from the sidewalk into funny little kitchens, where women, in soiled calico dresses, appeared to iron all day long. It was the poorer quarter of what is known in Richmond as "Church Hill," a portion of the city which had been left behind in the earlier fashionable progress westward. Between us and modern Richmond there were several high hills, up which the poor dripping horses panted on summer days, a railroad station, and a broad slum-like bottom vaguely described as the "Old Market." Our prosperity, with our traditions, had crumbled around us, yet there were still left the ancient church, with its shady graveyard, and an imposing mansion or two inher-

Shockoe Bottom, ca. 1908. A similar "slum-like" market area provided Ben Starr refuge in *The Romance of a Plain Man.*

ited from the forgotten splendour of former days. The other Richmond—
that "up-town" I heard sometimes mentioned—I had never seen, for my
early horizon was bounded by the green hill, by the crawling salmon-
coloured James River at its foot, and by the quaint white belfry of the
parish of old St. John's.[36]

Shockoe Bottom, the "broad slum-like bottom" separating Church Hill
from the western part of the city, held Richmond's oldest produce market, where
Ben Starr eventually went to seek work and refuge from an unhappy home.
Shockoe Bottom also accommodated Main Street Station, an 1899 railroad hub,
and the homes of many of Richmond's poorer residents. A few blocks to the
west, Richmond's thriving red light district held sway amid the faded glory of
once-prominent hotels.[37]

Saint John's Church, the site of Patrick Henry's famed "Liberty or Death"
speech, anchored the Church Hill neighborhood. The brick antebellum town
houses of city leaders and tobacco barons jostled with humbler frame houses
around the old church. The Adams–Van Lew house, which stood between
Twenty-third and Twenty-fourth Streets on Grace Street until it was demolished
in 1911 for the construction of Bellevue School, is undoubtedly one of the mansions mentioned by Glasgow. This elegant and stately residence, built in 1801, was
one of several erected by Richard Adams on Church Hill and was the home of
the abolitionist and notorious Union sympathizer, Elizabeth Van Lew.[38]

In *The Romance of a Plain Man*, Ben Starr makes his brother take him to the
"big house" where Sally Mickelborough lives, the fictionalized Van Lew mansion.
Peering over the high wall, Ben imagines that he was "gazing upon an enchanted
garden." He beheld "a fine old mansion, with a broad and hospitable front, from
which the curved iron railing bent in a bright bow to the pavement. It was the
one great house on the hill, with its spreading wings, its stuccoed offices, its
massive white columns at the rear, which presided solemnly over the terraced
hillside."[39]

Glasgow creates striking contrasts between old gentility and the world of the
poor through her descriptions of the houses, factories, and haunts of the city.
Ben's wonder at the elegant life within the mansion is matched only by his striving to escape his "common" background. He takes the first step toward his goal
when he seeks a job in a tobacco factory down the hill from his home on
Church Hill.

I . . . set out down Twenty-fifth Street in the direction of the river. As I
went on, a dry, pungent odour seemed to escape from the pavement
beneath and invade the air. The earth was drenched with it, the crumbling

A postcard view of the Adams–Van Lew house on Grace Street in Church Hill

bricks, the negro hovels, the few sickly ailantus trees, exuded the sharp scent, and even the wind brought stray wafts, as from a giant's pipe, when it blew in gusts up from the river-bottom. Overhead the sky appeared to hang flat and low as if seen through a thin brown veil, and the ancient warehouses, sloping toward the river, rose like sombre prisons out of the murky air. It was still before the introduction of modern machinery into the factories, and as I approached the rotting wooden steps which led into the largest building, loose leaves of tobacco, scattered in the unloading, rustled with a sharp, crackling noise under my feet.[40]

This description of the foot of Church Hill, the so-called Tobacco Row along Cary Street just above the Richmond dock, could have been written yesterday. No tobacco is processed in Richmond north of the James today, but the odor still persists and many of the former warehouse and manufacturing buildings have been transformed into apartments and offices. Visually, the experience is much the same.

To the west of Shockoe Bottom looms Shockoe Hill, providing the perfect setting for Capitol Square, Richmond's distinguished civic sanctuary. Thomas Jefferson's capitol building, hailed as the first neoclassical municipal structure in the United States, is without doubt the most famous structure in Richmond, for the national importance of its historical events as well as its architectural significance and for its historical prominence. Glasgow vividly depicts the Capitol, the governor's mansion, and their surroundings in *The Voice of the People*. In describing the Capitol, she sets up the tension between tradition and modernism in this political novel: "The Capitol building at Richmond stands on a slight eminence in a grassy square, hiding its gray walls behind a stretch of elms and sycamores, as if it had retreated into historic shadow before the ruthless advance of the spirit of modernism. In the centre of the square ... the grave old building remains the one distinctive feature of a city where Iconoclasm has walked with destroying feet."[41] The square itself is a retreat into a more distinguished and noteworthy past, symbolized by the great bronze equestrian statue of Washington by Thomas Crawford surrounded by other Revolutionary heroes: "In Capitol Square one forgets to-day and relives yesterday. Beneath the calm eyes of the warlike statue of the First American little children chase squirrels across the grass, and infant carriages with beruffled parasols are drawn in white and pink clusters beside the benches. Jefferson and Marshall, Henry and Nelson are secure in bronze when mere greatness has decayed."[42]

The description of the Executive Mansion also emphasizes the serene retreat into a lost world:

To the left of the Capitol a gravelled drive leads between a short avenue of lindens to the turnstile iron gates that open before the governor's house. Here, too, there is an atmosphere of the past and the picturesque. The lawn, dotted with chrysanthemums and rose trees, leads down from the rear of the house to a wall of grapevines that overlooks the street below. In front the yard is narrow and broken by a short circular walk, in the centre of which a thin fountain plays among long-leaved plants. The house, grave, gray and old-fashioned—the square side porches giving it a delusive suggestion of length—faces from its stone steps the thin fountain, the iron gates, beyond which stretches the white drive beneath the lindens, and the great bronze Washington above his bodyguard of patriots.[43]

Glasgow again in her political novel *One Man In His Time* uses Capitol Square to suggest tension between the old and new Richmond. Stephen Culpeper, a young scion of the Old Guard, observed the governor's mansion and "frowned as his eyes fell on the charming Georgian front, which presided like a serene and spacious memory over the modern utilitarian purpose that was devastating the Square. Alone in its separate plot, broad, low and hospitable, the house stood there divided and withdrawn from the restless progress."[44] In the square itself, "clustering traditions had fled in the white blaze of electricity; the quaint brick walls, with their rich colour in the sunlight, were beginning to disappear beneath the expressionless mask of concrete." Just as surely as electricity and concrete had engulfed Capitol Square, "Democracy, relentless, disorderly, and strewn with the wreckage of finer things, had overwhelmed the world of established customs" that had sustained Culpeper and his ancestors for generations.[45]

There are many other neighborhoods, homes, and sites in Ellen Glasgow's novels that a native of Richmond would recognize immediately, either specifically or generically. A small frame house on Pine Street in *The Builders* calls to mind the feast of wooden cottages on Oregon Hill, built in large part for the artisans and industrial laborers of the Tredegar Iron Works, and the "look of desiccated gentility" on Leigh Street from *Life and Gabriella* could be any one of the remaining unrestored houses along Clay or Marshall Street in the eastern Jackson Ward neighborhood.[46] Glasgow's novels not only evoked the character of the inner city's nineteenth-century neighborhoods, but also moved westward beyond Monument Avenue to the most modern and affluent suburbs along Cary Street and Three Chopt and River Roads. After all, Richmond is the place she knew best, and she knew it very well.

Ellen Glasgow's final neighborhood not only figures in several of her novels but is also one of the most venerable, prestigious, and frequented sites in the city today—Hollywood Cemetery. In *The Romantic Comedians* Judge Honeywell puts a lily on Cordelia's grave, an Easter tradition that continues today. "A remarkable character, a wonderful mother, he murmured softly, with his gaze on the Italian tombstone, where even the marble angel, he observed with a wanton flight of fancy, wore the enchanting contour of youth."[47]

Inspired by the immensely popular development of tranquil parklike cemeteries first in Europe and then in Boston, Philadelphia, and New York, Hollywood Cemetery's founders, William Henry Haxall and Joshua Jefferson Fry, developed in 1847 a beautiful hillside tract, Harvie's Woods, just beyond the modest homes of Tredegar's workers on Oregon Hill. The cemetery boasts not only one of the best collections of iron and stone funerary architecture and sculpture in the nation, but also perhaps the most illustrious concentrated gathering of presidents, Confederate soldiers, heroes and generals, authors, fire captains, governors and other elected officials, the wealthy and the not-so-wealthy. On a high ridge overlooking the cemetery's entrance valley is the Glasgow family's prominent burial plot where Ellen Glasgow is entombed together with her cherished Sealyham, Jeremy. "Tomorrow to fresh woods and pastures new" reads the Miltonic inscription in raised script on the handsome Art Moderne headstone that marks her grave—a fitting, more contemporary and refreshing sculptural statement in contrast to the nineteenth-century obelisks and other symbols that surround her.[48]

FIFTEEN

Remembering Ellen Glasgow

I n the autumn of 1993 and early in 1994, Tricia Pearsall and Welford D. Taylor interviewed seven individuals who had known Ellen Glasgow in various capacities and who remembered her with surprising clarity. Five of the interviews were conducted by Pearsall, one by Taylor, and one by both of them.

Mary Tyler Freeman McClenahan, one of Richmond's most important civic leaders, is the daughter of Douglas Southall Freeman (1886–1953), who was editor of the Richmond News Leader, *Pulitzer Prize–winning biographer of Robert E. Lee and George Washington, and longtime friend of Ellen Glasgow.*

TRICIA PEARSALL: We're sitting on the patio of the home of Mary Tyler Freeman Cheek McClenahan who, as a child, was an acquaintance of Miss Glasgow through her father.

MARY TYLER CHEEK MCCLENAHAN: My father . . . was a great admirer of hers. She was very kind to him, helping him in many ways. She would come to our house for lunch or dinner, and she was always just so kind to me, as was her friend James Branch Cabell. . . .

I remember once when I was just entering adolescence and was in that most awkward of all stages, not being either a child anymore or a young lady . . . and I sat next to her at lunch.

In the middle of lunch, she put her hand on mine, and she said, "My dear, you have such beautiful red lights in your hair."

And I thought afterward that only a most highly imaginative novelist could have found anything nice to say about this homely little adolescent beside her.

That absolutely made my whole month. . . .

I thought, well, if Miss Glasgow thinks—if Miss Ellen thinks—that I have red lights in my hair, I must be all right after all.

•••

She really was such a charming person. She handled her deafness with, I thought, such grace.

But Father was once asked by the *Saturday Review of Literature* to write a piece about her. He did. In it he mentioned her deafness in a very kindly, graceful way. But . . . he took her the article before he sent it in. She said, "Oh, Douglas, I know it's foolish, but I wish you wouldn't mention my deafness, because whenever it is mentioned, it is like a knife twisted in my heart."[1]

So she never could accept it in her heart, but she certainly accepted it in a practical way. She had . . . a graceful little horn that she sat on a platform. I suppose it was about six inches in diameter, maybe a little more. It sat up about eight inches or so. She would just put that in front of you when you sat at table or wherever, and it never interfered. It never bothered.

•••

PEARSALL: Did she carry this with her when she came to lunch or dinner?

MCCLENAHAN: Yes, she did. I was trying to think how she did carry it. But she must have put it just in her handbag because it wasn't that large. She probably had a capacious handbag, as many of us do today.

She was lovely—I just loved her from the very beginning. It was always considered an enormous privilege to go to her house for tea.

•••

PEARSALL: Can you sort of go through what it was like going up the steps, ringing the doorbell, what sort of feeling you got when you entered the house?

MCCLENAHAN: Well, it was completely hospitable. You didn't—I didn't feel that it was very different from any other house of that quality. It was just—The cakes and things were always delicious. She was just very, very kind.

•••

PEARSALL: I have talked to a lot of people who must have been in between the ages of ten and fourteen or fifteen who visited her home with their mothers. So apparently it was okay to bring children?

MCCLENAHAN: I think she always invited children, if she wanted them. She was elegantly fashionable. She was never extreme in any way. But she was always attractively dressed and in dark colors. I remember, I was trying to think if I had ever seen her in anything light. It was usually dark blue or black. I don't ever remember seeing her in any light colors. Of course, most of the time she was out, she wore a hat; ladies did. . . . And gloves. . . . Miss Ellen was a lady, and it was obvious when you saw her that she was a lady. . . . She always looked very nice and appropriately dressed, but she never attempted to dazzle the way some ladies do.

PEARSALL: From the way you have described her and from my conversation with others, she must have been very sensitive and could be a very warm, involving human being?

MCCLENAHAN: She was. She was very sensitive. She was very easily hurt. And perhaps that was tied to the fact that she had a great deal of sympathy for the young and for the vulnerable, and certainly that was part of her love for animals. They were unprotected and she had that. Her sensitivity was a very large part of her.

Her interest in helping younger writers like my father was enormous. When Father finished his *R. E. Lee* and it was going to be reviewed on the first page of the *New York Times*, the *Times* suggested, or maybe it was Scribners who suggested—I don't know who it was—suggested a famous historian to review the book. Father called Miss Ellen and said, "Can you help me? I really would like to have Stephen Vincent Benét review the book."

Miss Ellen said, "Well, why would you want a poet when you have written history?"

Father said, "There was so much poetry about Robert E. Lee that I would like a poet to review it."

He did. Father and Mr. Benét became great friends. It was eventually he who insisted that Father be tied to his desk until he finished the Washington— "chained" to his desk is what he said—until he finished the book.

What Miss Ellen did immediately was to get in touch with her friend Irita Van Doren. It was Mrs. Van Doren who arranged for Stephen Vincent Benét to do the review. Out of that developed a great friendship between Father and Irita.[2]

Irita was a great friend of Miss Ellen's. Miss Ellen had a wonderfully creative way of relating to the people that she loved and wanted to help. It was a very, very, very, very generous thing for her to do.

•••

She did have a sense of humor. She was always a very, very charming lady.

I wish so, so much that her letters to Mr. Anderson had not been burned, but they were burned at his command, as you know. That is a loss because that would reveal a lot about her that we still don't know.

She, like any artist, she had a very complicated inner life that very few people ever reached—in fact, perhaps no one ever did. Perhaps she never let anyone into her inner sanctum.

Zayde Rennolds Dotts knew Ellen Glasgow mainly through her mother, Mrs. Edmund A. Rennolds, a contemporary and close friend. Mrs. Dotts also retains her own memories of Glasgow.

TRICIA PEARSALL: Tell us: you went for tea one time?

ZAYDE RENNOLDS DOTTS: Yes, we went for tea once. She was upstairs on the second floor on the chaise. As we walked in the front door, there was a "mammy" there with a white fichu on and an apron, just sitting. I don't know whether she was on call or what. I think Ellen Glasgow was then an older lady. Maybe she wasn't feeling well.

The rooms were big and square and high-ceilinged. Of course, I was a little girl; maybe they looked bigger then.

Upstairs there was just regular old-timey southern furniture. She was on a chaise. There seemed to be two rooms run together. There was a big screen in one corner. It was just a normal southern bedroom for that time.

PEARSALL: When you first went for tea, when you were relatively small, this must have been a fairly intimidating experience. Or . . . were there other people there?

DOTTS: I can't remember anyone else being there. . . . Of course, Miss Glasgow was deaf. She held a "thing" out. You had to talk into it. That was a little bit intimidating. Also she talked quite loud. She had quite a loud voice, being deaf.

But I don't remember it being intimidating. . . .

PEARSALL: You said that she did go to visit you all at the farm?

DOTTS: Yes, up in Duchess County, New York, we have a farm. I distinctly remember her coming by. We were having tea again in the living room and sitting on the sofa. She was on her way to Castine, Maine.

She was telling my grandmother that she had all of these characters running around in her head, and that she just had to write one more book.

I just seem to remember dark hair pulled back in a sort of bun. She had on a longish dress. It was in the '30s, when they wore them longer, and some kind of white jabot or something inside. I remember that the little black "thing" she held sort of matched her dress, because another awful great big "thing" had to be pinned to her dress.

PEARSALL: Part of her hearing device?

DOTTS: Part of the hearing, yes.

Sarah Anderson Easter is the daughter of James Anderson, Glasgow's cook and major-domo. Ms. Easter, along with her nine brothers, often assisted her father in his duties at One West Main.

TRICIA PEARSALL: You weren't born here [at One West Main]?

SARAH ANDERSON EASTER: No.

PEARSALL: But two of your mother's children were?

EASTER: Her two oldest children.

PEARSALL: They were born in the carriage . . .

EASTER: Carriage house outside.

•••

PEARSALL: We're in Miss Glasgow's dining room, the dining room of the house at One West Main. Can you just tell us a little bit about what went on here?

EASTER: The china closet was here [at the north corner of the east wall]. The dining room table is the same [in the middle]. The sideboard was there [at the south corner of the east wall]. A screen was over there right behind that chair [against the south wall] with a serving table behind it where the maid put her vegetables before she brought them to the table. A chair here and a chair there and a bell up under the table.

PEARSALL: Explain the bell up under the table.

EASTER: When she wanted something served again, she would just press her foot on [the bell], and it rang in the kitchen. They came to the door.

PEARSALL: You said Miss Glasgow would eat . . .

EASTER: Right there [at the south end of the table]. . . . Miss Bennett was right there close to her [on her right].

•••

PEARSALL: Did they have all their meals here? Breakfast?

EASTER: No. Breakfast, Miss Ellen had hers in bed. The chauffeur took hers to her every morning.

PEARSALL: She would have lunch and . . .

EASTER: 1:30 lunch and 6:30 supper.

PEARSALL: . . . You said she had a lot of visitors, but never more than one or two at a time.

EASTER: At one time.

PEARSALL: Who were some of the people who would come to supper?

EASTER: Miss Lizzie Crutchfield, Miss Roberta Wellford.

PEARSALL: This was where she kept all of her books. You all kept . . .

EASTER: House. My daddy did.

PEARSALL: Did you come over every day?

EASTER: Yeah. We had to come over every day from school.

•••

PEARSALL: Did you have to work while you were here?

EASTER: My first job here was ironing napkins for two dollars a week on a block in that same room back there. She had a cat named Bobby my brother sold her for five cents that had no tail. . . .

My daddy stayed here to keep the dog for her while she was gone.

PEARSALL: Jeremy?

EASTER: No, Bonnie. The last one.

PEARSALL: He would stay here . . . every day?

EASTER: . . . He stayed all night.

PEARSALL: During the week?

EASTER: Yes. Come home on weekends. But he come back on Saturday nights, come back Sunday, and come back Sunday night.

PEARSALL: One of the ladies that we interviewed said that when she came to visit with her mother, there was a chambermaid or somebody sitting out here to receive coats.

EASTER: The chambermaid was Mrs. Blanche Mail. The upstairs maid was Miss Mattie Coleman. The woman that did the serving was Irene Gesper. The man that brought up the coal was Mr. Jim White. And the chauffeur was Nathaniel Model.

PEARSALL: Your father, James Anderson, was the cook?

EASTER: He was the one that ran it.

PEARSALL: . . . You said Colonel Anderson came for dinner?

EASTER: Yes. My daddy had to make three breads when he came.

PEARSALL: What three breads?

EASTER: Sally Lunn, hoecakes, and light bread.

PEARSALL: All for Sunday evening?

EASTER: It didn't have to be a Sunday. Any night in the week. With lamb hash.

•••

PEARSALL: You said she was very petite?

EASTER: She was very. . . . She wore a [size] three shoe. . . . She used to sleep in gloves at night. . . . To keep her hands soft.

PEARSALL: She typed with gloves?

EASTER: Uh-huh. . . . She used to wear colored stockings to bed.

PEARSALL: Was that just to keep warm?

Easter: I guess so. Because the lady used to iron them. Now we're in the pantry of Ellen Glasgow's home. Right here was where the telephone was with a stool on a model-top stand.

PEARSALL: Was that the telephone for the whole house?

EASTER: No. They had ones upstairs. This was for downstairs, really. . . .

PEARSALL: The number?

EASTER: 33118.

PEARSALL: Did she have a favorite menu?

EASTER: No. She liked split-down-the-back chicken, and she liked Sally Lunn bread. She was crazy about oysters. But they had to use cream. He made her eggnog out of nothing but cream.

PEARSALL: We're upstairs now. We're going into the room that was Miss Glasgow's study. Did she have lots of books on these shelves?

EASTER: Oh, yes. . . . And papers and everything. Anything you wanted, she had it here. . . . We didn't come in here often.

PEARSALL: She worked regular hours? She was very disciplined?

EASTER: She worked to suit herself, you know. She worked every day. It wasn't special hours.

PEARSALL: Did she work on weekends?

EASTER: No, no, no. Read the paper all the weekend.

PEARSALL: What papers?

EASTER: Well, what was it? *New York Times* and then all the papers from New York, stock market papers, and all those things.

PEARSALL: She actively followed the stock market?

EASTER: Sure.

PEARSALL: Did she ever have people visit her or come up to see what she was working on or anything like that in this room?

EASTER: No. I never saw anybody in this room.

•••

PEARSALL: So the room behind was like a sitting room?

EASTER: She had a dressing room back going all the way across the back. The secretary and the nurse's room was Anne Virginia Bennett['s].

PEARSALL: What were her duties exactly?

EASTER: She was her nurse and her secretary. She paid all the bills and saw that the food was ordered and saw that everybody got paid and everything like that.

•••

This is where Nathaniel found her in bed that morning.

•••

He came to bring her breakfast, knocking on the door, and she didn't answer. It was Thanksgiving morning [1945].

•••

PEARSALL: You said that she lay in state here?

EASTER: Until the day of the funeral. She got an orchid every day, hair fixed every day. All she did was kind of primp it up. Everybody wasn't free to come.

PEARSALL: It was only for special friends?

EASTER: Then the last day, they carried her downstairs and put her in the back parlor. Then she went to Hollywood [Cemetery].

Pocahontas Wight Edmunds (1904–1999), a Richmond writer, enjoyed an acquaintance with Ellen Glasgow that began in the 1930s.

EDMUNDS: Well, I kind of contrived seeing her, because I have always been a bookworm and wanted to know about authors and whether the characters in the book were real and things like that. So I was up to something.

I was one of some Richmond college students who volunteered to help the

Community Fund by each choosing a charity. I am scared of animals. I chose the SPCA. And the others kind of snickered and shrugged.

. . . She met me at the SPCA building. Then I got off on the wrong foot because I said, "Miss Glasgow, the public thinks of the SPCA as a sentimental thing. Since there is a rabies scare going on, looking in everybody's mind, I think we can get special publicity."

"Sentimental? I am known all over the world as the most unsentimental woman anywhere. I don't think anybody will think anything I'm connected with is sentimental."

Virginius Dabney (1901–1995), Pulitzer Prize–winning editor and historian, knew Miss Glasgow for many of the thirty-three years that he edited the Richmond Times-Dispatch. *He was often a guest when she entertained at One West Main Street. He graciously complied when Anne Virginia Bennett requested him to write an obituary for Miss Glasgow's beloved Jeremy, and some years later he served as a pallbearer at the author's funeral. His autobiography,* Across the Years, *contains a section on Miss Glasgow and reprints Jeremy's obituary in an appendix.*

VIRGINIUS DABNEY: . . . I knew her pleasantly. She was not an intimate friend, but she was quite nice to me and invited me to many of her parties.

WELFORD D. TAYLOR: . . . Did she entertain often?

DABNEY: Fairly often, yes. Especially when writers came to town. She was very deaf, you know. She had a great long thing that looked like a telephone. She'd say something and would hold it out to you to reply. You'd better come through with a reply, too. She was very unhappy about her deafness. She never got over that.

•••

TAYLOR: I want to ask you about her famous party in 1936, when the Modern Language Association of America had its meeting in Richmond.

DABNEY: I was there.

TAYLOR: Is that so? Well, so you were there with Thomas Wolfe and Allen Tate and all the Fugitives and Agrarians. . . . But of course, the more interesting party, I daresay, was the one in 1935 . . . [on] Gertrude Stein's arrival in Richmond.

•••

DABNEY: There was a reporter on the *Times-Dispatch* who wrote some very amusing stuff, and I know he interviewed her once or twice. I think she told him that she felt Virginia was uninhabited.

TAYLOR: . . . Well, I gather that the entertaining for her consisted of two events, did it—a dinner and . . .

DABNEY: If there was a dinner I didn't know it. I just was invited to the cocktail party.

TAYLOR: . . . Was there a large crowd, do you recall?

DABNEY: Yes, there were quite a few people . . . fairly crowded her house pretty well, . . . at least fifty.

TAYLOR: A goodly number. Did you have a chance to talk with Miss Stein and—as Bennett Cerf used to call her—"Toklas"? Did you have a chance to talk to them both?

DABNEY: Well, when I got that book [*The Autobiography of Alice B. Toklas*] autographed they were both together and . . . you saw what she put in there ["to Mrs. and Mr. Virginius Dabney"]. . . . It's exactly what you'd expect [from her].

TAYLOR: Was she gracious in conversation?

DABNEY: Well, more or less. She was a very peculiar individual, and you never knew what she was going to say next. Or what her attitude would be. She wasn't unpleasant or . . .

TAYLOR: I see. . . . But how about Stein and Glasgow? I don't suppose they could converse very . . .

D: I didn't hear them converse . . . everyone was standing around, and it wasn't the easiest to follow the conversation.

•••

TAYLOR: Did you ever ask Miss Glasgow to contribute anything to the paper while you were editor?

DABNEY: I don't think I did. I don't remember it, anyway.

TAYLOR: Was she considered a hot spot of news? I'm sure she was a very newsworthy subject.

DABNEY: No, not unless she had a party or something, or a published new book; that was news.

TAYLOR: But I meant feature articles . . . that sort of thing, you wouldn't do . . .

DABNEY: I don't think so.

TRICIA PEARSALL: So she never wrote letters to the editor, or anything?

DABNEY: I don't recall she ever wrote one.

•••

PEARSALL: You were a pallbearer at Glasgow's funeral.

DABNEY: Yes.

PEARSALL: Was it a large gathering? Or was it intimate . . . just family?

DABNEY: There weren't many people. It was by invitation. . . . Henry Anderson wasn't invited, but he came anyway.

•••

TAYLOR: I guess Anne Virginia [Bennett] was probably the moving force behind choosing the guests?

DABNEY: Yes, she asked me to be a pallbearer, and she asked me to write the obituary of Jeremy.

PEARSALL: When Glasgow's books were published, did she attend festivities at Miller and Rhoads or other bookstores, or did she have receptions at home?

DABNEY: I don't recall her doing it, but she may have. I don't remember any events in connection with her books.

TAYLOR: I don't suppose she made many public appearances.

DABNEY: No, I don't think so. Being deaf was very embarrassing to her.

Carrington Tutwiler Jr. is the son of Ellen Glasgow's sister Rebe.

CARRINGTON TUTWILER: To me she was a grande dame whom I never caught or was aware of in an informal moment. I would see her probably only at mealtimes, and by mealtimes I mean dinner. Breakfast she, of course, always had in her room. Luncheon, she might have had by herself. Dinner was a formal occasion in the dining room served by two waitresses and prepared by James [Anderson], the colored chef, in the kitchen.

The conversation would be always dominated by her. In other words, she was the presence at the table. What was said was said by her. This was, of course, partly necessitated by the fact that she was deaf even at that age.

Her hearing aid at that time was comparatively primitive by today's standards. It consisted of a microphone on top of a case about the size of a Coca-Cola bottle, perhaps, sitting in a glass cup, a sterling silver glass cup, on the table beside her which was connected by a cord to the hearing phone in her ear. In order to be understood by her, it was necessary to speak directly into the microphone. Consequently, she could speak to only one person at a time at the table. This would apply to dinner parties as well as to informal meetings.

She was quite deaf, really quite deaf at that time and could not hear a thing without the microphone on. . . . .

Her impression was a formal and formidable one to a young man such as I was. We met very seldom on one or two occasions when she invited me to spend the weekend perhaps with her in Richmond.

WELFORD TAYLOR: . . . Well, of course you grew up to become a man of letters yourself. . . . you have written about her library and about books that she personally owned.

•••

TUTWILER: . . . let me say that I came to know Ellen better after her death than I did during her lifetime . . . because I had the privilege of doing a bibliography of her library. Fortunately, I had that opportunity because Mother inherited that library. That bibliography was published by the Bibliographical Society of the University of Virginia. . . .

•••

This was the most extraordinary fact I think about her reading, probably to a greater extent than any other distinguished writer that you know of. Her education was formed by her reading. She never went to any school or any college whatsoever. She was self-educated entirely. Of course, she had conferences with her sister Cary and with Cary's husband [George Walter McCormack]. But in general, she started off as an enthusiastic, romantic young girl reading romantic literature, as you might expect, but far more [widely] than you might expect, particularly going into Greek and Roman philosophy, early Renaissance philosophy. She read extensively such writers as Plotinus, Marcus Aurelius. Her reading in those writers is attested by her markings and annotations in those books and many others. She had no direction, so far as I know, at that time. She had no friends who were interested in this. This is entirely, with the exception of her sister Cary, this is entirely a self-education.

As time passed, she grew beyond that early stage into a later one coming down into nineteenth-century biology, psychology, history. And in the end almost every branch of knowledge that you would find in a college was shown in her library.

When I say almost every branch, I mean that quite literally. For example, if I may quote a few items.[3] "Fiction: English fully represented in all periods; all major and many minor authors in standard sets. European realists in sets, including Proust and Mann. American fiction well represented through 1940.

"Drama: Ibsen and Shaw complete. Jacobean and miscellaneous twentieth-century authors represented.

"Poetry: English and American heavily represented through 1940. Arnold, Clough, Wordsworth in sets; almost no significant omissions.

"Philosophy: very heavy representation. Stoics; Jowett's six-volume Plato; neo-Platonists; Bacon; Kant, Hegel, Spinoza; Berkeley, Locke, Hume complete; Santayana complete in the Triton edition." And I would say that Santayana was one of her greatest loves.

TAYLOR: Well, now, a great many of these authors were considered, were certainly controversial, at the least, or radical, at the worst, in the view of a great many . . .

TUTWILER: The great majority of them were unknown, I would think, in Richmond.

TAYLOR: Quite so. . . .

TUTWILER: Not only those of the authors I have cited, but "Buddhism, Hinduism collections.

"History: European and American covered in standard works: including Buckle, Lecky, Gibbon. Toynbee's *Study* complete. Special concentrations in French and Scottish history. Anthropology, sociology, psychology: selective representation. Frazer's *Golden Bough* in eight-volume edition; Freud, Jung; Sumner;

George; special items on the history of ethics and religion, including White's *War-fare of Science and Religion.*" That is only one of many items in that special area.

"Science: Darwin, Huxley." Both of those had a tremendous influence, I think, on her novels, particularly the earliest ones.

"Fine Arts: items representing special interests, including Vasari complete; studies of Leonardo, Botticelli, Whistler, Conder; English Cathedral architecture; ceramics.

"Travel: extensive collection, especially Italy, Florence, England, London through 1940, including Lucas, Hare, Symonds.

"Virginiana: very strong representation, including such items as Freeman (complete, autographed) and Meade's *Churches.*

"Special interests: criminology. Small but good collection, especially true crime, including Roughead, and extensive collection of key mystery and detective novels, from Wilkie Collins to Freeman Croft, Joseph Shearing. Certain minor novelists, such as Rider Haggard and Maurice Hewlett fully represented.

"Association and presentation copies: items from many contemporaries, including Mary Johnston, Marjorie Kinnan Rawlings, Carl van Vechten, James Branch Cabell.

"Reference: very full collection of writers on writing; all available standard reference works, including the large Oxford English Dictionary.

"Significant omissions: theology; science, other than Darwin; music." The mention of anything on music is, I think, obvious and explainable.

TAYLOR: Yes, quite so.

TUTWILER: Moreover, science was not heavily recommended. This self-education did not I think include anything in mathematics. There was no way that it could have. And the biological sciences, because she could have had no laboratory experience whatsoever.

TAYLOR: Absolutely, yes.

TUTWILER: So the remainder of this is simply an amplification of that outline of the areas of which she did. This is the history of her education.

TAYLOR: While we're on the subject of her library, . . . you have unique knowledge of perhaps a most important event in the history of that library, that is, on the day following her death in 1945, you went with your mother to Richmond to survey the library. . . .

TUTWILER: I think I had gone down several years before she died. It was my last year in grad school, which would have been probably 1934. At that time, out of curiosity, I would have made a very careful examination of her library. I did notice one or two things in it that I noticed were missing after her death.

TAYLOR: What kinds of things would have been missing?

TUTWILER: Books on the psychology of sex, particularly Freud's works with that title.

TAYLOR: I see, yes.

TUTWILER: Jung. Books that you would not expect to find in a private Richmond library [or] house at that time.

TAYLOR: I see. So they had been removed?

TUTWILER: Yes.

TAYLOR: I see.

TUTWILER: There is one other thing I would like to mention that was not a book but was also in the library. Hanging over the fireplace in the library was a large picture of a chained dog. It was the most sad, most depressing thing you could possibly imagine. A full-size dog painted, chained to a heavy stone beside him, and looking so mournfully into your face as you looked at it.

Now when I went down there the second time—I mean after my [aunt's] death—that picture had been removed.

TAYLOR: By her?

TUTWILER: I don't know. Perhaps by Mother, [although] I can't say that. What became of it I don't know. Whether they gave it away or they destroyed it, I just don't know.

I realize it was there because Ellen saw it in a way as emblematic of her life. She always considered herself chained in a way by her isolation.

Frances Shield is the niece of Colonel Henry Anderson, who was a prominent Richmond attorney, influential figure in national Republican politics, and longtime friend of Ellen Glasgow.

TRICIA PEARSALL: We're here today at One West Main. . . . Mrs. Shield, thanks for coming. I am particularly interested . . . you did not grow up in Richmond?

FRANCES SHIELD: No, I was born in Farmville, Virginia, Prince Edward County, and lived there until I was eleven, when my family moved to Richmond.

PEARSALL: Do you remember hearing your family talk much about your uncle[4] and his relationship with Miss Glasgow? He was a very prominent Richmonder, a lawyer, very active in civic . . .

SHIELD: He was. But in my childhood in Farmville, my recollection of him was [that] he would come in his beautiful Pierce Arrow touring car with a very handsome chauffeur who was half Indian, and he would come loaded with all kinds of toys and presents for all the family up there. . . . He was very devoted to his mother.

I came here [One West Main] several times. Back then ladies would call on each other at an appointed time. I came here once, maybe twice, with my mother to call on Miss Glasgow. I was sitting in the front parlor on a horsehair sofa like a little girl sat in those days. Miss Glasgow walks in with this trumpet that you had to speak into for her to hear. She was stone deaf. That was very awkward for her.

You would visit about twenty minutes and then leave.

But Miss Glasgow never went out to dinners and things like that. . . . She was very uncomfortable with this ear trumpet. . . .

There was one remark that always amused me. My uncle had English servants in his house, an English cook [Violet Mangon] and her husband, who was a butler. Mrs. Mangon told my mother once, said she had read one of Miss Glasgow's books, because the servants know everything. She said to my mother, "How could a maiden lady know what she knows and put in a book?" Well, my mother, knowing her brother, knew perfectly well why Miss Glasgow knew the things she did.

PEARSALL: Your impressions of Miss Glasgow. . . . Did she make you feel at ease?

SHIELD: No, very uncomfortable. As a child it was very rigid and very cold. I was glad to leave with my mother. . . . she was very straight, very rigid, and the conversation was very stiff. It was just a proper call. My mother was very fond of people. She thought it was the thing for her to do.

•••

PEARSALL: Do you recall what recollection of her or her relationship with your uncle you first remember?

SHIELD: I don't remember very much about her, actually, until I went to live with him, when I was nineteen. . . .

It always interested me that he, every Sunday morning, would write a note at his desk there in the library (I used to tease him a great deal), send it down by the chauffeur to Miss Glasgow here at the house to say—I think they said—"Dear Ellen, I would like to dine with you this evening." . . . The note would come down by his chauffeur. The chauffeur would wait. She would write a note back saying whether it was convenient or not for him to come to supper. This went on up until her last illness.

It was interesting to me that Miss Glasgow kept every single note or letter that he ever wrote. All those notes, those Sunday morning notes, are all in the Alderman Library [at] the University of Virginia. I went up there once to read them. So he always signed them himself, "Sincerely, Henry W. Anderson." He was very conscious of not putting anything on paper.

PEARSALL: . . . that was affectionate?

SHIELD: Being a lawyer. He was a very private man. He didn't put anything of his feelings on paper.

PEARSALL: He would often then come Sunday to One West Main for supper? . . . Did you ever come with him?

SHIELD: No. I think they still enjoyed their conversations together. They had been friends for so many years. I think the bitterness in Miss Glasgow was still there, but I think my uncle was a very loyal person. I think he enjoyed her company.

PEARSALL: So this was kind of an intellectual friendship?

SHIELD: That's right. I think so.

PEARSALL: [Rather] than actually any passion or romantic sort of . . . ?

SHIELD: Well, it may have been earlier in their lives. I think she interpreted it that way.

PEARSALL: Do you recall his ever telling you—or I'm sure there's a lot of rumor and innuendo about their relationship prior to his visit to Romania during World War I. Were they officially engaged as such, or do you know?

SHIELD: It has always been interesting to me because Miss Glasgow, I think, thought that she was engaged to him. I asked him once, because a nineteen-year-old young girl and a sixty-five-year-old bachelor, I had a lot of fun with him. He had a great sense of humor. I teased him a great deal about all of the beautiful women, ladies in his life. There were a great many. I was named for one of them, Lady Frances Hadfield.[5] So I would tease him about it.

I asked him once, "Weren't you engaged to Miss Glasgow?" He said no, he wasn't. . . . I don't think he thought he was ever engaged to her.

But in reading his letters—and they are all in the library—I came across a letter from my grandmother, his mother, . . . in which she said that she was delighted to know that Henry was engaged I thought, "Uh-huh." . . . I don't really think that his mother, Martha Henry Anderson, ever really thought he was going to marry Miss Glasgow.

I asked him once or twice why he never married. He said, well, when he first came to Richmond from Washington and Lee, he was a very poor young man. He started out practicing law with a very distinguished gentleman here in Richmond, Mr. [Robert Bland] Munford. He said there was one perfectly beautiful young lady here in Richmond whose father was very wealthy, and he said, "I was too poor to ask her to marry me." So he just never did marry.

•••

He helped her a great deal in writing one or two of her books. I don't think she ever gave him credit for it, not that he cared. It must have been a very interesting relationship intellectually.

PEARSALL: Now, Colonel Anderson was also a friend of Arthur Glasgow[6]?

SHIELD: Yes. He stayed with my uncle when he came to Richmond instead of staying here. He knew how difficult she was.

PEARSALL: Now, the question that I guess everybody asks you concerning the letters that Miss Glasgow wrote to Colonel Anderson . . . that he requested that these letters be burned or destroyed?

SHIELD: Not to me. Not to anybody. He never spoke about it. But within the last few weeks of his life, I was very stressed and distressed because I adored him. He was just wonderful to me.

In a closet there next to his bedroom, . . . there was quite a large package of letters wrapped in brown wrapping paper and string. Written on it—the brown paper—in his handwriting was, "To be burned at my death," and he signed it. Evidently he couldn't bring himself to burn those letters. So I sat there and read them those last two or three weeks of his life because I was just sitting there. So I read all of the letters. My sister was there too. We decided that we should honor his wishes. So we did burn them.

Well, after his death and people found out about it, . . . they wanted to tar and feather me because I had burned literature. Well, as I said before, my uncle was a very private man. I was going to be completely loyal to him. I was not going to expose anything about his personal life. What I'm saying today is what everyone knew about the relationship of my uncle with Miss Glasgow. That's all I remember. And so I burned them.

•••

I hesitated to do this interview because I wanted to be perfectly loyal to my uncle. And still I thought I owed it to him to say that he found Miss Glasgow very disagreeable, very rude at times, and most of the time [she] felt that he was inferior to her . . . both socially and intellectually.

•••

PEARSALL: The letters she wrote to Colonel Anderson, were these letters written when he was in Romania, [or] were they just the casual correspondence they maintained here in Richmond?

SHIELD: They went over a long period of time. It was all the letters, I think, that she had written through the years. She never destroyed, as I said, a single note of his. . . . I think all of her notes and letters were in this. They were talking about different things that they had written from Maine and written from different places and written to him when he was abroad. And he traveled a great deal. He was out of Richmond most of the time on law cases and railroads and things. This is correspondence that went on between two friends.

But she always signed it "Devotedly, Ellen"; whereas, he always signed his letters, "Sincerely, Henry W. Anderson." She was . . . very bitter about his not marrying her.

PEARSALL: Oh?

SHIELD: Yes. You can see that in the book, *The Woman Within*. She was very bitter about it. She was very bitter about the Queen Marie of Romania.[7] She said some pretty ugly things. "You were so impressed with this," you know. She belittled him a lot when he came back. She had heard about it.

PEARSALL: In the letters she belittled him?

SHIELD: Yes. Personally, yes.

PEARSALL: His relationship with the Queen Marie of Romania has received all sorts of, I guess, again, gossip, innuendo, what have you. Did he ever really talk about her very much?

SHIELD: Yes. He told me once she was the most beautiful woman he had ever seen. His house [had] just, I reckon, a dozen or more beautiful portrait photographs of her, and all in different dress, her peasant dress of Romania and her royal jewelry and so forth.

•••

PEARSALL: The house . . . you came here a couple of times. Do you have any impressions? . . .

SHIELD: Yes. It was sort of dark and dreary and stiff. Because I was a teenager, I couldn't wait to leave because it was very depressing to me.

PEARSALL: What about her animals? Were they around all the time?

SHIELD: My uncle gave her the first dog she ever had. . . . Jeremy, yes. That was her interest in the SPCA. She left all her money to the SPCA. Jeremy was buried out here in the garden. He gave her that dog. I think it was a great companion for her. I think after that she always had a dog.

There was one moving instance when I was living with him. They exchanged very handsome presents at Christmas time. I have several pieces of silver that she gave him. So on Christmas morning, the usual note came down. He was going to take her Christmas present. Well, he came home. It was one of the few times I ever saw my uncle really upset and so angry. I sort of laughed at him.

He was a very sweet man. He wasn't this time. He said, "Ellen is the most disagreeable woman I have ever known in my life." I said, "What on earth happened?" He said, "Well, I brought her a very handsome present." It was a beautiful leather toilet case, which ladies carried in those days, with all silver fittings and monogrammed inside. He said she opened it and said, "You gave me one just like it ten years ago." He considered that extremely rude. He was just furious, really. He was very angry about it. But I laughed at him. He soon got over it.

•••

Well, you can understand her frustrations in a way with having been deaf since a child, not very pretty really, not very attractive, and all she had was her intellect. . . . You could understand her frustrations and her lashing out at people.

Notes

Works Frequently Cited in the Notes

Writings by Ellen Glasgow

Barren Ground (New York: Doubleday, Page and Company, 1925).

The Battle-Ground (New York: Doubleday, Page and Company, 1902).

A Certain Measure: An Interpretation of Prose Fiction (New York: Harcourt, Brace and Company, 1943).

The Collected Stories of Ellen Glasgow, ed. Richard K. Meeker (Baton Rouge: Louisiana State University Press, 1963).

The Descendant (New York: Harper and Brothers, 1897).

In This Our Life (New York: Harcourt, Brace and Company, 1941).

Letters of Ellen Glasgow, ed. Blair Rouse (New York: Harcourt, Brace, and Company, 1958).

Life and Gabriella (New York: Doubleday, Page and Company, 1920).

The Miller of Old Church (New York: Doubleday, Page and Company, 1911).

One Man in His Time (New York: Doubleday, Page and Company, 1922).

The Romance of a Plain Man (New York: The MacMillan Company, 1909).

The Romantic Comedians (New York: Doubleday, Page and Company, 1926).

The Sheltered Life (New York: Doubleday, Doran and Company, 1932).

They Stooped to Folly (New York: Doubleday, Doran and Company, 1929).

Vein of Iron (New York: Harcourt, Brace, 1935).

Virginia (Garden City, New York: Doubleday, Page and Company, 1913).

The Voice of the People (New York: Doubleday, Page and Company, 1900).

The Woman Within (New York: Harcourt, Brace and Company, 1954).

Critical Works on Ellen Glasgow

E. Stanly Godbold Jr., *Ellen Glasgow and the Woman Within* (Baton Rouge: Louisiana State University Press, 1972).

Susan Goodman, *Ellen Glasgow: A Biography* (Baltimore and London: The Johns Hopkins University Press, 1998).

M. Thomas Inge, ed., *Ellen Glasgow—Centennial Essays* (Charlottesville: University Press of Virginia, 1976).

Frederick P. W. McDowell, *Ellen Glasgow and the Ironic Art of Fiction* (Madison: The University of Wisconsin Press, 1960).

Pamela R. Matthews, *Ellen Glasgow and a Woman's Traditions* (Charlottesville: University Press of Virginia, 1994).

Julius Rowan Raper, *Without Shelter: The Early Career of Ellen Glasgow* (Baton Rouge: Louisiana State University Press, 1971).

———, *From the Sunken Garden: The Fiction of Ellen Glasgow, 1916–1945* (Baton Rouge: Louisiana University Press, 1980).

———, *Ellen Glasgow's Reasonable Doubts: A Collection of Her Writings* (Baton Rouge: Louisiana State University Press, 1988).

Blair Rouse, *Ellen Glasgow* (New Haven: College and University Press, 1962).

Dorothy M. Scura, ed., *Ellen Glasgow: The Contemporary Reviews* (Cambridge: Cambridge University Press, 1992).

————, ed., *Ellen Glasgow: New Perspectives* (Knoxville: The University of Tennessee Press, 1995).

Linda W. Wagner, *Ellen Glasgow: Beyond Convention* (Austin: University of Texas Press, 1982).

CHAPTER 1: THROUGH A GATE AND INTO ANOTHER LIFE
Catherine Rainwater

1. *Barren Ground*, 496.

2. Edgar E. MacDonald and Tonette Bond Inge, *Ellen Glasgow: A Reference Guide* (Boston: G. K. Hall, 1986).

3. Holman's works calling for more attention to Glasgow's art include "The Southerner as American Writer," in *The Southerner as American*, ed. Charles Grier Sellers Jr. (Chapel Hill: The University of North Carolina Press, 1960), 180–199; "*Barren Ground* and the Shape of History," *South Atlantic Quarterly* 77 (spring 1978): 137–145; "A *Mea Culpa* for Glasgow Scholars," *Ellen Glasgow Newsletter* 9 (October 1978): 2; and "The Tragedy of Self-Entrapment: Ellen Glasgow's *The Romance of a Plain Man*," in *Toward a New American Literary History: Essays in Honor of Arlin Turner*, ed. Louis J. Budd, Edwin H. Cady, and Carl L. Anderson (Durham: Duke University Press, 1980), 154–163.

4. See sections devoted to Glasgow in the annual *American Literary Scholarship* (Durham: Duke University Press) throughout the late 1970s and the 1980s for examples of this refrain.

5. Raper, *Ellen Glasgow's Reasonable Doubts,* 71, 78, 82.

6. See Glasgow's essays on Southern literature included in Raper's *Ellen Glasgow's Reasonable Doubts*.

7. Rouse, *Ellen Glasgow,* 139.

8. See Otis W. Coan and Richard G. Lillard, *America in Fiction: An Annotated List of Novels That Interpret Aspects of Life in the United States*, 2d ed. (Stanford, Calif.: Stanford University Press, 1945); and Henry Bamford Parkes, *The American Experience: An Interpretation of the History and Civilization of the American People* (New York: A. A. Knopf, 1947).

9. Allen Tate, "The New Provincialism: With an Epilogue on the Southern Novel," *Virginia Quarterly Review* 21 (spring 1945): 262–272.

10. C. Hugh Holman, "Ellen Glasgow and the Southern Literary Tradition," in *Virginia in History and Tradition*, ed. R. C. Simonini Jr. (Farmville, Va.: Longwood College, 1958), 85–105.

11. Josephine Lurie Jessup's doctoral dissertation "The Faith of Our Feminists: Edith Wharton, Ellen Glasgow, Willa Cather" (Vanderbilt University, 1948), was later published as a book. See *The Faith of Our Feminists: A Study in the Novels of Edith Wharton, Ellen Glasgow, Willa Cather* (New York: Richard R. Smith, 1950). Other forward-looking dissertations on Glasgow's women, including some in French and German, are listed in MacDonald and Inge's *Reference Guide*.

12. McDowell, *Ironic Art of Fiction,* 9.

13. See John Edward Hardy, "Ellen Glasgow," *Hopkins Review* 5 (summer 1952): 22–36; and Blair Rouse, "Letter to Editor," *Hopkins Review* 6 (fall 1952): 4.

14. See *Hopkins Review,* 5:35.

15. See, for example, Alfred Kazin's struggle with himself over Glasgow's merit in "The Lost Rebel," in *The Inmost Leaf: A Selection of Essays* (New York: Harcourt, Brace and Com-

pany, 1955), 136–141, an essay that led to a dispute about Glasgow between Kazin and Donald J. Adams in the latter's "Speaking of Books," *New York Times Book Review*, 30 October 1955, p. 2; "Elegy and Satire: Willa Cather and Ellen Glasgow," in *On Native Grounds: An Interpretation of Modern American Prose Literature* (Boston: Harcourt, Brace and Company, 1942; Garden City, N.Y.: Doubleday and Company, Inc., Anchor Books, 1956), 181–196. See also Louis D. Rubin Jr., *No Place on Earth: Ellen Glasgow, James Branch Cabell and Richmond-in-Virginia* (Austin: University of Texas Press, 1959); and *The Faraway Country: Writers of the Modern South* (Seattle: University of Washington Press, 1963).

16. See Raper, *Ellen Glasgow's Reasonable Doubts*, 74–75.

17. Marianne DeKoven, *Rich and Strange: Gender, History, Modernism* (Princeton, N.J.: Princeton University Press, 1991), 11.

18. See the author's "Ellen Glasgow's Outline of History in *The Shadowy Third and Other Stories*," in *The Critical Response to H. G. Wells*, ed. William J. Scheick (Westport, Conn., and London: Greenwood Press, 1995), 125–138; "Consciousness, Gender, and Animal Signs in Ellen Glasgow's *Barren Ground* and *Vein of Iron*," in Scura, *New Perspectives*, 204–219; and "Narration as Pragmatism in Ellen Glasgow's *Barren Ground*," *American Literature* 63 (December 1991): 664–682.

19. Wayne Lesser, "The Problematics of Regionalism and the Dilemma of Glasgow's *Barren Ground*," *Southern Literary Journal* 11 (spring 1979): 3–21; and J. E. Bunselmeyer, "Ellen Glasgow's 'Flexible' Style," *Centennial Review* 28 (1984): 112–128.

20. See Rouse, *Ellen Glasgow*, 138.

21. Judith B. Wittenburg, "The Critical Fortunes of *Barren Ground*," *Mississippi Quarterly* 32 (fall 1979): 591–609.

22. E. Stanly Godbold Jr., "A Biography and a Biographer," *Ellen Glasgow Newsletter* 32 (spring 1994): 4–5.

23. See Raper, *From the Sunken Garden;* and Susan Goodman's "Competing Visions of Freud in the Memoirs of Ellen Glasgow and Edith Wharton," *Colby Library Quarterly* 25 (December 1989): 218–226. See also Josephine Donovan's *After the Fall: The Demeter-Persephone Myth in Wharton, Cather, and Glasgow* (University Park: Pennsylvania State University Press, 1989).

24. See for example Matthews, *Ellen Glasgow and a Woman's Traditions;* Will Brantley, *Feminine Sense in Southern Memoir: Smith, Glasgow, Welty, Hellman, Porter, and Hurston* (Jackson: University Press of Mississippi, 1993); William J. Scheick, "The Narrative Ethos of Glasgow's 'A Point in Morals,'" *Ellen Glasgow Newsletter* 30 (spring 1993): 1, 3–4; Dorothy M. Scura, "A Knowledge in the Heart: Ellen Glasgow, the Women's Movement, and *Virginia*," *American Literary Realism* 22 (winter 1990): 30–43; and her edited collection of essays, *Ellen Glasgow: New Perspectives* (Knoxville: The University of Tennessee Press, 1995), which includes an essay by Terence Hoagwood on the intertexts of Glasgow's poetry, 59–73; Lucinda H. MacKethan, *Daughters of Time: Creating Woman's Voice in Southern Story* (Athens, Ga., and London: The University of Georgia Press, 1990); Julius Rowan Raper, "Once More to the Mirror: Glasgow's Technique in *The Sheltered Life* and Reader-Response Criticism," in *Modern American Fiction: Form and Function*, ed. Thomas Daniel Young (Baton Rouge: Louisiana State University Press, 1989); and "Inventing Modern Southern Fiction: A Postmodern View," *Southern Literary Journal* 22 (spring 1990): 3–18.

25. The University Press of Virginia has recently published *The Romantic Comedians* (1995), *The Sheltered Life* (1994), *Vein of Iron* (1995), and *The Woman Within* (1994).

Chapter 2: Ellen Glasgow and Southern History
E. Stanly Godbold, Jr.

1. C. Vann Woodward, *Origins of the New South, 1877–1913* (Baton Rouge: Louisiana State University Press, 1951), 431.
2. Raymond H. Pulley, *Old Virginia Restored: An Interpretation of the Progressive Impulse, 1870–1930* (Charlottesville: University Press of Virginia, 1968).
3. Allen W. Moger, *Virginia: Bourbonism to Byrd, 1870–1925* (Charlottesville: University Press of Virginia, 1968).
4. Julius Rowan Raper, *Without Shelter: The Early Career of Ellen Glasgow* (Baton Rouge: Louisiana State University Press, 1971).
5. Ibid., ix–x.
6. Godbold, *Ellen Glasgow and the Woman Within.*
7. *The Voice of the People,* 60; *In This Our Life,* 463.
8. *Virginia,* 67–69.
9. *The Romantic Comedians,* 62.
10. H. L. Mencken, "Two Southern Novels," in "The Library," *American Mercury* 18 (October 1929): 251.
11. Pamela R. Matthews, *Ellen Glasgow and a Woman's Traditions* (Charlottesville and London: University Press of Virginia, 1994); Dorothy M. Scura, ed., *Ellen Glasgow: New Perspectives* (Knoxville: The University of Tennessee Press, 1995); Susan Goodman, *Ellen Glasgow: A Biography* (Baltimore and London: The Johns Hopkins University Press, 1998).
12. Edward L. Ayers, *The Promise of the New South: Life After Reconstruction* (New York: Oxford University Press, 1992).

Chapter 3: Ellen Glasgow's Civil War Richmond in *The Battle-Ground*
Dorothy M. Scura

1. This essay is a revision of an earlier one, "Ellen Glasgow's *The Battle-Ground*: Civil War Richmond in Fiction and History," which appeared in *Rewriting the South: History and Fiction,* ed. Lothar Hönnighausen and Valeria Gennaro Lerda (Tübingen und Basel: A. Francke Verlag, 1993), 185–196. Duplicate parts are reprinted here with permission. The quotation is from Emory M. Thomas, *The Confederate State of Richmond: A Biography of the Capital* (Austin and London: University of Texas Press, 1971), 31.
2. *The Battle-Ground*; C. Vann Woodward, ed., *Mary Chesnut's Civil War* (New Haven and London: Yale University Press, 1981); Thomas, *The Confederate State of Richmond*; Shelby Foote, *The Civil War: A Narrative,* vol. 1, *Fort Sumter to Perryville* (New York: Random House, 1958), 1:815.
3. *The Woman Within,* 38.
4. *A Certain Measure,* 19 (second quotation), 21 (first quotation).
5. Ibid., 8 (first quotation), 13 (third quotation), 24 (second quotation), 25 (fourth quotation).
6. Ibid., 3.
7. *The Battle-Ground,* 70.
8. Ibid., 30–31.
9. Ibid., 478, 493, 510.
10. Ibid., 512.
11. Ibid., 362.

12. Ibid., 367.

13. Ibid., 376.

14. Ibid., 357, 358, 359, 360.

15. Ibid., 361.

16. Ibid., 361–362, 366.

17. Scura, *Contemporary Reviews*, 62, 65, 66.

18. Edmund Wilson, *Patriotic Gore: Studies in the Literature of the American Civil War* (New York: Oxford University Press, 1962); Daniel Aaron, *The Unwritten War: American Writers and the Civil War* (New York: Alfred A. Knopf, 1973), 289–290.

19. Sheldon Van Auken, "The Southern Historical Novel in the Early Twentieth Century," *Journal of Southern History* 14 (May 1948): 157–191 (quotation on 171); Ernest E. Leisy, *The American Historical Novel* (Norman: University of Oklahoma Press, 1950), 19, 162; Robert A. Lively, *Fiction Fights the Civil War: An Unfinished Chapter in the Literary History of the American People* (Chapel Hill: The University of North Carolina Press, 1957), 12.

20. C. Hugh Holman, *The Immoderate Past: The Southern Writer and History* (Athens: The University of Georgia Press, 1977), 41, 49, 50; McDowell, *Ironic Art of Fiction*, 67.

21. R. H. W. Dillard, "On Ellen Glasgow's *The Battle-Ground*," in *Classics of Civil War Fiction*, ed. David Madden and Peggy Bach (Jackson, Miss., and London: University Press of Mississippi, 1991), 64 (second quotation), 67 (first quotation), 80, 81 (third–fifth quotations).

22. Two earlier editions of the Chesnut material are Isabella D. Martin and Myrta Lockett Avary, eds., *A Diary from Dixie, as Written by Mary Boykin Chesnut, Wife of James Chesnut, Jr., United States Senator from South Carolina, 1859–1861, and Afterward Aide to Jefferson Davis and a Brigadier-General in the Confederate Army* (London: William Heinemann, 1905; New York: D. Appleton and Company, 1905), and Ben Ames Williams, ed., *A Diary from Dixie by Mary Boykin Chesnut* (Boston: Houghton Mifflin Company, 1949). See Woodward, *Mary Chesnut's Civil War*, xxvii–xxix, and C. Vann Woodward and Elisabeth Muhlenfeld, eds., *The Private Mary Chesnut: The Unpublished Civil War Diaries* (New York and Oxford: Oxford University Press, 1984), xxvi–xxvii, for information about the unreliability of the texts of both editions noted above.

23. Wilson, *Patriotic Gore*, ix (third quotation), 278, 279 (first and second quotations); Woodward and Muhlenfeld, *The Private Mary Chesnut*, xviii.

24. Woodward and Muhlenfeld, *The Private Mary Chesnut*, 96 (first quotation), 123 (third quotation), 135 (second quotation).

25. Woodward, *Mary Chesnut's Civil War*, 498, 500.

26. Ibid., 477.

27. Woodward and Muhlenfeld, *The Private Mary Chesnut*, 105.

28. Woodward, *Mary Chesnut's Civil War*, 515–516, 589.

29. Woodward and Muhlenfeld, *The Private Mary Chesnut*, 42.

30. Thomas, *The Confederate State of Richmond*, 87, 99.

31. Ibid., 68, 69.

32. Foote, *The Civil War*, 1:445–446, 449.

33. Ibid., 1:513, 515.

34. Ibid., 1:518–519.

35. Ibid., 1:815.

36. *A Certain Measure*, 24.

Chapter 4: From Joan of Arc to Lucy Dare
Pamela R. Matthews

1. Glasgow's agricultural metaphors look ahead to the Fugitives' future emphasis on agrarianism. In her essay on the Southern Renaissance, Carol Manning argues that many Southern women writers anticipated the region's literary awakening. See Carol S. Manning, "The Real Beginning of the Southern Renaissance," *The Female Tradition in Southern Literature*, ed. Carol S. Manning (Urbana: University of Illinois Press, 1993), 37–56.
2. The interview with Glasgow is "No Valid Reason Against Giving Votes to Women: An Interview," reprinted in Raper, *Ellen Glasgow's Reasonable Doubts*, 24, 25.
3. The story is in manuscript in the Ellen Glasgow Papers, Accession no. 5060, University of Virginia Library, Charlottesville. It was first published in the *Mississippi Quarterly* 49 (spring 1996): 202–209. E. Stanly Godbold Jr. dates the story closer to the mid-1880s. See Godbold, *Ellen Glasgow and the Woman Within,* 25, 26, 33.
4. See Anne Goodwyn Jones, *Tomorrow Is Another Day: The Woman Writer in the South, 1859–1936* (Baton Rouge: Louisiana State University Press, 1981), xi, 26; and Anne Firor Scott, *Making the Invisible Woman Visible* (Urbana: University of Illinois Press, 1984), 223.
5. See Glasgow, "No Valid Reason," 23; Jones, *Tomorrow Is Another Day*, 13–14; Scott, *Making the Invisible Woman Visible*, 179.
6. "A Modern Joan of Arc," ed. Pamela R. Matthews, in *Mississippi Quarterly* 49 (spring 1996): 204.
7. Ibid., 205.
8. Ibid., 205, 208.
9. Ibid., 208.
10. Ibid.
11. Godbold, *Ellen Glasgow and the Woman Within,* 25.
12. Lynette Carpenter has discussed "Dare's Gift" from a feminist perspective, highlighting, as I do here, the unreliable male narrators and the prisonlike qualities of the house. See "The Daring Gift in 'Dare's Gift,'" *Studies in Short Fiction* 21 (spring 1984): 95–102; and "Visions of Female Community in Ellen Glasgow's Ghost Stories" in *Haunting the House of Fiction: Feminist Perspectives on Ghost Stories by American Women*, ed. Lynette Carpenter and Wendy K. Kolmar (Knoxville: The University of Tennessee Press, 1991), 117–141.
13. Glasgow, "Dare's Gift," in *The Collected Stories of Ellen Glasgow*, 90. In his introduction to *The Collected Stories*, Richard K. Meeker discusses literary parallels between Glasgow and Poe, evident in several of Glasgow's short stories, 12–15.
14. Ibid., 90.
15. Diane Price Herndl, in *Invalid Women: Figuring Feminine Illness in American Fiction and Culture, 1840–1940* (Chapel Hill and London: The University of North Carolina Press, 1993), provocatively and thoroughly discusses the parallel histories of female invalidism and cultural contexts for both women and men.
16. "Dare's Gift," 99, 101.
17. Ibid., 103.
18. Ibid., 104.
19. Ibid., 106.
20. Ibid., 117.

21. Glasgow, "No Valid Reason," 25.

CHAPTER 5: MINING THE *VEIN OF IRON*
Helen Fiddyment Levy

1. *A Certain Measure,* 169.
2. Glasgow's phrase from *A Certain Measure,* 177. Although this statement has been taken as representative of a certain self-pity characteristic of Glasgow's difficult last years, it nonetheless contains elements of truth. Much Southern literary criticism has indeed downplayed her contribution. See, for example, such critical works on modern Southern literature as Richard Gray, *The Literature of Memory: Modern Writers of the American South* (Baltimore: Johns Hopkins University Press, 1977), and Richard H. King, *A Southern Renaissance: The Cultural Awakening of the American South, 1930–1955* (New York: Oxford University Press, 1980). Gray, for example, goes so far as to lump Welty, Gordon, and Porter under the chapter heading, "Back to the Old Plantation," and Glasgow—strange conclusion indeed!—is seen as ultimately nostalgic, celebrating "the virtues of the old patriarchy" (33). Even such a recent collection as *Southern Literature and Literary Theory* (1990), claiming as its intent the application of recent theoretical approaches to Southern studies, finds room in an anthology with twenty chapters for articles on only three women authors, Grace King, Zora Neale Hurston, and Alice Walker. We search the index in vain for the name of Ellen Glasgow, but once again the usual male literary subjects are rounded up and their works asked to perform sprightly new critical dances: Robert Penn Warren—two chapters, William Faulkner—three chapters, Allen Tate—two chapters. The work of Linda W. Wagner in *Ellen Glasgow: Beyond Convention* and that of Anne Goodwyn Jones in *Tomorrow Is Another Day,* as well as the equable, sensitive appraisal of such critics as Julius Rowan Raper and the late C. Hugh Holman offer welcome exceptions to this trend. Two recent discussions should also be noted. Elizabeth Jane Harrison's *Female Pastoral* has a chapter on Glasgow's connection to the pastoral tradition, and Suzanne Clark's *Sentimental Modernism* dissects the assumptions of the Modernist critics, particularly the New Critics. Many of these assumptions parallel the beliefs of the Nashville Agrarians in cultural outlook, and, indeed, such figures as Robert Penn Warren, Allen Tate, and John Crowe Ransom find themselves at the vanguard of both movements. The effect of this redoubtable group on both literary criticism and Southern literature perhaps goes far to explain the shared classification or neglect in much Southernist criticism of such diverse women as Eudora Welty, Caroline Gordon, Ellen Glasgow, and Katherine Anne Porter. Jefferson Humphries, ed., *Southern Literature and Literary Theory* (Athens: University of Georgia Press, 1990); Linda W. Wagner, *Ellen Glasgow: Beyond Convention* (Austin: University of Texas Press, 1982); Anne Goodwyn Jones, *Tomorrow Is Another Day: The Woman Writer in the South, 1859–1936* (Baton Rouge: Louisiana State University Press, 1981); Elizabeth Jane Harrison, *Female Pastoral: Women Writers Re-Visioning the American South* (Knoxville: University of Tennessee Press, 1991); Suzanne Clark, *Sentimental Modernism: Women Writers and the Revolution of the Word* (Bloomington: Indiana University Press, 1991).
3. Nina Baym's witty title for her groundbreaking essay, "Melodramas of Beset Manhood: How Theories of American Fiction Exclude Women Authors," *American Quarterly* 33 (spring 1981): 123.
4. *A Certain Measure,* 169.
5. Lucinda H. MacKethan's *Daughters of Time: Creating Woman's Voice in Southern Story* (Athens,

Ga., and London: The University of Georgia Press, 1990) argues that completing a process of individuation, and thus achieving a degree of cultural separation, grants the Southern women she discusses, Eudora Welty, Zora Neale Hurston, and Ellen Glasgow, a distinctive style. Resting on an oral tradition, this voice bears many commonalities with the "speakerly voice" that Henry Louis Gates Jr. associates with Hurston in *The Signifying Monkey: A Theory of Afro-American Literary Criticism* (New York: Oxford University Press, 1988). Only after the process of separation is complete, MacKethan posits, is the female author empowered to approach the communal attitudes of her past. In contrast, my argument rests on the assumption that the Southern woman writer must learn how to eschew the individualistic, competitive messages of the "mainstream" literary community, messages conveyed in the elaborated, abstract language codes of the bureaucratic center. In their maturity these women produce works that insist on female creativity as arising directly from the female tradition exemplified by the elder wise women, often the grandmother, and her well-tended garden and thrifty kitchen. I would insist that this characterization represents an ideal based on the reclamation of the communal tradition, rather than a celebratory tribute.

6. The manse may be seen as a representation of the female family in all its creative aspects, uniting and sheltering the generations of the family within its walls.

7. *A Certain Measure,* 173.

8. Noted by Julius R. Raper in *From the Sunken Garden,* 167. In addition, Glasgow's discussion of her writing process on *Vein of Iron* is expressed in explicit and detailed birth imagery: "As long as a book has the life of reverie alone, it is possessed by the author; and through the stages of pre-natal development, it is attached by some vital cord to the writer's unconscious being" (*A Certain Measure,* 180). The link between biological identity and female art in the essay mirrors the connection between gender and creativity portrayed symbolically in the novel. In making this argument, I have had to confront Glasgow's words in *The Woman Within* that she found in the writing of *Barren Ground* "a code of living that was sufficient for life or for death" (271). The last chapter, however, contains these words, "In the past few years I have made a thrilling discovery ... that until one is over sixty one can never really learn the secret of living" (282). Given Glasgow's contradictory statements in the autobiography, I have turned to the characterization and plots of her last novels to locate the nexus of her final beliefs.

9. *Vein of Iron,* 23.

10. The identification of the rock and the eagle with Grandmother brings to mind Thea Kronborg, the earth-goddess, creator of Cather's *Song of the Lark* (1915), and her physical description closely resembles that of Aunt Eliza in Katherine Anne Porter's "The Fig Tree" in *The Collected Stories of Katherine Anne Porter* (1965), and Almira Todd in Sarah Orne Jewett's *The Country of the Pointed Firs* (1896).

11. *A Certain Measure,* 168. In *Natural Symbols,* Mary Douglas insists on the connection of social attitudes toward the body with the shape of its modes of communication. In her schema, traditional communities, which strongly emphasize the group and prescribed behavior, give rise to ritualistic utterance, a form of communication that insists on group solidarity. As we know, such traditional societies, such as the older Southern arrangements, can seriously restrict the lives of the marginalized individuals. Thus, such women writers' attempt to idealize the maternal home is quite visionary; they attempt to merge the comfort of the stable community with the nurture of individual difference. (They are all located "up home" or in "Shut-In Valley" or "located on no map" or "off the coast.") The

emblematic figure who allows this revolutionary language and social vision to emerge is the elder wise woman, a figure who both conserves and creates. Mary Douglas, *Natural Symbols: Explorations in Cosmology*, new ed. (London: Routledge, 1996).

12. *Vein of Iron*, 21.

13. My discussion of the relation of competitiveness and cooperation is drawn from Mary Douglas's *Natural Symbols*. Douglas connects ritual and language with the underlying social attitudes toward hierarchy and social control. I assume a persistent suspicion manifested toward the female body and its reproductive cycles in our rationalized large-scale social structures. That assumption rests on the writings of Max Weber and Sara Ruddick. For a fuller methodological discussion, see my *Fiction of the Home Place: Jewett, Cather, Glasgow, Porter, Welty, and Naylor* (Jackson: University Press of Mississippi, 1992), 13–23.

14. *A Certain Measure*, 183.

15. Ibid.

16. In Julia Kristeva's *Powers of Horror*, the critic notes the fear of female defilement that lies at the heart of much male language, "Fear of the archaic mother turns out to be essentially fear of her generative power. It is this power, a dreaded one, that patrilineal filiation has the burden of subduing." Like several other Southern women of the modern era, Glasgow writes through this horror to accept and claim this generative female power for her own. The sense of loss, both cultural and individual, the *horror* underlying the paternalistic social arrangements in Kristeva's formulation, is assuaged. Julia Kristeva, *Powers of Horror: An Essay on Abjection* (New York: Columbia University Press, 1982), 77.

17. Wagner, *Ellen Glasgow: Beyond Convention*, 95.

18. *Vein of Iron*, 428.

19. Ibid., 425.

20. Ada's fictional history begins as John's ends with the figure of the idiot, directionless, instinctive, irreducible humanity unmitigated by the wise woman's nurturing and generous hand. Both of these passages emphasize the effects of the missing provident, creative female presence on both men and women. Without this figure, social relations have no order, no shelter, no creativity. The wise woman's efforts and memories raise humanity above its most instinctive level.

21. *Vein of Iron*, 456.

22. Ibid., 457.

23. *A Certain Measure*, 178–179. See Linda Wagner's informative discussion of the function of style in drawing characterization in *Ellen Glasgow: Beyond Convention*, 103–107.

24. *Vein of Iron*, 167. Such women authors as Eudora Welty, Gloria Naylor, and Willa Cather, among others, explicitly locate their early literary inspirations as arising from the voices of female family members and the female community.

25. See *The Woman Within* for her conscious attitudes toward her father, Francis Glasgow.

26. Godbold, *Ellen Glasgow and the Woman Within*, 213–214.

27. *A Certain Measure*, 175.

28. Jane Tompkins's commentary in *Sensational Designs* on the cultural work women's literature undertook in the nineteenth century has relevance here. Like the nineteenth-century women's novelists, Glasgow attempts to effect a change in emotional sensibilities and ultimately a change in social attitudes and actions; she therefore appropriates strategies found in earlier women's novels, notably the conventional symbolism—the emotional language, the belief in spirituality, and the didactic intent. Jane P. Tompkins,

Sensational Designs: The Cultural Work of American Fiction, 1790–1860 (New York: Oxford University Press, 1985).

CHAPTER 6: NOVELIST ELLEN GLASGOW'S FEMINIST REBELLION IN VIRGINIA
Catherine G. Peaslee

1. H. L. Mencken, *Prejudices* (1919), quoted in the *Christian Science Monitor*, 12 April 1993, p. 13.
2. Godbold, *Ellen Glasgow and the Woman Within*, 91.
3. *The Romance of a Plain Man*, 94–95.
4. Ibid., 398.
5. *A Certain Measure*, 65–66.
6. Michael B. Chesson, *Richmond After the War, 1865–1890* (Richmond: Virginia State Library, 1981), 3.
7. Rosalind Miles, *The Women's History of the World* (New York: Harper and Row, 1989), 200.
8. Suzanne Lebsock, *"A Share of Honour": Virginia Women, 1600–1945* (Richmond: Virginia Women's Cultural History Project, 1984), 25.
9. Louise Belote Dawe and Sandra Gioia Treadway, "Hannah Lee Corbin: The Forgotten Lee," *Virginia Cavalcade* 29 (autumn 1979): 70–77; Jo Freeman, *The Politics of Women's Liberation: A Case Study of an Emerging Social Movement and Its Relation to the Policy Process* (New York: David McKay Company, Inc., 1975), 13.
10. Freeman, *Politics of Women's Liberation*, 266; Lebsock, "Share of Honour," 115.
11. Anne Firor Scott. *The Southern Lady: From Pedestal to Politics, 1830–1930* (Chicago: The University of Chicago Press, 1970), 219; Sandra Gioia Treadway, *Women of Mark: A History of The Woman's Club of Richmond, Virginia, 1894–1994* (Richmond: The Library of Virginia, 1995), 18, 60–63.
12. *Ellen Glasgow Newsletter* 19 (1983): 6.
13. Ibid., 2.
14. Raper, *Ellen Glasgow's Reasonable Doubts*, 16.
15. *The Woman Within*, 186.
16. Raper, *From the Sunken Garden*, 16.
17. *Life and Gabriella*, 511.
18. Raper, *Ellen Glasgow's Reasonable Doubts*, 26.
19. Ibid., 21.
20. Ibid., 17.
21. Ibid., 26.
22. Ibid., 21.
23. Ellen Glasgow to Lila M. Valentine, 17 September 1920, Lila Meade Valentine Papers, Virginia Historical Society, Richmond.
24. Monique Parent-Frazee, "Ellen Glasgow as Feminist" in Inge, *Centennial Essays*, 307–308.
25. Raper, *Ellen Glasgow's Reasonable Doubts*, 3.
26. *The Woman Within*, 187.
27. Ibid., 163.

CHAPTER 7: WHAT ELLEN GLASGOW MEANT BY "AVERAGE"
Mark A. Graves

1. *A Certain Measure*, 75.
2. Daniel Joseph Singal, *The War Within: From Victorian to Modernist Thought in the South,*

1919–1945 (Chapel Hill: The University of North Carolina Press, 1982), 12.

3. Bertram Wyatt-Brown, *Honor and Violence in the Old South* (New York: Oxford University Press, 1986), 35.

4. *The Voice of the People*, 7 (quotation), 23, 43, 46, 117–118.

5. Ibid., 434.

6. Ibid., 119.

7. McDowell, *Ironic Art of Fiction,* 91.

8. *The Romance of a Plain Man*, 183.

9. *The Miller of Old Church.*

CHAPTER 8: WITHOUT THE GLORY OF GOD
Susan Goodman

1. *A Certain Measure,* 109–110.

2. *The Woman Within*, 15, 16, 85–87.

3. Ibid., 13 (first quotation); *A Certain Measure,* 90 (second quotation); Wagner, *Ellen Glasgow: Beyond Convention,* 7–8; Godbold, *Ellen Glasgow and the Woman Within,* 27.

4. *The Woman Within*, 16.

5. For additional information about Francis Glasgow's association with the Tredegar Iron Works, see Charles B. Dew, *Ironmaker to the Confederacy: Joseph R. Anderson and the Tredegar Iron Works*, 2d ed. (Richmond: The Library of Virginia, 1999), 16, 108, 168–169, 235, and esp. 252.

6. The first myth can be summed up by Glasgow's own observation that the less a woman knew about life, the "better prepared she would be to contend with it" (*A Certain Measure,* 90). A woman's charm lay in her innocence (or ignorance), her ability to suffer in silence, her piety, and her devotion to everyone but herself; in return, they worshiped her. See Anne Firor Scott, *The Southern Lady: From Pedestal to Politics, 1830–1930* (Chicago: University of Chicago Press, 1970), 5, 7. See also Jacqueline Jones, *Labor of Love, Labor of Sorrow: Black Women, Work, and the Family from Slavery to the Present* (New York: Basic Books, 1985); Elizabeth Fox-Genovese, *Within the Plantation Household: Black and White Women of the Old South* (Chapel Hill: The University of North Carolina Press, 1988); Catherine Clinton, *The Plantation Mistress: Woman's World in the Old South* (New York: Pantheon Books, 1982); Carol Bleser, ed., *In Joy and in Sorrow: Women, Family, and Marriage in the Victorian South, 1830–1900* (New York: Oxford University Press, 1990); and Barbara Welter, "The Cult of True Womanhood: 1820–1860," *American Quarterly* 18 (summer 1966): 151–174. The second myth romanticized plantation life: "We are slaves to our slaves," many a Southerner lamented. The system prospered on silence and on women's playing "their parts of unsuspecting angels to the letter," Mary Boykin Chesnut, *A Diary from Dixie,* ed. Ben Ames Williams (Boston: Houghton Mifflin Company, 1949), 122, 163–164.

7. *A Certain Measure*, 163.

8. *The Woman Within*, 243–244 (first quotation), 270–271 (third quotation); *A Certain Measure,* 213 (second quotation). For general information on Calvinism, I have relied on Victor B. Howard, *Conscience and Slavery: The Evangelistic Calvinist Domestic Missions, 1837–1861* (Kent, Ohio: Kent State University Press, 1990); Jon Pahl, *Paradox Lost: Free Will and Political Liberty in American Culture, 1630–1970* (Baltimore: Johns Hopkins University Press, 1992); Alister E. McGrath, *A Life of John Calvin: A Study in the Shaping of Western Culture* (Oxford: B[asil] Blackwell, 1990); Marshall Gordon, *Presbyteries and Profits:*

Calvinism and the Development of Capitalism in Scotland, 1560–1707 (New York: Oxford University Press, 1980); Alastair Duke, Gillian Lewis, and Andrew Pettegree, eds. and trans., *Calvinism in Europe, 1540–1610: A Collection of Documents* (Manchester, Eng.: Manchester University Press, 1992). For a discussion of Modernism that pertains to this essay, see William R. Hutchison, *The Modernist Impulse in American Protestantism* (Cambridge: Harvard University Press, 1976), and Suzanne Clark, *Sentimental Modernism: Women Writers and the Revolution of the Word* (Bloomington: Indiana University Press, 1991). For an analysis of the new phase of Glasgow's writing career, see Raper, *From the Sunken Garden.*

9. Although Glasgow creates the impression that she recorded thoughts and feelings as they spontaneously occurred, the manuscript reveals that analysis did come later. The first typed draft shows many working revisions from words and phrases to whole sections on Harold S. that have been typed over with rows of *X*'s. Glasgow seems to have read the draft several times, making small changes, usually word substitutions, which are marked with ink and pencil. The second draft is a copy of the first with modifications in punctuation, the additions of dates, and the reordering of sentences. Ellen Glasgow Papers, Accession no. 5060, Box 5, University of Virginia Library, Charlottesville (hereafter cited as UVA); Ernest Hemingway, "Preface," in *A Moveable Feast* (New York: Charles Scribner's Sons, 1964).

10. Georges Gusdorf, "Conditions and Limits of Autobiography," in *Autobiography: Essays Theoretical and Critical,* ed. James Olney (Princeton, N.J.: Princeton University Press, 1980), 36–37.

11. *The Woman Within*, 227; *Barren Ground*, 460.

12. *The Woman Within*, 289.

13. Ibid., 91.

14. Ibid., 56 (third quotation), 130 (first quotation), 227 (second quotation).

15. Mary Grimley Mason, "Introduction," in *Journeys: Autobiographical Writings by Women*, ed. Mary Grimley Mason and Carol Hurd Green (Boston: G. K. Hall, 1979), xiii; *The Woman Within*, 16, 275.

16. Ibid., 227; James Olney, "The Ontology of Autobiography," in his *Autobiography: Essays Theoretical and Critical* (Princeton, N.J.: Princeton University Press, 1980), 244.

17. *The Woman Within*, 3–4.

18. Carroll Smith-Rosenberg, "The Female World of Love and Ritual: Relations between Women in Nineteenth-Century America," *Signs: Journal of Women in Culture and Society* 1 (autumn 1975): 1–29; Jacques Lacan, *Écrits: A Selection*, trans. Alan Sheridan (New York: Norton, 1977), 107, 281–291; *The Woman Within*, 3 (first quotation), 14 (second quotation), 168 (third quotation). See also Terry Eagleton, *Literary Theory: An Introduction* (Minneapolis: University of Minnesota Press, 1983), 151–193 and 166 esp.; and Melanie Klein, *Love, Guilt, and Reparation, and Other Works, 1921–1945* (London: The Hogarth Press and the Institute of Psycho-Analysis, 1975), 334. Klein describes the creative writer as impelled by the desire to rediscover the mother. See also Susan Suleiman, "Writing and Motherhood," in *The Mother Tongue: Essays in Feminist Psychoanalytic Interpretation*, ed. Shirley Nelson Garner, Claire Kahane, and Madelon Sprengnether (Ithaca, N.Y.: Cornell University Press, 1985), who quotes Klein on 357.

19. *A Certain Measure*, 111.

20. James Hogg, *The Private Memoirs and Confessions of a Justified Sinner* (1824; reprint, London: Cresset Press, 1947), 39.

21. *The Woman Within*, 4, 285.

22. Raper, *Ellen Glasgow's Reasonable Doubts,* 123 (first quotation); *The Woman Within,* 5 (third quotation), 8 (second quotation), 271 (fourth quotation); Ursula Brumm, *American Thought and Religious Typology* (New Brunswick, N.J.: Rutgers University Press, 1970), 33.

23. Brumm, *American Thought and Religious Typology,* 168.

24. *The Woman Within,* 123, 195.

25. *A Certain Measure,* 113–114; Virginia Woolf, *A Writer's Diary: Being Extracts from the Diary of Virginia Woolf,* ed. Leonard Woolf (New York: Harcourt, Brace and Company, 1954), 60; *The Woman Within,* 67.

26. *The Woman Within,* 25.

27. Ibid., 289, 290.

28. *A Certain Measure,* 148; Glasgow recorded the epigram in Notebook No. 3, Ellen Glasgow Papers, Accession no. 5060, Box 6, UVA; Virginia Woolf, *A Room of One's Own* (New York: Harcourt Brace Jovanovich, 1989), 98.

29. See Carol Edkins, "Quest for Community: Spiritual Autobiographies of Eighteenth-Century Quaker and Puritan Women in America," in *Women's Autobiography: Essays in Criticism,* ed. Estelle C. Jelinek (Bloomington: Indiana University Press, 1980), 41; and Anthony Storr, *Solitude: A Return to the Self* (New York: Free Press, 1988).

30. *The Woman Within,* 279, 296.

31. Ibid., 3, 226.

32. *A Certain Measure,* 94, 155, 199, 264.

33. Max Weber, *The Protestant Ethic and the Spirit of Capitalism,* trans. Talcott Parsons (London: George Allen and Unwin Ltd., 1952), xii; *Barren Ground,* 7–8, 159. For a discussion of race and religion, see Joseph R. Washington, *Anti-Blackness in English Religion, 1500–1800* (Lewiston, N.Y.: E[dwin] Mellen, 1984), esp. 482–488.

34. *Barren Ground,* 44.

35. Ibid.

36. Ibid., 121.

37. *The Woman Within,* 41.

38. *Barren Ground,* 53.

39. *The Woman Within,* 244; *Barren Ground,* 44, 239–240; *A Certain Measure,* 155.

40. *Barren Ground,* 198.

41. *A Certain Measure,* 156, 159; *Barren Ground,* 170.

42. *Barren Ground,* 340.

43. Annette Kolodny, *The Land Before Her: Fantasy and Experience of the American Frontiers, 1630–1860* (Chapel Hill: The University of North Carolina Press, 1984), 3–14; David R. Williams, *Wilderness Lost: The Religious Origins of the American Mind* (Selinsgrove, Pa.: Susquehanna University Press; London and Toronto: Associated University Presses, 1987), 12.

44. *Barren Ground,* 299, 336; *A Certain Measure,* 158–159.

45. *The Woman Within,* 197; *A Certain Measure,* 160.

46. Ellen Glasgow, manuscript of *The Woman Within,* Ellen Glasgow Papers, Accession no. 5060, Box 5, 74, UVA.

47. *The Woman Within,* 138–139; *Barren Ground,* 459–460.

48. *Barren Ground,* 8 (first quotation), 27 (third quotation), 410; *Vein of Iron,* 50 (second quotation), 111 (fourth quotation); *A Certain Measure,* 160; *The Woman Within,* 289.

49. Ibid., 296; Henry James to Grace Norton, 28 July [1883], *The Letters of Henry James,* ed. Percy Lubbock (New York: Charles Scribner's Sons, 1920), 1:101.

50. *The Woman Within*, 125; *Barren Ground*, 497.

51. *The Woman Within*, 281.

52. Ibid., 280.

Chapter 9: The Invisible Stigma in Ellen Glasgow's *The Descendant*
Linda Kornasky

1. Rouse, *Ellen Glasgow*, 20.

2. Wagner, *Ellen Glasgow: Beyond Convention*; Marcelle Thiebaux, *Ellen Glasgow* (New York: Frederick Ungar Publishing Company, 1982).

3. Monique Parent Frazee, "Ellen Glasgow as Feminist," in *Ellen Glasgow: Centennial Essays*, 183.

4. Kathryn P. Meadow-Orlans, "Social and Psychological Effects of Hearing Loss in Adulthood: A Literature Review," in *Adjustment to Adult Hearing Loss*, ed. Harold Orlans (San Diego, Calif.: College-Hill Press, 1985), 35–36.

5. These emotions include depression, isolation, irritability, fatigue, nervousness, embarrassment, fear of others' stigmatization, and paranoia or suspiciousness. Frequently cited maladjustment behavioral strategies include overcompensation (extremely extroverted social behavior), denial of hearing loss and the consequent refusal to make necessary changes, retreat from society, somatic complaints, and exploitation of others. For a typical, traditional analysis of these emotions and "maladjustment" strategies, see Peter Hobart Knapp, "Emotional Aspects of Hearing Loss," *Psychosomatic Medicine* 10 (July–August 1948): 203–222.

6. James G. Kyle, Lesley G. Jones, and Peter L. Wood, "Adjustment to Acquired Hearing Loss: A Working Model," in *Adjustment to Adult Hearing Loss,* 119–138.

7. *The Woman Within*, 113.

8. Furthermore, even after she received a positive confirmation of hearing loss, Glasgow's passage to the second stage was complicated by the inefficient diagnostic ability of audiologists and the limits of hearing-aid technology during the turn of the century and first half of the twentieth century.

9. *The Woman Within*, 103.

10. Ibid.

11. Of course, this strategy did have negative results as it made Glasgow vulnerable to charges of pettiness and unprofessionalism.

12. *The Woman Within*, 113.

13. Wagner, *Ellen Glasgow: Beyond Convention*, 12.

14. For instance, Kyle, Jones, and Wood affirm that an amazing 97 percent of hearing-impaired people read books "every day or regularly, compared with 60 per cent of hearing people." *Adjustment to Adult Hearing Loss,* 133.

15. *The Woman Within*, 152, 157, 181.

16. Raper, *Without Shelter,* 63, 82.

17. *The Descendant*, 65, 172, 175–176, 177.

18. Ibid., 187, 240, 242.

19. Ibid., 186.

20. Ibid., 188.

21. Ibid., 223.

22. *A Certain Measure*, 196.

23. *The Woman Within*, 152.

CHAPTER 10: LIVING WITHOUT JOY
Benita Huffman Muth

1. *A Certain Measure*, 154. All references in this chapter are to the first edition of *Barren Ground* (Garden City, N.Y.: Doubleday, Page and Company, 1925).
2. *Barren Ground*, 13, 36, 41, 100; Raper, *From the Sunken Garden*, 90.
3. *Barren Ground*, 168.
4. Ibid., 199.
5. Ibid., 235.
6. Ibid., 239, 299.
7. Ibid., 238 (second quotation), 239, 246 (first quotation).
8. Jan Zlotnik Schmidt, "Ellen Glasgow's Heroic Legends: A Study of *Life and Gabriella*, *Barren Ground*, and *Vein of Iron*," *Tennessee Studies in Literature* 26 (1981): 126.
9. *Barren Ground*, 344–347; M.-L. von Franz, "The Process of Individuation," in *Man and His Symbols*, ed. Carl G. Jung (Garden City, N.Y.: Doubleday and Company Inc., 1964), 181.
10. Annette Kolodny, *The Lay of the Land: Metaphor as Experience and History in American Life and Letters* (Chapel Hill: The University of North Carolina Press, 1975), 4 (second quotation), 8 (first quotation); Beth Harrison, "Ellen Glasgow's Revision of the Southern Pastoral," *South Atlantic Review* 55, no. 2 (May 1990): 48.
11. Ibid., 56; *Barren Ground*, 285.
12. Harrison, "Ellen Glasgow's Revision of the Southern Pastoral," 57; *Barren Ground*, 376.
13. Ibid., 107, 308.
14. Mary Castiglie Anderson, "Cultural Archetype and the Female Hero: Nature and Will in Ellen Glasgow's *Barren Ground*," *Modern Fiction Studies* 28 (autumn 1982): 387.
15. *Barren Ground*, 340, 341.
16. Ibid., quotations on 231, 305, 326, 333.
17. Ibid., 103–104, 371.
18. Ibid., 331, 394.
19. Ibid., 336, 337.
20. Ibid., 504–506.
21. Ibid., 509–510.
22. Ibid., 510.
23. Raper, *From the Sunken Garden*, 97; *Barren Ground*, 511.

CHAPTER 11: FROM JORDAN'S END TO FRENCHMAN'S BEND
Edgar MacDonald

1. The writer is indebted to Richard K. Meeker's introduction to *The Collected Stories of Ellen Glasgow*, and to Julius Rowan Raper's essay, "The Words for Invisible Things," in Raper's *From the Sunken Garden*. Meeker's collection includes the seven stories published in *The Shadowy Third and Other Stories* (1923), four others from magazines not included in that volume, and "The Professional Instinct," which was not published in Glasgow's lifetime. Meeker's introduction is enlightening, especially his discussion of post-Darwinian romanticism, and he makes an especially telling case for the influence of Poe on the four "ghost" stories with their first-person narrators. He likewise comments on Glasgow's use of garden imagery and on the influence of Henry James and Joseph Conrad. Raper, Glasgow's most sympathetic interpreter, brings deep

psychological insight to these products of her midlife decade of emotional and aesthetic crisis. He extends the Poe influence to Faulkner and sees Glasgow as standing "squarely in the doorway through which the tradition of Southern writing passes from the often barren past into the fruitful modern period."

2. *The Woman Within*, 228.

3. Ibid., 227.

4. *Letters of Ellen Glasgow*, 352.

5. Raper, *From the Sunken Garden*, 70.

6. Meeker, "Introduction," *The Collected Stories of Ellen Glasgow*, 18.

7. Raper, *From the Sunken Garden*, 61.

8. Matthew Arnold, "Stanzas from the Grande Chartreuse," in *The Poems of Matthew Arnold*, ed. Kenneth Allott (London: Longman; New York: Norton, 1972), 288 (first quotation); Arnold, "The Forsaken Merman," in *The Poems of Matthew Arnold*, 95–100; *The Woman Within*, 213 (second quotation).

9. *The Woman Within*, 234–235.

10. Henry Seidel Canby, "A Changing Order," in *New York Evening Post Literary Review*, 1 July 1922, p. 771, in Scura, *Contemporary Reviews*, 213; Raper, *From the Sunken Garden*, 51.

11. *Letters of Ellen Glasgow*, 352.

12. Ellen Glasgow felt the strictures of the short story form, aware that only the novel gave her the amplitude "to trace the process of cause and effect." Meeker, "Introduction," *The Collected Stories of Ellen Glasgow*, 6.

13. Undated letter quoted in Godbold, *Ellen Glasgow and the Woman Within*, 125.

14. Hunter Stagg, "*The Shadowy Third*," *New York Tribune*, 18 November 1923, sec. 9, p. 23, in Scura, *Contemporary Reviews*, 230.

15. Meeker, "Introduction," *The Collected Stories of Ellen Glasgow*, 14.

16. In *Barren Ground*, Ellen Glasgow would have Pedlar's Mill on "Whippernock River," Whippernock being the name of Henry Anderson's ancestral acreage in Dinwiddie County.

17. *Phases of an Inferior Planet* (New York: Harper and Brothers, Publishers, 1898).

18. *The Woman Within*, 227.

CHAPTER 12: ELLEN GLASGOW'S *IN THIS OUR LIFE*
David W. Coffey

1. See, for example, Godbold, *Ellen Glasgow and the Woman Within*, 279.

2. Ellen Glasgow to Bessie Zaban Jones, 16 June 1942, *Letters of Ellen Glasgow*, 302.

3. Godbold, *Ellen Glasgow and the Woman Within*, 280.

4. For an analysis of the four drafts of Koch's script for *In This Our Life* as well as a consideration of feminist issues in the translation of Glasgow's novel to the screen, see Serafina Kent Bathrick, "Independent Woman, Doomed Sister," in *The Modern American Novel and the Movies,* ed. Gerald Peary and Roger Shatzkin (New York: Frederick Ungar Publishing Company, 1978), 143–155.

5. Ibid., 147.

6. *The Woman Within*, 42–50.

7. Ibid., 52–53.

8. Godbold, *Ellen Glasgow and the Woman Within*, 247.

9. Glasgow to Jones, *Letters of Ellen Glasgow*, 302.

10. *Richmond Afro-American*, 18 July 1942, p. 11.

11. Thomas Cripps, *Slow Fade to Black: The Negro in American Film, 1900–1942* (New York: Oxford University Press, 1977), 370.

12. *Richmond Times-Dispatch*, 22 May 1942, p. 10; *Richmond News Leader*, 25 May 1942, p. 7.

13. *Richmond Afro-American*, 23 May 1942, p. 11.

14. Ibid., 11 July 1942, p. 11.

15. Scott Hammen, *John Huston* (Boston: Twayne Publishers, 1985), 12.

16. John Huston, *An Open Book* (New York: Alfred A. Knopf, 1980), 81.

17. Ellen Glasgow, *Beyond Defeat: An Epilogue to an Era,* ed. Luther Y. Gore (Charlottesville: The University Press of Virginia, 1966).

CHAPTER 13: ELLEN GLASGOW: GAPS IN THE RECORD
Julius Rowan Raper

1. The University Press of Virginia has begun remedying this unfortunate lack with a series of Glasgow novels, plus *The Woman Within*, printed in handsome editions suitable for the classroom.

2. Scura, *Contemporary Reviews*.

3. John Raper Ormond, "Some Recent Products of the New School of Southern Fiction," *South Atlantic Quarterly* 3 (July 1904): 285–289; Archibald Henderson, " Recent Novels of Note," *Sewanee Review* 12 (October 1904): 462–464; W. J. Cash, *The Mind of the South* (New York: Alfred A. Knopf, 1941); C. Vann Woodward, *Origins of the New South, 1877–1913* (Baton Rouge: Louisiana State University Press, 1951), 434.

4. The University Press of Virginia Glasgow series made *The Sheltered Life* a priority.

5. *The Descendant*.

6. Pearce Bailey, *Diseases of the Nervous System Resulting from Accident and Injury* (New York: Appleton, 1898; reprint, New York: Appleton, 1906). Originally published in 1898 under the title *Accident and Injury: Their Relations to Diseases of the Nervous System*.

7, Raper, *Without Shelter,* 104–106, 210–211.

8. Edgar E. MacDonald, "An Essay in Bibliography," in Inge, *Centennial Essays,* 222–223.

9. Matthews, *Ellen Glasgow and a Woman's Traditions*, 54.

10. Frances W. Saunders, "Glasgow's Secret Love: 'Gerald B' or 'William T?' " *Ellen Glasgow Newsletter* 31 (fall 1993): 1.

11. Ibid., 3.

12. "Saunterings," *Town Topics: The Journal of Society* 54 (13 July 1905): 1.

13. Matthews, *Ellen Glasgow and a Woman's Traditions*, 54.

14. Ibid., 53–55.

15. Raper, *Without Shelter,* 204, 207.

16. Matthews, *Ellen Glasgow and a Woman's Traditions*, 52.

17. Raper, *From the Sunken Garden,* 12–13.

18. Julia Kristeva, *Black Sun: Depression and Melancholia* (New York: Columbia University Press, 1989), 13–15, 145–146.

19. Ann Belford Ulanov, "Transference/Countertransference: A Jungian Perspective," *Jungian Analysis*, ed. Murray Stein (LaSalle, Ill. and London: Open Court, 1982), 75.

20. *The Woman Within*, 153–157; Raper, *Without Shelter,* 144–145.

21. Goodman, *Ellen Glasgow: A Biography*, 79–81, 83, 262–269 n. 10 (quotations on 81 and 83).

22. Raper, *Without Shelter,* 47–50.

CHAPTER 14: ELLEN GLASGOW'S RICHMOND
Tricia Pearsall

1. This discourse was first presented as a slide address for the Glasgow Festival, 16 October 1993. Ruth Jones Wilkins's master's thesis, "Ellen Glasgow's Virginia: The Background of Her Novels," was the source for site identifications and corresponding references in Glasgow's novels. Wilkins credited interviews with the author's friends and family as well as Glasgow's writings in correlating specific fictional scenes with precise place references. In her preface Wilkins noted the assistance of Rebe Glasgow Tutwiler, the youngest of Ellen Glasgow's nine siblings; Anne Virginia Bennett, a trained nurse who became the novelist's secretary and companion; and Caroline "Carrie" Coleman Duke, a friend since childhood. Ruth Jones Wilkins, "Ellen Glasgow's Virginia: The Background of Her Novels" (master's thesis, University of Richmond, 1951).
2. Characters in *Vein of Iron* and *In This Our Life*.
3. For an overview of these changes in Richmond's neighborhoods, see Christopher Silver, *Twentieth-Century Richmond: Planning, Politics, and Race* (Knoxville: The University of Tennessee Press, 1984), and Richmond City Planning Commission, *A Master Plan for the Physical Development of the City* (Richmond: City Planning Commission, 1946).
4. The Valentine Museum/Richmond History Center's photograph collection and the research and photographs of preservationist Mary Wingfield Scott provided valuable information on the significant residences along Franklin and Main Streets. Jack Zehmer, then-executive director of the Historic Richmond Foundation, shared slides for the address from his personal collection. Photographs documenting One West Main's interior during Ellen Glasgow's life and the same spaces during her parents' occupancy hang in the Glasgow house. These images were a gift to the Association for the Preservation of Virginia Antiquities from Glasgow's niece, Josephine Glasgow Clark.
5. Mary Wingfield Scott, *Houses of Old Richmond* (Richmond: The Valentine Museum, 1941; reprint, New York: Bonanza Books, [1972]), 209.
6. Charles B. Dew, *Ironmaker to the Confederacy: Joseph R. Anderson and the Tredegar Iron Works*, 2d ed. (Richmond: The Library of Virginia, 1999), 16, 108, 153–154.
7. *The Voice of the People*, 366.
8. My family (my husband and two sons) and I have lived in the Glasgow house since 1986 and have undertaken extensive repairs and general maintenance.
9. *Autobiography of Thomas Rutherfoord, Esq. Of Richmond, Virginia, 1766–1852* (Richmond: Maylocks Publications, 1986); Mary Wingfield Scott, *Old Richmond Neighborhoods* (Richmond: Whittet and Shepperson, 1950), 150–155.
10. Scott, *Old Richmond Neighborhoods*, 198.
11. Scott, *Houses of Old Richmond*, 193–194.
12. *The Sheltered Life*, 4.
13. Scott, *Old Richmond Neighborhoods*, 198–199; *Houses of Old Richmond*, 148; Wilkins, "Ellen Glasgow's Virginia," 72. Although Scott's *Old Richmond Neighborhoods* gives Crenshaw's address at 21 West Main Street, the address was actually 11 West Main according to her files at the Valentine Museum and to the contemporaneous Richmond city directories.
14. *The Sheltered Life*, 5.
15. Scott, *Old Richmond Neighborhoods*, 198–199.
16. Ibid., 201, 204; William H. Gaines Jr., *A History of Grace and Holy Trinity Episcopal Church, 1858–1987* (Richmond: Grace and Holy Trinity Episcopal Church, [1987]), 7, 13.

17. Scott, *Old Richmond Neighborhoods,* 150–155; *Houses of Old Richmond*, 150, 183.

18. Dew, *Ironmaker to the Confederacy*, esp. 107, 115–120, 179, 318.

19. Scott, *Houses of Old Richmond*, 230–234.

20. *Vein of Iron*, 295.

21. Scott, *Old Richmond Neighborhoods*, 170–172; Robert P. Winthrop, *Architecture in Downtown Richmond* (Richmond: Whittet and Shepperson Printers, 1982), 144; Bill Wasson, "City Approves Razing Church," *Richmond Times-Dispatch*, 13 October 1992, B-3; Virginia Churn, "In 'correctness of detail,' Church Is 'one of best,'" *Richmond Times-Dispatch*, 1 November 1992, K-4.

22. Scott, *Houses of Old Richmond*, 210–211; "Joseph Reid Anderson, of Richmond, Virginia," in Philip Alexander Bruce, Lyon Gardiner Tyler, and Richard L. Morton, *History of Virginia, Volume VI, Virginia Biography* (Chicago and New York: The American Historical Society, 1924), 636.

23. Scott, *Old Richmond Neighborhoods*, 163.

24. *The Romantic Comedians*, 15.

25. Drew St. J. Carneal, *Richmond's Fan District* (Richmond: The Council of the Historic Richmond Foundation, 1996), 68, 76–77, 79–80, 82, 154–155; *The Romance of a Plain Man*, 237.

26. *The Romantic Comedians,* 10.

27. *Vein of Iron*, 273.

28. *They Stooped to Folly*, 94.

29. Wilkins, "Ellen Glasgow's Virginia," 6.

30. Ibid., preface; Scott, *Old Richmond Neighborhoods*, 191; Marguerite Crumley and John G. Zehmer, *Church Hill: The St. John's Church Historic District* (Richmond: The Council of Historic Richmond Foundation, 1991), 101, 122.

31. *Vein of Iron*, 275.

32. Ibid., 278.

33. Winthrop, *Architecture in Downtown Richmond*, 228.

34. Wilkins, "Ellen Glasgow's Virginia," 67; *One Man in His Time*, 58–59.

35. Scott, *Old Richmond Neighborhoods*, 194; *Houses of Old Richmond*, 286–287.

36. *The Romance of a Plain Man*, 3.

37. Harry Kollatz Jr., "'Send the Rascals to the Tall Timber': Adon Allen Yoder," *Virginia Cavalcade* 46 (summer 1996): 44–45.

38. Scott, *Houses of Old Richmond*, 68–69; Crumley and Zehmer, *Church Hill*, 56–57.

39. *The Romance of a Plain Man*, 31.

40. Ibid., 102.

41. *The Voice of the People*, 321.

42. Ibid., 322.

43. Ibid.

44. *One Man in His Time*, 3.

45. Ibid., 1–2.

46. Wilkins, "Ellen Glasgow's Virginia," 58, 62.

47. *The Romantic Comedians*, 5.

48. Mary H. Mitchell, *Hollywood Cemetery: The History of a Southern Shrine* (Richmond: Virginia State Library, 1985; reprint, Richmond: The Library of Virginia, 1999), 5–7. According to Sarah Easter, daughter of Ellen Glasgow's cook James Anderson, Anne Virginia Bennett choose the headstone and organized the brief service at One West Main, which was apparently much more elaborate than what Glasgow had requested.

A telephone conversation with Dan Morris, a former employee of the Frank Bliley Funeral Home, revealed that the funeral workers were requested to unearth the dog's copper casket from the back garden at One West Main. In so doing, they pierced the coffin and had to reseal it before slipping it into the casket with her. Hollywood Cemetery prohibits the burial of pets.

CHAPTER 15: REMEMBERING ELLEN GLASGOW

1. Douglas Southall Freeman, "Ellen Glasgow: Idealist," *Saturday Review of Literature* 12 (31 August 1935): 11–12.
2. See *Letters of Ellen Glasgow,* 161.
3. Carrington C. Tutwiler Jr., *Ellen Glasgow's Library* (Charlottesville: Bibliographical Society of the University of Virginia, 1967), 3–5.
4. On Henry Watkins Anderson, see *Dictionary of Virginia Biography: Volume One, Aaroe to Blanchfield* (Richmond: Library of Virginia, 1998), 136–138.
5. Frances Wickersham Hadfield, an American by birth, was married to Sir Robert Abbott Hadfield, an English steel manufacturer. See Anne Hobson Freeman, *The Style of a Law Firm: Eight Gentlemen from Virginia* (Chapel Hill: Algonquin Books, 1989), 236 n. 4, and, on Sir Robert Hadfield, *Dictionary of National Biography, 1931–1940,* ed. L. G. Wickham Legg (Oxford: Oxford University Press, 1949), 384–386.
6. Arthur Graham Glasgow (1865–1955), Ellen's older brother, who lived in England for most of his life.
7. While serving as head of the American Red Cross delegation to Romania during World War I, Anderson had enjoyed a deep friendship with the country's widowed queen, Marie.

Notes on Contributors

David W. Coffey is Instructor of Virginia History at the Virginia Military Institute, director of the Ruth Anderson McCulloch Branch of the Association for the Preservation of Virginia Antiquities in Lexington, Virginia, and author of "Into the Valley of Virginia: The 1852 Travel Account of Curran Swaim," *Virginia Cavalcade* (1990), and "Reconstruction and Redemption in Lexington, Virginia," in *After the Backcountry: Rural Life in the Great Valley of Virginia, 1800–1900*, edited by Kenneth E. Koons and Warren R. Hofstra, and published by the University of Tennessee Press in 2000.

E. Stanly Godbold, Jr., Professor of History at Mississippi State University, is author of *Ellen Glasgow and the Woman Within* (1972), *Christopher Gadsden and the American Revolution* (1982), and *Confederate Colonel and Cherokee Chief: The Life of William Holland Thomas* (1990).

Susan Goodman is Professor of English at the University of Delaware. She is the author of *Ellen Glasgow: A Biography* (1998), *Edith Wharton's Inner Circle* (1994), and *Edith Wharton's Women: Friends and Rivals* (1990). She has recently written an introduction to Ellen Glasgow's 1902 Civil War novel, *The Battle-Ground*, published by The University of Alabama Press in cooperation with the United States Civil War Center (2000).

Mark A. Graves is an Instructor in the Department of English, Foreign Languages, and Philosophy at Morehead State University. He formerly taught at Bowling Green State University and Michigan State University. His publications on Wilfred Owen, Ellen Glasgow, Josephine W. Johnson, John Dos Passos, and American playwright George Kelly have appeared in journals such as *English Language Notes*, *Ellen Glasgow Newsletter*, *Mid America: Yearbook of the Society for the Study of Midwestern Literature*, *CLAJ* (College Language Association journal), and *Theatre Annual*. He is the author of *George Kelly: A Research and Production Sourcebook* (1999) and co-editor of *An Encyclopedia of American War Literature* (2001) with Philip K. Jason, of the United States Naval Academy.

Linda Kornasky is an Assistant Professor of English at Angelo State University in San Angelo, Texas. Hearing impaired herself, she is currently working on a study of disabled American writers' autobiographical and fictional representations of deafness and other sensory disabilities.

Helen Fiddyment Levy, Lecturer of English at George Mason University, is the author of *Fiction of the Home Place* (1992), which contains a discussion of Ellen Glasgow. She has also written articles on Ellen Glasgow, Willa Cather, and Gloria Naylor.

George C. Longest is Associate Professor of English at Virginia Commonwealth University. He is the author of *Three Virginia Writers: Mary Johnston, Thomas Nelson Page, and Amélie Rives Troubetzkoy: A Reference Guide* (1978), and *Genius in the Garden: Charles F. Gillette & Landscape Architecture in Virginia* (1992).

Edgar MacDonald, Senior Cabell Scholar at Virginia Commonwealth University, is the author of numerous works on Ellen Glasgow, including "Glasgow, Cabell, and Richmond," in *Ellen Glasgow: Centennial Essays* (1976), and the co-editor of *Ellen Glasgow: A Reference Guide* (1986).

Pamela R. Matthews, Assistant Professor of English and former director of Women's Studies at Texas A&M University, is the author of *Ellen Glasgow and a Woman's Traditions* (1994) and editor of Glasgow's letters, forthcoming from the University Press of Virginia.

Benita Huffman Muth is a Visiting Assistant Professor at Westminster College. She recently received her Ph.D. from The University of North Carolina at Chapel Hill and has formerly taught at Tennessee Wesleyan College and The University of North Carolina at Chapel Hill.

Tricia Pearsall and her husband own and reside at One West Main Street, Richmond. She is Director of Minimester and Community Outreach at St. Catherine's School and teaches Glasgow for the St. Catherine's Senior Summer Program (a summer school for senior citizens).

Catherine G. Peaslee, who lives in Charlottesville, Virginia, founded and was the publisher and editor of the *Charlottesville Observer* prior to her retirement. She is a longtime student of Ellen Glasgow, has written many articles about Glasgow, and is currently working on a biography of Glasgow.

Catherine Rainwater, Professor of English at St. Edward's University in Austin, Texas, is president of the Ellen Glasgow Society and editor of the *Ellen Glasgow Newsletter.* Her articles on Glasgow appear in such journals as *American Literature, Tennessee Studies in Literature,* and *Mississippi Quarterly.* Her most recent book is *Dreams of Fiery Stars: The Transformations of Native American Fiction,* published by the University of Pennsylvania Press in 1999.

Julius Rowan Raper, Professor of English and American literature at The University of North Carolina at Chapel Hill, is author of numerous works on Ellen Glasgow, including *From the Sunken Garden: The Fiction of Ellen Glasgow, 1916–1945* (1980) and *Without Shelter: The Early Career of Ellen Glasgow* (1982). He also edited *Ellen Glasgow's Reasonable Doubts* (1988), a collection of her nonfiction.

Dorothy M. Scura, Professor of English at the University of Tennessee, Knoxville, is editor of *Ellen Glasgow: New Perspectives* (1995), *Ellen Glasgow: The Contemporary Reviews* (1992), *Evelyn Scott: Recovering a Lost Modernist* (2001), and *Conversations with Tom Wolfe* (1990). She has published articles on Glasgow, Mary Johnston, Doris Betts, Evelyn Scott, and Constance Cary Harrison in such journals as *Mississippi Quarterly, Virginia Magazine of History and Biography, American Literary Realism,* and *Southern Humanities Review.*

Welford Dunaway Taylor is James A. Bostwick Professor of English at the University of Richmond and former Chairman of the English Department. He is the author and editor of numerous works on American literature and culture, including *Southern Odyssey: Selected Writings by Sherwood Anderson* (1997), which he co-edited with Charles E. Modlin. His most recent work is *The Woodcut Art of J. J. Lankes* (1999).

INDEX

Italic numbers refer to illustrations. The novel wherein the character appears is given after the character's name in the index. Titles of works followed by a date in parentheses are those of Ellen Glasgow. A select bibliography of works by and about Glasgow can be found on pages 173–174.

Regarding Ellen Glasgow: Essays for Contemporary Readers, was designed by Sara Daniels Bowersox, of the Library of Virginia. Page layout was produced using a Power Macintosh G3 and QuarkXpress 4.11. Text was composed in Bembo. Printed on acid-free uncoated natural high-bulk paper 55-lb. text by Sheridan Books, Ann Arbor, Michigan.